# "*Francis, Repair My Church*"

# *"Francis, Repair My Church"*

## Pope Francis Revives Vatican II

John Edgar Raub

WIPF & STOCK · Eugene, Oregon

"FRANCIS, REPAIR MY CHURCH"
Pope Francis Revives Vatican II

Copyright © 2014 John Edgar Raub. All rights reserved. Except for brief quotations in critical publications or reviews, no part of this book may be reproduced in any manner without prior written permission from the publisher. Write: Permissions. Wipf and Stock Publishers, 199 W. 8th Ave., Suite 3, Eugene, OR 97401.

Wipf and Stock
An Imprint of Wipf and Stock Publishers
199 W. 8th Ave., Suite 3
Eugene, OR 97401

www.wipfandstock.com

ISBN 13: 978-1-62564-977-5

Manufactured in the U.S.A.                    12/08/2014

Dedicated to my wife, Ann.
During these past thirteen years, you have both summarized and increased all the blessings of my first sixty-eight years.

"All the people of God, seen as a whole, are infallible."
"The culture of prosperity has deadened us."
"Unfettered capitalism . . . the new tyranny."

—POPE FRANCIS


Disguised, he feeds the hungry,
Protects the environment,
Denounces judgment of gays,
Accepts atheists,
Opposes frivolous church spending.

—JOHN RAUB

# Contents

# Contents

# Foreword

I WAS A PRIEST in active ministry from 1962 to 1972, during and immediately following the Second Vatican Council (1962–65). I entered the monastery in 1972 and left in 2000. The changes in attitude, atmosphere, and mentality of the clergy—and especially the hierarchy—were immediately evident. Parish life reflected these changes.

In 2000, the church was no longer that of Pope John XXIII and Vatican II. While in the monastery, I had heard from my priest friends in the parishes as early as the 1980s that the shift in emphasis had begun. This de-emphasis was definitely coming from "on high." Church officials were subtly, but surely, putting a damper on the spirit of the Council.

In the early 1990s, a priest friend and I had the following exchange. One of us began, "Well, the revolution is over . . ." and the other finished, "yes, and we lost." We still debate about who had the punch line; regardless, the "revolution" was the spiritual revolution by Pope John XXIII and his Council. And it was over.

Through the years, there has been little spiritual oxygen to keep the Council's fire alive. By 2000, I saw only a few smoldering embers left in parish life. The fire and light, the spirit, and the joy of the Council were gone.

Even sadder, most of the people living in the heavy and burdensome atmosphere were too young to realize the change that had taken place. They had experienced neither the restrictions of the years before the Council, nor the joys and freedom of the years immediately following. Quite literally, most Catholics today are not old enough to realize what they are missing. They are satisfied with the crumbs, because they never tasted the cake.

Very few are still around who tasted the cake. I was blessed: I lived in those days, and I was in the right place at the right time. The cake was delicious!

There are not many eyewitnesses left—those who were present before, during, and after the Council. Not many are left to tell of the Council's spiritual revolution and of its slow passing. Not many can ask, "What happened to Vatican II?"

This book is not meant to be a scholarly presentation with every statement minutely documented. I am of that age where I can identify with Samuel Butler's remark, "Life is one long process of getting tired." I am getting tired! This book is merely the reflections of an old man who by fate found himself in the midst of theologically exciting and grace-filled times. I am speaking largely from memory, and it has served me surprisingly well! This is not a doctoral dissertation, heavily referenced with sources and footnotes. Besides, most of my personal sources have departed and left me with their words. What follows comes from my head (such as it is) rather than libraries.

My memory, however, is not infallible, and any mistakes are accidental. I have tried to be as truthful as I can be. At this stage in life, what else is important? I am an average person, on all levels, but I was thrust into events in the church's life and met exceptional people along the way. I consider it all a gift.

Looking back, I have had two main interests in life: theology and spirituality. Since I have been married, I have added a third—my wife.

Certainly, throughout my schooling, including college, I was just one of the boys, indistinguishable from the herd. I would have been greatly surprised if someone told me that I had religious leanings. I might even have been insulted—I did not especially care for "religious people." I respected priests, but I didn't idolize them and never thought I wanted to be a priest until shortly before my college graduation.

At that time, I was asking myself: What do I want to do with my life? I decided that I wanted to do something that would benefit people. Doctors, teachers, social workers and others benefit people, but I thought the priesthood would be the most beneficial vocation. So I began seven more years of college to study to be a priest. It was a difficult path! I was especially poor in languages, though I signed up to study Latin, Greek and Hebrew! Truth be told, I didn't really even care that much for school, but I attended for twenty-three consecutive years.

I was not a good student. My home diocese turned me down because of poor grades, even though I had graduated from a respected university. At that time, seminarians were told that because there were so many priests, they probably would never get to be a pastor. So I went to another diocese that was in need of priests.

If you find the following too detailed concerning theological questions and spiritual infighting, you may be right. The spiritual life and its underlying theology should not be complicated. It should be free from strain, simple, and unsophisticated.

Two events reminded me of the simplicity of Christ's message. I am still in contact with my former abbot, and he recently asked me a rhetorical question: "Why do we make religion so complicated?" He went on to answer: "All we have to do is go about our daily lives trying to be as unselfish as possible. It really is that simple."

Through the centuries we have turned something that was intended to be uncomplicated into a labyrinth of laws, customs, and do's/don'ts that would confuse a Wall Street lawyer. Those who listened to that Galilean preacher were not intellectually sophisticated. If he had made things complicated, they would not have followed. Through the years, obviously, there have been accessories added that complicate the simple message of Christ.

That message was brought home to me a few years ago as I was riding with a physician who was taking his sons to school. As each got out, the father said to him, "Remember, do something kind for someone today." I thought, "In all my years of schooling and theological training, no one has ever said that to me. If they had, they would have been doing me a great favor." If you find parts of this book too complicated and polemic, just remember, "Do something kind for someone today," and you will be living the gospel, the good news of Jesus Christ.

# Preface

IN 2013, THE CHURCH elected a pope. Like his namesake, St. Francis, he has thrown his lot in with the poor. Already, Pope Francis is referred to as the Pope of the Poor, condemning the "greed of the marketplace." He has warned against the glorification of individual rights to the neglect of caring for the common good, against the economic exultation of the "I" rather than "we." He has warned of the excesses of capitalism.

He washed the feet of criminals in a prison: a Muslim and a woman. As a cardinal in Brazil, he knelt before a congregation of six thousand Protestants and had Protestant pastors lay hands on him in prayer. He has reiterated the oft-forgotten traditional Catholic teaching that "atheists could find themselves in paradise." These small gestures have sent a big message.

Added to these gestures were his kind words toward homosexuals: "Who am I to judge?" Contrary to Ecclesiastes, there may indeed be something new under the sun! Those five words—"who am I to judge"—contradict two thousand years of judgment and hatred against gay people.

What a difference a few seemingly casual remarks can make. What a difference one man can make in just a few months. Pope Francis already has created a climate very different from one we had been experiencing for much too long.

The pope's inspiring style is a matter of form rather than doctrine. Francis is not about to radically change major doctrines, but he is very much about changing attitudes about how those doctrines are expressed. Some have said that this pope may "not change the words, but he is certainly changing the music." His call for a more understanding response to questions about homosexuality, birth control, and abortion has not been typical of the church in recent years. This pope knows that it is counterproductive—and not Christlike—to present a teaching in a negative or combative way.

Francis' words indicate a willingness to appreciate that well-meaning people may differ in their understanding of these questions. We don't have to agree with them, but neither do we have to damn them to hell because of their honestly held beliefs. For too long, that damning attitude of negativity has been ruling the church and poisoning the atmosphere. It seems this pope is eager now to facilitate a return to the more positive days after Vatican II.

This book is about the need for that change in atmosphere. We have been in a law and policy mode, and we need a return to the spirit and people mode that was prevalent following the Council. This book is saying, "Let's drop the negativity." If I understand Pope Francis correctly, that is what he is saying: "Let's drop the negativity; let's replace judgment with love."

In 1962, in preparation for the Vatican II Council, Pope John XXIII said he wanted to "open the church windows to let some fresh air in." Through the years, the windows that were thrown open at the Council have been slowly, but surely, closing. In the words of my bishop friend, "We have been going backwards."

For too many years, now, the church has again been stuffy. Many are praying for Pope Francis to provide some much-needed oxygen. So far, he has exceeded even the most positive expectations.

Francis belongs to the Jesuit order. Their founder, St. Ignatius of Loyola, said, "The only way we know about God, is through people." The pope has taken those words to heart; consistently, he has shown himself to be a people pope, rather than an institutional pope. Few popes throughout history have stirred the pot as much as Francis. Pope John XXIII (1958–1963), the grace behind Vatican II, is one of those few, and even he did not stir as vigorously.

Francis has publicly condemned the Vatican's "centric view": "Leaders of the church have often been narcissistic, often been flattered and sickeningly excited by their courtiers. That court is the leprosy of the Papacy."[1] To most Catholics it is unthinkable, close to blasphemy, that a pope would call the leaders of the church "narcissistic."

I don't think there is a bishop in this country that would not severely censure a priest making such a statement. In recent years, the litmus test for priests had not been how they served people but whether they were 150 percent company men.

1. Scalfari, "The Pope."

On several occasions, the pope has condemned "clericalism." On one occasion, he went so far as to say that when he meets such a cleric, he "becomes anti-clerical." Note, however, that he didn't say "anti-priest." There is a huge difference between a priest and a cleric. A priest is first a human being; a cleric is first a "churchman." At this time in history, an anti-clerical pope is just what the church needs.

The pope has denounced economic policies that promote "the idolatry of money" and pointed out the fallacy of trickle-down economics, which, in his words, have "never been confirmed by facts." The economic Right is disturbed that he has urged business and political leaders "to be protective of the environment." Wall Street must have quaked at the pope calling unfettered capitalism "the new tyranny unleashed on the world." If nothing else, Francis may cause us to examine economic views that for years have been thought to be "good" and in accord with the gospel. We may find our economic views are far from the gospel message.

The story I like best about Francis concerns his talk with Eugenio Scalfari, a famous Italian journalist who also happens to be atheist. The pope called him—personally, not through an aide. When Scalfari answered the phone he heard, "This is Pope Francis."[2] How many people in all of history can say they ever received such a phone call? The pope suggested that they "get together."

They met later at "Francis' place," and the pope met him with a hug. The pope let him in on a secret: "God is not a Catholic." He went on, "I believe in God, not in a Catholic God."[3]

That settles it—the pope is a heretic!

Francis has set out to do some hard work. He has taken to himself the words of Christ, which tradition says were spoken to St. Francis: "Francis, repair my church."

In the first decade of the thirteenth century, Francis was praying in a broken-down chapel near the town of Assisi in Italy. Three times he heard the words, "Francis, repair my church." Thinking that the words were instructing him to repair the dilapidated structure, he began to repair the church building. Later he realized that he was being called to spiritually repair the Christian church. In the year 1211 he began the religious order that took his name—the Franciscans—who are still active. Even today, they are known for their care for the poor and their efforts for peace. Francis

2. Ibid.
3. Ibid.

became the poorest of the poor, and he visited the Muslim sultan in an effort to end the Crusades.

Among Catholics and Protestants, Francis has become the most beloved saint. He is the poor man who has talked with birds and loved "Sister Sun" and "Brother Moon." He perfectly exemplified the words of Ps 148, which says, "every wild and tame animal, all reptiles and birds, come praise the Lord!" As such, he was the first environmentalist. My wife and I, like many others, have a St. Francis statue in our garden. I am waiting for the day to see a St. Francis statue on Wall Street. I think it is significant that this pope chose the name Francis as he begins to revive Vatican II. Did Pope Francis, as did his namesake, also hear, "Francis, repair my church?"

That Christ wants his church to be repaired may sound strange to us. It shouldn't. The church is always in need of reform. "Ecclesia semper reformanda est" is true for all ages.

*Viva il Papa!*

I left the active priesthood and entered the Abbey of Gethsemani in 1972. There, I was a priest-monk for twenty-eight years. I have not served in the active ministry for over forty years. My knowledge of present parish life comes from my priest friends and my experience being a layperson sitting in the pews for the past fourteen years. Being a layperson for the first time in fifty years has been educational for me.

I do not want to criticize what priests are doing today. As in sports, if you are not playing the game, don't stand on the sidelines and shout instructions to the players. However, Pope Francis has changed the climate completely, opening the way for objective assessment of the church. More than any pope in memory, he has put the spotlight on the church's dark areas. He has given a very severe critique of our present situation. He has spoken pointedly of the areas where the church has not lived up to the ideals of the gospel promoted by Vatican II. In his words, "We have to find a new balance, otherwise even the moral edifice of the church is likely to fall like a house of cards, losing the freshness and fragrance of the gospel."[4]

His evaluation comes from his love of the church and his desire that the church more faithfully fulfill the call to serve her people. His words are not meant to discourage but to encourage. Similar to Pope Francis' approach, I am not criticizing as much as I am revealing the church. I rejoice at the church's successes in serving people, not in the church's failures.

---

4. Spadara, "Big Heart."

# Acknowledgments

Father James Bacik (MS Fordham University, PhD Oxford), who has taught at Catholic Theological Union, Notre Dame, Fordham, and University of San Francisco. For years, he was professor of humanities at Toledo University.

David Burrell (CSC Notre Dame University, Hesburgh professor emeritus in Philosophy and Theology) for his assistance and suggestions. Any theological errors are mine, not David's or Jim's.

William Lammers, my brother-in-law, for his reading and encouragement.

Laura Poncy and all the people at Wipf and Stock Publishers, especially Mary Roth.

Jennifer Stevens for her proofreading, technical, and editorial advice.

# My Religious Background

IN 1972, AT THE age of thirty-nine, I entered a Trappist monastery. While in the monastery, I did not experience the church as a Catholic layperson would, so I was not familiar with what was happening in the parish churches. I returned to society twenty-eight years later. The difference between what I had experienced as a Catholic before I entered the monastery in 1972 and when I left in 2000 was marked. Out of the monastery now for fourteen years, I find myself asking, what happened to the Spirit of Vatican II? The atmosphere has changed completely.

I had twenty-three consecutive years of Catholic education, culminating in my ordination to the priesthood in 1962 for a diocese in the midwest. After doing parish work, I was assigned to religious education; I taught theology. Following ordination, I had seven summers in graduate school: five at Notre Dame for theology, one at Akron University and one at Kent State University—both for education.[5] Notre Dame was influential in my priestly and monastic vocations.

While in the active ministry, I initiated the adult Religious Education Program for the Diocese and wrote the textbook used in the program. I was appointed principal of a Catholic high school. While there, we had more than 1,800 students enrolled.

In 1972, I left the active ministry to fulfill a fifteen-year desire to be a monk. I entered a Trappist monastery, where I lived a very happy and grace-filled twenty-eight years. They were not fault-free, of course. I left the monastery in 2000 with mutual respect and affection. I return often to visit my friends, my former abbot being one of my closest. After leaving monastic life, I met a widow. I received my dispensation, and we were married.

---

5. I had also attended Notre Dame before entering seminary; I received a degree in business in 1956.

## My Religious Background

Presently I am in my eighty-first year as a Catholic. I have lived forty-four years in religious life, thirty-eight of those as a priest. No one ever had a more satisfying priesthood, and for that I am grateful. I enjoyed both my active and contemplative experiences. I can summarize my active ministry and monastic life by saying, "I had fun and laughed a lot."

# Introduction

ABOUT TEN YEARS AGO, my wife and I visited a retired bishop who was living in a nursing home. To the core he was a Vatican II bishop. In the 1960s he started a teachers' union for all the Catholic schoolteachers in the diocese, one of the first in the country. He marched with Martin Luther King Jr. at Selma in 1965. He understood why the council was so necessary and what it was saying.

When I was in the active ministry, he was my immediate boss. We remained good friends, and he would come to see me in the monastery. While visiting him in the nursing home I asked, "What do you think about the direction the church is taking today?" This was his reply: "The church is going backward. Today we are caught up in rules and regulations, and we have forgotten about serving people."

In essence, he was saying that a negative, defensive church has replaced the openness, charity, and general goodwill created by the Second Vatican Council in the early 1960s. Old age offers the freedom to speak the truth!

When leaving, we agreed that I, though I was a layman, would give him my blessing. It was a case, in many people's eyes, of an inferior giving a blessing to a superior. But the bishop never thought in terms of superior and inferior Christians, and our last visit was a grace-filled moment for all three of us. He has since died, and I thought much about him while writing this book. I have tried to be as truthful in my old age as the bishop was in his.

I know he would be pleased at how Pope Francis, in such a short time, has revived the spirit of Vatican II. What follows is a review of what transpired between the end of that Council in 1965 and the arrival of Pope Francis. This was almost fifty years that I experienced very intensely. There is ample evidence that during that time the church had indeed "gone backward" and "forgotten about serving people." Now a new spring has arisen, as Pope Francis revives Vatican II.

While being truthful, I also need to be respectful. I have great affection for those I lived and worked with in the active ministry and later in the monastery. As a priest in high school work, I was privileged to be associated with outstanding individuals, priests and nuns, laypeople, and students. Later, in monastic life, that privilege continued with the monks.

I do not want to offend priests or monks, as I hold both in high esteem. I want the story of my active priesthood and my monastic life to be a story of gratitude. It has been a story of grace upon grace. That life of grace has continued during my thirteen years of marriage. To have one grace-filled vocation is a gift; to have had three is a gift incalculable.

# 1

# The Church, Past and Present

## My Active Ministry

THE SECOND VATICAN COUNCIL brought tremendous changes that affected how priests carried out their ministry. To give just one example, in the council documents, the common name "church" was often replaced with the expression "people of God." This linguistic shift was earthshakingly significant. When the word "church" was used, it conjured up the church hierarchy and structures with its rules and obligations. "The church says," or, "The church has spoken" (*Roma locutus est*) was the historical format for proclaiming church laws. For most people, the word church signifies a structure or institution, but not people. By using the term "people of God," the image of "church" became personal and alive. It applied a human face to the institutional church, and we began to realize that we, and those next to us, *are* the church.

It was from the council that "compassionate Catholicism" emerged. Serving people became important, and the priests were to be the carriers of that message of service. And for the first time in church history, other religious traditions began to be respected. Efforts were made to connect with people of other Christian traditions and even with non-Christians, whereas before, in Good Friday services, the church had prayed for the "faithless Jews." In the 1960s, Pope John XXIII dropped that derogatory line from the liturgy. I remember that even as a young person that "prayer" in church made me cringe. But it didn't seem to bother the priests who were leading the liturgy. And why should it have? For years, hostile language directed toward people of other faiths was the accepted practice.

At the Council of Trent (in the mid-1600s), all the positions taken by the Protestants were named. Then it was added that anyone who holds these positions, *"anathema sit,"* which in English is roughly "let him go to Hell." After Vatican II, however, we called Protestants our "separated brethren" and shared pulpits with Protestant ministers. That was a big change!

Before the council, those of non-Christian faith were below contempt. The church didn't tell them to go to hell, because the church believed they were already there. Anti-Semitic violence through the ages is the saddest mark on Christian history. It seemed that the only point that Catholics and Protestants agreed upon was their hatred of the Jews:

> St. Augustine: "How hateful to me are the enemies of your Scripture. How I wish that you would slay them [the Jews] with your two-edged sword, so that there should be none to oppose your word."[1]

> Martin Luther: "Jewish homes should be destroyed, their synagogues destroyed."[2]

> John Calvin: "The Jews' rotten and unbending stiff-neckedness deserves that they be oppressed unendingly and without measure and that they die in their misery, without pity from anyone."[3]

> St. John Chrysostom ("Golden Mouth"): "The synagogue is a place of meeting for assassins of Christ."[4]

In 1492, Catholic Spain expelled all Jews who refused to be baptized. In Germany, the soil that gave nourishment to the right-wing insanity of the Nazi era was fertile for centuries. Germany was a Christian country, about half Protestant and half Catholic. Yet in the 1930s, Germany, Catholic Spain, and Italy all went Fascist.

The Christian Orthodox record was just as despicable. Under the Russian czars, anti-Jewish pogroms were the rule. Roman and Orthodox Catholics, along with the majority of Protestant churches, all have a hideous record of anti-Semitism. The Jews were "Christ killers"—scripture "proved it." In Matthew's Gospel: "Let his (Christ's) blood be upon us and

---

1. Augustine, *Confessions*, 12:14.
2. Luther, "On the Jews and Their Lies," in *Luther's Works*.
3. Cited in Falk, *Jew in Christian Theology*.
4. Cited in Hay, *Thy Brother's Blood*.

our children." As Hitler asked: "Why should the church criticize our treatment of the Jews? The church had them living in ghettos for centuries."

Pope John Paul II repeatedly condemned and apologized for the church's shameful treatment of the Jews throughout history. He had seen it firsthand in Poland, where he saw the Jewish ghettos long before the Germans came.

Pope John Paul II is greatly regarded by the Jews, but Pope Pius XII is greatly scorned. It was he who signed the Concordance between the church and Nazi Germany in the 1930s. His refusal to condemn the Holocaust, or to even mention it, is incomprehensible to many still today. That papal silence is another story, which will not be fully told until the church opens all the archives of that period.

This aside on the history of Christian anti-Semitism is an important backdrop to understanding the extent of the Vatican II radicalism. It was truly revolutionary, and in no way is that more evident than in the church's attitude toward non-Christians. At the council, for the first time in church history, Jews and Muslims were referred to as "our brothers" because we all have the same father, "our Father Abraham." The council also mentioned atheists with respect and consideration. Such consideration was practically unheard in previous council documents.

The younger priests led the way in this ecumenical movement with Protestants and non-Christians, treading on new ground. It was difficult for older Catholics, including older priests, to have "a feel" for ecumenism. We younger people felt at home with its spirit.

My ministry typified the type of ministry prevalent following the Second Vatican Council among young priests. We were the young Turks! It was a time of change, and we worked hard, with long hours. Adults had to be updated in their theology and spirituality. High school students needed education. (In the mid-1960s, more students attended Catholic schools than ever had before or have since.)

We preached the social gospel, stressing that to be a Christian meant more than spending one hour in church Sunday morning.

We were involved in issues that priests never had been involved in before. We questioned the morality of the Vietnam War, proposing that it was not Christian to say, "my country, right or wrong." Many of our people had never been taught that before. The peace activists, Father Daniel Berrigan and the monk/priest Thomas Merton, were our idols—both had been harassed for their anti-war activities in their own times. Father Berrigan was even on the FBI's Ten Most Wanted list.

For us, having Richard Nixon, Spiro Agnew, and J. Edgar Hoover against you was a badge of honor and a sure sign that you were preaching the gospel. Their behavior was anything but gospel-like. Former Attorney General John Mitchell was in jail. Agnew and Nixon could have been in jail, and Hoover should have been in jail for his harassment of Martin Luther King Jr. and other civil rights supporters—many priests among them.

Social justice meant justice for farm workers, so we protested the unfair labor practices of the large lettuce and grape corporations. No self-respecting young priest ate lettuce or grapes as long as workers were being deprived.

During those days, one of the great joys was leading the liturgy. Rather than being frowned upon, innovation was encouraged, and people were excited about worshiping in their own language. For the first time in history, young people felt they were a welcome part of worship. The clergy and laity wanted young people to understand and participate in the Mass.

I was privileged to be a part of young people's liturgy during my high school work. Every morning we would roll a table, an "altar," out onto the gym floor where there had been a game, a dance or bingo the night before, and we would have Mass for the students. In the mid-1960s, we had more than 1,800 students plus seventy faculty, so at times, we would have 1,900 people in that gym. All would be sitting, not kneeling, in the bleachers.

In the early fall, when it was still hot, liturgy was a very "earthy" experience. The Mass was optional. The first period of the day was study hall, and kids could either go to study hall or Mass. It was edifying how many gave up their study hall to attend Mass. They were amazingly well behaved. Whether they were devotional or just afraid of me is another question.

We had a school mascot, a dog, who would roam the halls all day. He would lie over in the corner and sleep, and never once did he come up for communion. Everyone else did, though; every human soul in the gym took communion. As we had only fifty-five minutes to get them in and out of there, we skipped the formalities.

Was that Mass "high church"? Not really. There was no incense, no cassocks. The servers often were girls, and that was long before the church allowed girls to be "altar boys." One day two girls walked up to the altar, and presto! We had altar girls. I didn't interrupt Mass to stop them, and none of the faculty objected. Maybe breaking the rule of boy servers was that girl's conversion into the ways of righteousness. Historically, that is the way liturgical rules have been changed. People just do things differently.

Another example of people changing church laws is the law concerning women having their heads covered while attending Mass or entering a church. Before the 1960s you never saw a woman in a Catholic church without a hat or scarf. The practice was based on St. Paul's words, "a woman must have her head covered while praying" (1 Cor 11:13). The Bible says so! This law presented a problem. Our girls didn't wear hats to school, so would they be able to attend Mass bareheaded? If they did, how serious was that sin? To comply with church law, the girls purchased lace doilies to cover their heads at the school Masses. If a girl forgot to bring her doily, she put a handkerchief on top of her head.

It was an ungodly sight, to be saying Mass and looking out over the "congregation," with those nine hundred girls with those doilies perched precariously on their heads! What nonsense we endured following man-made religious laws. The girls gradually stopped covering their heads, and it became a non-issue. Females having their heads covered went out of practice.

A priest told me he was saying Mass in France, and a woman in the congregation was changing a baby's diaper. When services were not being held, a street woman would come in to get out of the cold and change her clothes in the confessional. Then she would wash her things in the holy water font. She was very considerate and would wait until the church was empty to come in and tidy up. The word liturgy literally means "the work of the people." The French Mass with the woman and baby was truly the work of the people; the street woman and all like her are the church; the kids sitting on bleachers in a sweaty gym are the church. The clergy must never forget that truth.

The young clergy had fun! The gospel of joy was "in." We laughed a lot. We laughed with the anti-establishment TV show *Laugh In*. We laughed at the bigoted Archie Bunker of *All in the Family*. We laughed at ourselves.

In our exuberance we, like young King David, felt free enough to dance naked before the Ark of the Covenant. We were convinced we were ushering in a new era of tolerance and acceptance, both in the church and society.

If there ever was a case of the "inmates taking over the asylum," that was it. But ironically, our craziness did create, for a time, a kinder and more caring asylum. That was a "long time ago." To paraphrase a Pete Seeger song:

> Where have all the young men gone?
> Long time passing.

Where have all the young men gone?
Long time ago.

The attitude of "people before rules" became prevalent after the council. Spirit, rather than law, was the prevalent mindset, and priests were to be examples of Christ's spirit.

While I agreed with that emphasis, I must confess that in one stage of my career, I violated the "people before rules" attitude. It was the late 1960s and early 1970s, and I was a principal of a large Catholic high school. The school had a long tradition of excellence going back to the early 1900s, and I was determined that reputation was not going to be tarnished under my watch. The school's reputation became more important to me than any particular student's welfare.

I was wearing two hats, my bad-guy hat while a school principal and my good-guy hat while dealing with adults. I justified my ways at school by thinking they were "only kids." I felt I had to keep them in line so that teachers would have a teachable atmosphere. Also, I was too young to be a principal of such a large school, and I wanted to make everything and everyone perfect. Youthful idealism can be blinding and sometimes unkind.

Looking back at those times, I often sided with the school rather than with the troublesome student. I got my priorities confused and too often was harsh. I regret some of my behavior and my bad temper, and there are situations I would redo if I could. Making things difficult for kids is not something to look back upon with pride when you're in your eighties.

The mid-1960s were difficult times in high school work. Anti-war feelings, the civil rights movement, the changes in the church, and the beginning of the drug culture were all reflected in student life. Our high school was not far from Kent State University, the site of the 1970 shootings, which have been labeled "The May Fourth Massacre." Thirteen students were shot, four of them died, and I knew one of the students who was wounded.

The evening of the shooting, I was with him and the other casualties in the hospital's intensive care unit. One of my closest priest friends had been in the emergency room as the wounded were brought in. "There was blood everywhere," he said. "I didn't want to get in the way, so I anointed and gave absolution to all thirteen and got out of there. There wasn't time to ask if each was a Catholic. Besides, most of them couldn't speak."

In those days, a priest didn't look in a rulebook to see who could be served. He just tried to be Christlike.

A year later, I had a similar situation at our school. A father came to the school and shot his son and himself. After I anointed them, I went to their home to tell his wife. I found that he had also shot her and their younger son. Like my priest friend, I didn't ask questions. I administered to them. All four died.

I relive those experiences every time there is a school shooting. I get more and more angry at the insanity of our country's gun laws. When it comes to guns, why are we the least sane of the first-world nations? There are approximately 300 million guns in circulation in our country. As of November 2013, there were around 315 million people in the United States, including the children and the elderly. Is it any wonder that our murder rate is off the charts? Every year, there are twice as many bullets manufactured as there are people in the world. The munitions industry is more "productive" than God! In my frustration, I wrote to President Barack Obama. Much to my surprise, he responded with a two-page, personal letter. It read in part:

> Dear John:
>
> Thank you for taking the time to write. I am deeply saddened to learn of the pain you have experienced. I have heard from many Americans regarding firearms policy and gun violence in our Nation, and I appreciate your perspective. From Aurora to Newtown to the streets of Chicago, we have seen the devastating effects gun violence has on our American family.
>
> Like the majority of Americans, I believe the Second Amendment guarantees an individual right to bear arms. Yet, even as we acknowledge that almost all gun owners in America are responsible, when we look at the devastation caused by gun violence, we must ask ourselves whether we are doing enough.

I also received a letter from the First Lady. I found both the President's and First Lady's responses to be compassionate, fair, and well balanced.

I do not find the National Rifle Association compassionate, fair, or well balanced. The NRA is correct in proclaiming that the Constitution allows civilians to bear firearms, but after that, they lose any semblance of honesty or even common sense.

What kind of firearms did the framers of the Constitution have in mind? They had the only firearms they knew: a musket, which could shot one ball a minute, two if you were fast. The Second Amendment allows for that type of firearm, and, in 1776, such a provision made sense—people hunted game for food. Allowing a citizen to have a firearm was important for survival. Daniel Boone needed a firearm!

It is obvious that when the framers of the Constitution allowed for civilians to carry firearms, they had muskets in mind, not machine guns, automatic weapons or assault rifles. To stretch the meaning of the founding fathers from muskets to weapons that can shoot more than five hundred bullets a minute, with each bullet having infinitely more killing power than a musket ball, is just that—a stretch. It's a stretch into insanity or dishonesty, or both!

I have been present at shooting deaths in a high school. I have seen college kids shot with military rifles. Military bullets make big holes. I continually ask myself, "How long will this sickening love affair between Americans and guns continue?"

While the slaughter of the innocent increases, the NRA loudly proclaims the "freedom" granted to them by the Constitution. Is it truly freedom to be able to walk into a gun show or get online and, with no background check, purchase weapons capable of wiping out small towns? Is it freedom or callousness, maybe sinful indifference?

Every attempt by President Obama to correct this insane license for Americans to walk around armed like Rambo is blocked. Congress—waving the American flag and consorting with the munitions dealers—defeats the bill.

Wikipedia gives the following statistics concerning the homicide rate worldwide. Most countries forbid their citizens to carry guns, and the difference between those countries and ours is shocking. The homicide rate per every 100,000 people is as follows:

Hong Kong: .03

Japan: .06

Spain: .06

England: .25

Poland: .25

Italy: 1

Germany: 1

America: 9

America's homicide rate is nine times greater than that in Germany and Italy, thirty-six times greater than that in England and Poland and fifty-six times greater than that in Japan and Spain.

I don't understand those figures. The "cruel" Spanish kill bulls. We kill people! How can we explain that contrast? Are Americans innately more violent than the Japanese and the Spaniards? Or does it have more to do with the ridiculously easy access to guns?

The pro-gun platform says that reducing access to guns will not stop the killing because criminals will still get guns. The statistics above prove just the opposite; denying access to guns does reduce the killing.

Japan is a much more crowded country than the United States, yet our killing rate is fifty-six times higher than theirs. Why do other countries have such a lower rate of homicides? Because in other countries you can't stop into the corner store and buy a gun. Why is that so difficult to understand? We kill more primarily because we have more guns.

There may be another influencing factor to why our killing rate is off the charts — money, old-fashioned greed. "The love of money is the root of all evil" (1 Tim 6:10). Historically, the greatest reason for shedding blood can be followed back to money. I suspect the killing will continue as long as an obscene amount of money is being made in the gun and ammunition business.

In America, it does not appear that pattern is going to change anytime soon; at least, not if the NRA and the munitions industry supported by their political lackeys have their way. Too much money is being made! At the root of the matter, it seems as if we may not have a gun problem as much as a money problem!

Is America's gun question really about the Constitution? Is defending the "freedom granted by the Constitution" merely a convenient cover for greed? I have asked myself that question since that night forty-four years ago in the hospital near Kent, Ohio.

The day after the Kent State shootings, two neighboring high schools called off classes for fear that student uprisings would breed dysfunction. We stayed open and had a normal school day. To control any possible unrest, I felt I had to keep a tight lid on the school. I practiced absolute dictatorship over those poor teenagers in "bondage," running the school like something between a Marine boot camp and the Bataan Death March. My mentors? Captain Bly and Attila the Hun!

I did have a great advantage, however, in our school's outstanding faculty. We had seven priests, about twenty-five sisters, and forty male and female lay teachers. Everyone worked hard. The faculty, the priests and nuns, and the office personnel worked selflessly, going far beyond the call of duty. No principal ever had a better faculty or kids to work with. I accommodated the adults; I dominated the kids.

They were excellent teachers, and we had a lot of fun with each other and the students. The priests lived in a faculty house, and acted like the Marx brothers at the zoo—all day long. This carried over into the school, and the kids were sucked up in the "healthy craziness."

I once had a parent ask: "What are you people doing there? My kids can't wait to go to school. They say they have fun." So I knew the kids were happy, no matter how dictatorial I was. Many people, especially the parents, applauded my efforts. From their perspective, I was a success.

Personally, however, I was beginning to feel I was "gaining the whole world but suffering the loss of my soul." I was getting caught up in power. Granted, it was for the good, but power nevertheless. I was involved in "good power."

Thanks be to God, I began to see that "good power" is an oxymoron. Power is the antithesis of the gospel, and it is intoxicating. We like to feel powerful, and that "liking" is the soul's destruction. Lord Acton rightly states, "Power tends to corrupt. Absolute power corrupts absolutely."

I began to revisit the attraction to monastic life that I had sixteen years before, when I entered the seminary in 1956. Thomas Merton, the famous monk author, wrote: "The very essence of monastic life is the renunciation of the capacity to exercise power. A monk does not want to be a self that is a source of power that can move (others). Monks are not 'movers and shakers.' (In this sense) monastic life is useless, not pragmatic. A monk's life is not for producing results, even spiritual results."[5] Merton's idea of spiritual power being the most insidious is akin to Edmund Burke's idea that "the greater the power, the more dangerous the abuse." Certainly having spiritual power over people is the most dangerous of all.

I found Merton's approach to the idea of power to be unique among spiritual writers and speakers. He renounces even "spiritual power," and, in this, he parts ways with most religious thinkers. Instead of seeing monks as those who spend their lives praying to make the world better, he sees their spiritual life as one of total receptivity. When it comes to God, monks don't do anything; rather, they receive everything. His idea of monasticism as being passive and receptive is similar to the Buddhist idea. He thought favorably of Buddhism and had met the Dalai Lama.

5. *Tape 9.*

While I was in the monastery, the Dalai Lama visited twice. Once, he brought about a dozen monks with him, and they stayed for a week, living and meditating with us. We didn't worry about theological differences; we were all communing with the same God called by different names. Catholic monks and Buddhist monks have much in common and get along well. In fact, they get along better than most Christian denominations get along with each other.

Also in the monastery, I worked with those who came for a spiritual retreat. There were about ninety or so each week, and only about two-thirds were Catholic. A few were referred to themselves as "nonbelievers" or called themselves agnostic. Agnostics don't say there is or is not a God; they are neutral on the subject, and I respect their honesty. After hearing some of the things that they were told about God in their youth, I understood why they were agnostic. Indeed, I wondered that they were not out-and-out atheist. Sadly, we Christians don't advertise God very well, often clothing him with our bigotry and ignorance.

Many who call themselves atheists aren't really denying God; they are denying the "God" that is taught by some Christians. For the sake of intellectual honesty, one would almost have to renounce that kind of "God." Einstein believed in a supreme reality. He did not object to God, but he did object to the way people try to explain God. He was too bright and honest to accept the foolishness rampant in the common explanation of God. In his time, Jesus rejected the common understanding of God and paid the consequences.

I am confident that the biggest threat to Christianity is not the atheist, but the misguided Christian. How many people do you know who left the church because of what an atheist said or did? Probably none. But how many have left the church because of what a Christian said or did? That number is beyond counting. Active priests frequently hear, "Father, I was a Catholic, but I had this experience and I left the practice of religion altogether." Notice they didn't say, "I left God" or "I abandoned spirituality." They just leave the negativity that is so often associated with the practice of religion.

People leave the church because they see the church as usurping power. This is why the witness of monks as being powerless is necessary for a church that is always tempted to employ power. Churches want to use power for the sake of God, even though "power for the sake of God" is a contradiction in terms.

In a later chapter, we will speak more about monastic spirituality. The "monk's God" respects free will to an alarming degree. God is a free Being who extends that freedom to his/her creatures. God "lets be." We see people using their free will for destructive purposes toward themselves and others (Hitler, etc.), and we cannot understand why God doesn't use his power to change destructive wills. I think the answer is that God is "the Being who lets be." This non-forceful God is the God of the monks. They pattern their spirituality after the God who "lets be."

Monks are very much in tune with Pope Francis—they don't try to convert anyone, they do not proselytize. The pope said, "Our goal is not to proselytize, but to listen to people."[6] A monk is primarily a listener. His job is to listen while others are busy doing.

## Yesterday's Church

In the years following the council, the emphasis was on the Eucharist being a celebration of the community and for the community. The priest is the representative and symbol of the community: what he does, the community does; what the priest says, the community says. It is said that the priest represents Christ; that is true, but that statement is incomplete and misleading. The priest represents Christ because he represents the community, and the community is the body of Christ.

Liturgical rules and laws are important, but they must always be seen as a means to better the celebration of the community gathered around the altar. Church laws are secondary to the needs of the people. That is as it was in the church immediately following the council.

One Saturday evening in 1970, two nuns and I visited a couple who lived in the country. Snow began to fall, and we knew that our friends would never be able to get to Mass the next morning. The charitable thing to do was to have Mass for them that evening at their home.

We didn't have altar wine, the Missal, altar bread, a chalice, or vestments. And none of us saw any problem with those limitations. After all, we had people, the essential ingredient for Mass. The hostess cut bread into small squares. We had wine and a Bible for the readings. I knew the Eucharistic Prayer, at least substantially. I missed some words, but not the essential ones. Sitting around the dining room table, which became for us the "table of the Lord," we celebrated our communion in Christ.

6. Scalfari, "The Pope."

While exchanging the Eucharist, I saw the dog sitting up begging. No, I did not give him communion. I do follow some rules. However, I did say to him, "I'm sorry I can't give you communion since you are not a Catholic in good standing." Sweet Jesus, just what do those words mean? Whoever came up with the line "Catholic in good standing" should be drowned in the holy water font during the Easter Vigil.

How easily we forget that Mass is for the people, by the people, and from the people. A priest who speaks about saying "his Mass" does not understand his relationship to the community gathered around the altar. It is not his Mass; it is our Mass.

Looking back on our snowy Saturday evening Mass, what is significant is that no one thought it unusual. We just understood that it was the charitable, Catholic thing to do. People, priests, and even the bishops of that time would have not taken notice because, in those days, the church's mindset was "people before policy."

That night in the 1970s, we put the needs and wishes of people before liturgical rules. The Mass is for the people, and we did not allow liturgical rules to distract us from that. If we had gotten caught up with the kind of bread, the type of wine, the vestments worn, we would have been falling into the same trap as did the clergy at the time of Christ.

Christ severely criticized the Pharisees for doing that very thing. It is the people, the body of Christ that matters, not the regulations.

I don't think priests today would have conducted that "snowed-in liturgy." Or if they had, they would be in serious trouble. There are so many rules concerning gestures, words, types of chalice, etc., that there is no way that even the Last Supper could passed the requirements for today's "legitimate Mass."

Priests today, however, may have to relax their rigidity. Recently, I read where Catholic traditionalists are criticizing Pope Francis for the simple way he celebrates Mass, for how he doesn't get caught up in the pomp of the ritual. He would have fit right in as a 1960s priest. (In fact, he was, having been ordained in 1969.) I don't know, though, if today's younger priests would fit right in. Today's younger clergy has a fondness for a more formal, High Church liturgy, and were appalled at Pope Francis' placing a prized soccer ball on the altar during the offertory at Mass. Far Right Catholics responded to the pope's actions as expected: "That is sacrilegious," and they referred to him as the anti-pope.

For Eucharist at the monastery, we used bread that beautifully expressed the theology of communion, that is, the oneness of people with each other and with Christ. At Mass, we used a large host, which was made by the monks in the shape of a large pizza. It was corrugated, making it easy for the celebrant to break off pieces so the ministers could distribute them.

That communion was both theologically and experientially correct in that you could see and experience that the community was sharing the one bread, the one Christ. As St. Paul said, "We are one body because we share the One Bread" (1 Cor 10:17). Notice St. Paul said One Bread, not individual wafers, which have about as much substance to them as cotton candy.

Church authorities eventually made us stop using that bread because it was "not the right type of bread." The monastery had to return to small individual hosts that neither look nor taste like bread. With these "official" hosts, a person needs two acts of faith; first, that it is bread and second, that it is Christ. For me, the first requires much more faith.

The monks had used a beautifully crafted and stained wooden chalice made by a monk. Today, that also is a liturgical "no-no," and church authorities made the monks go back to golden chalices. Why the church wants to put Christ in gold is a mystery to me. I imagine that the church today would not tolerate the Last Supper with poor bread, poor clothes, poor drinking cups, and poor people.

Legality wins again. Institutions must have laws, but it is the priority placed upon them that is of significance. Liturgical rules can be easily overemphasized, and when that happens, the Mass becomes a performance judged on its aesthetics.

Watching a priest preside at Mass, you can tell if he understands the role of the community in what he is doing. His mannerisms, gestures, tone of voice are indications of how he regards the community he faces. He is leading the people of God of which he is a part, not conducting a personal meditation. He must never see himself above, or separate from, the community.

When the altars were turned around in the 1960s, and the priests had to face the people, it was difficult for many priests and downright traumatic for some. I had only said Mass with my back to the people for a couple of years, so I had not been hardened in the old way. I welcomed the chance to communicate with the people.

With your back to the people, you were in your own little world, facing the wall. You could blow your nose, yawn, scratch, and motion to the altar boys and no one could see you. It was a "private Mass," and therein was the pitfall. It was not supposed to be the priest's private Mass. So when the priest faced the people, he realized all at once he had to be a communicator instead of a navel-gazer. He had to realize that it is our Mass, not his personal Mass.

When a priest would say, "I don't like saying Mass facing the people; people distract me," I would say to myself, "Buddy, I think your vocation is to be a scuba diver, not a priest." There was a different mentality between the older and younger priests as to just what the Mass was supposed to signify and what the people's role in their Mass should be.

All things considered, though, young and old priests got along amazingly well—they had their birettas, and we had our Steelers stocking caps. They didn't like folk Masses, and we didn't like indulgences, so they didn't come to our folk Mass, and we didn't go to their "Mother of Sorrow" novenas. We all decided to just "let be."

The priesthood was the common bond that tied us all together. Our theological differences didn't stop us from partying together. It is a healthy priesthood when priests can party together and have a good time; I hope priests today still do that, because that support group is very important to their spiritual life. One of the tragic results of today's priest shortage is the lack of opportunity for priestly camaraderie. That can spell trouble for priests of all ages, but especially for the young. Priests need other priests to share confidentialities, and they can't do that with laity—no matter how friendly and good they are.

## Today's Church

I have perceived a significant difference between the church I served until 1973 and the church I have experienced since my return to parish life in 2000. In the late 1960s and early 1970s, while still in the fervor of Vatican II, the church's emphasis was on enabling the "people of God" to reach their full potential as Christians.

Since then, and my older priest friends agree, the emphasis has been on preserving the church as an institution. Before Francis, you could feel the institutional atmosphere descending like a fog. I am speaking more about an organizational climate, about policies, than I am about individual clerical behavior. There have always been, and there will always be, good and dedicated bishops and priests who put people first and are dedicated to service. I believe many, if not all, of the church leaders had tightened down the lid on the spirit of the council.

Prior to Francis, the joy and spontaneity of the immediate post-council years appeared to have disappeared, even among the good and generous ordinary Catholics. Maybe my years in the active ministry were so happy that I was unrealistic in looking for that same happiness and enthusiasm in others. Upon returning from the monastery, I certainly did not see it.

Monks experience a greater sense of freedom than I saw in lay Catholics in general. The abbot tells the monks that they come to a monastery to "get free for the Lord." More than once, I heard my abbot say, "If, after prayer, this is what you think you should do, then you should do it." His advice echoes St. Augustine's famous words, "Love God and do what you will." Those words are not frequently spoken from our pulpits, for it is feared that they will lead to chaos. But true freedom is rooted in the love of God, who first loves us—otherwise we could never love him. So if God does not fear freedom, neither should we.

Legalism is the conviction that we are made good by following laws. Christ criticized that attitude by showing us that it is God's love, and not the observance of laws, that transforms us. Laws are indeed necessary, but they are not life-giving, and church-constructed laws must be subservient to God's love.

Before Francis, there was a legalism afloat in the church that was not present in the years immediately following Vatican II. Some examples of that legalism—that "rules before people" attitude—follow.

Recently, I was a patient in a hospital. Upon entering, I registered as a Catholic, and the next morning a Eucharistic minister came to my room. Before giving me communion, he asked, "Are you a Catholic in good standing?" I truly didn't know whether to laugh or cry! In thirty-eight years of giving and seventy years of receiving the sacrament I had never asked nor been asked that question. I thought: "Good Lord, in our zeal for correctness, has it come to this? It is time for me to die."

"Catholic in good standing" has become a magical phrase that automatically opens or closes the gates of heaven to the "worthy" or "unworthy," and that was a misguided question for a minister to ask someone who is lying sick in a hospital bed.

If I wanted to answer according to Canon Law, I would have said, "I have no canonical impediments, and to answer your question in any other sense would be inappropriate." That is an unkind, smart aleck answer and hard to articulate while sitting on a bedpan. So I merely sighed a weak, "Yes, I guess I am."

However, I didn't feel any resentment toward the Eucharistic minister. He was unaware that his question was ill advised. He was a good man who was just doing what he was told by people who should have known better.

Three months later, I had a chance meeting with that Eucharistic minister. My wife and I were serving spaghetti at our church's benefit supper, and I saw him coming down the line. He did not recognize me, as I do not look the same when I am clothed, without dangling tubes.

I was tempted to say, "I am sorry, but before I can give you spaghetti I have been instructed to ask, 'Are you a Catholic in good standing?'" I didn't, and I even served him a double portion. By doing so, did I violate my office of "spaghetti minister"? Was I encouraging "interfaith communion"? God forbid!

In the late nineties, I was the retreat master at the monastery. We had about ninety retreat participants a week; usually thirty or so were not Catholic, but communion was given to all who approached. The same was done while I was a diocesan priest in the seventies, but that spirit of acceptance has changed. I do not think the monastery has open communion any longer. Somewhere, some cassock-clad clerics—church lawyers who never did a day's work serving people in a parish—decided that such unconditional acceptance is not Christlike.

Once again, religious correctness has trumped charity. The Scribes and Pharisees mentality, present in every religion, has taken over, and law supersedes the love of Christ. Depressingly, such inquisitional questioning and exclusions are becoming common in today's church. A priest friend from Michigan related this story: "A dark-skinned woman approached to receive communion, and the priest asked her, 'Are you a baptized Catholic?'"

She was. She also was the only dark-skinned person in the church and the only one asked that question, which made it even more offensive. The woman was visibly shaken. My friend added, "I could tell you more horror stories, but what's the use?"

The most laughable story is about a woman wanting to have her throat blessed. She, also, was asked by the priest, "Are you a Catholic?" A person nearby said, "Father, she has a throat."

When Christ approached the Samaritan woman or the Roman centurion, he didn't ask, "Are you a Jew in good standing?" He knew they weren't, but he served them anyway—much to the dismay of the religious authorities.

Whatever happened to the idea that the church is "the refuge of sinners?" Christ welcomed sinners, but today we kick them out. One of Pope John XXIII's first public appearances was a visit to a prison and a reform school. He said, "You couldn't come to me, so I came to you." Upon becoming pope, Francis repeated that gesture.

"I came to you." In communion, it is well to remember that it is not that we first come to Christ but that Christ comes to us. Christ's love is larger than our puny hearts, and we must not hinder his coming. Christ comes to whom he wills, and he wills to come to all—disregarding our theological correctness. Thank God!

The church's first obligation is to follow the spirit of Christ, which translates into following the spirit, rather than the letter, of the law. Charity must always come before man-made rules.

As Pope Francis wrote in *The Joy of the Gospel* in November 2013: "A pastoral ministry in a missionary style is not obsessed with the disjointed transmission of a multitude of doctrines (rules) to be insistently imposed, which distracts from the Gospel's primary invitation to respond to the God of love who saves us."[7]

## Interfaith Communion

I sometimes see in funeral leaflets, "Only properly disposed Catholics (Catholics in good standing) may receive communion." This forbids my wife, who is a much better Christian than I, from receiving communion at my funeral. Death is the special time of union, yet at that unique time, the church forbids it.

The two objections usually given for interfaith communion—lack of understanding and lack of unity—are not only rationally flawed but also contrary to the spirit of Christ.

About lack of understanding, it is said that, "Protestants don't have the same understanding of the Eucharist as do Catholics." What is the average Catholic's understanding of the Eucharist? You can get as many answers to that question as there are people in the church. A ten-year-old Catholic receiving communion has an understanding that is incomplete, at best, yet we allow children to receive.

Some Catholics' understanding of the Eucharist is so bizarre that it approaches cannibalism. Do we really eat the liver, kidney, and toenails of

7. Francis, *Joy*.

Christ? To listen to some you would think so, and we allow such misinformed Catholics to receive communion while we refuse a knowledgeable Protestant.

To deny our separated brethren communion because they don't have the same understanding of the Eucharist as we do is uncalled for. It also may very well be a religious sin, which is always the worst kind.

Christ didn't drive people away because they didn't have a perfect understanding of him. Nobody had such an understanding—they didn't then, nor do they now. Do we think Christ is offended because everyone's understanding of the Eucharist does not measure up to the Council of Trent's explanation from the 1550s?

Christ and his disciples, not being Greek philosophers, could not have answered the question about the nature of the Eucharist the way the church does today. They, and the early Christians, did not know Aristotelian philosophy, whose terminology is presently used to explain the Eucharist.

In describing the Eucharist, the first time the words "substance, accidents, and transubstantiation" were used was by St. Thomas Aquinas in the thirteenth century. The Fourth Lateran Council in 1215 was the first time they were even mentioned by the church. It wasn't until the Council of Trent in the mid-sixteenth century that they became official.

For the majority of its history, the Catholic Church never used philosophical words such as "substance, accidents, and transubstantiation" in its teaching of the Eucharist. For centuries, Christians partook of the Eucharist never having heard these words, much less understanding them.

Why do we demand that Protestants understand these words today when most Catholics do not? Martin Luther believed in the real presence of Christ in the Eucharist, but he rejected using philosophical words to explain it. He said simply, "Christ is truly present in the Eucharist." That is the point of our faith, and that is good enough! If we are going to exclude from communion all those who don't have a philosophical understanding of transubstantiation, we will have to exclude legions of Catholics, including some clergy. Not to mention that we would have to exclude the apostles and Christ himself.

A person doesn't have to have a philosophy degree to receive communion. She doesn't have to understand how the presence comes about in philosophical terms. She just has to believe that, as Luther said, "Christ is truly present in the Eucharist." Those clergymen who demand more details and theological explanations have adopted the legalism of the clergymen of old—the Scribes and Pharisees: "Woe to you Scribes and Pharisees you shut up the Kingdom of heaven to men. Woe to you Scribes and Pharisees you strain out a gnat and swallow a camel" (Matt 23:4).

Denying interfaith communion because Protestants "don't understand communion the way Catholics do" is another example of not appreciating people's needs and situations, of being theologically correct rather than being Christlike. Toward the end of my priestly vocation, I was not making the mistake about interfaith communion. A better understanding of the sacraments and the importance of extending Christ's love enabled me to grow.

The second objection to allowing Protestants to take communion with Catholics is that communion is a sign of unity, of oneness, and that we can't share that sign of oneness until we are, in fact, one.

Some would say we couldn't share the Eucharist until we are all one Catholic Church. We *are* one, though—not on the institutional level, but on the spiritual and mystical level, which is the most significant. It is the mystical body of Christ that is one, and we can't fracture that body, that oneness of Christ. Communion is not understood or shaped in terms of the institution; the institution should be understood and shaped in terms of communion. Communion goes beyond institutional boundaries.

We can't harness the body of Christ. All baptized persons are in the body of Christ. The Didache, the oldest Christian writing after the New Testament, allows all "who have been baptized" to receive communion. That is significant. At that time, there was much disagreement about the Christian faith. Just as there are today, there were various understandings about Jesus and his message. This first Christian catechism insists that all be allowed to receive communion "who have been baptized." Why can't we be as inclusive today?

We must also remember when speaking of baptism, that there are three types: baptism of water, baptism of blood (those who were martyred before they were baptized), and baptism of desire, which is when a person wants to do what is right and follow God's will as he understands it. This is how a person who never heard of Christ or who follows another religion can experience salvation—through baptism of desire. We learned this in grade school when we were taught that salvation is available to all people. "Atheists can find themselves in paradise," as Pope Francis rightly said. The only strange thing about his words is that some people found them strange.

I suspect that there are many non-baptized people who are "more baptized," or more "in grace," than some who have had water poured over their heads. We should remember that when we want to exclude people from communion. We must never judge the state of a person's soul, nor God's love for them.

The body of Christ is larger and more inclusive than the institutional church, and salvation is not limited to those in the visible church. Those outside the institutional church are also "in Christ," and being in Christ is what communion signifies.

Whenever we visit my priest friends, they invite my "heretical" wife to receive communion, which she does. Christ's spirit, his mystical body, extends beyond the institution of the church. We can't limit Christ's love with our structures and laws or our stupid intellects and arrogant exclusivity. As my wife is in the mystical body of Christ, she is thus in the church.

Finally, the most compelling argument against the church's forbidding interfaith communion is the example of Christ. Christ welcomed all. He accepted those who were most violently opposed by the Jews and especially the religious authorities of the time. Christ accepted the Gentiles, who always were referred to as Gentile sinners, and Samaritans, who were called traitors. Christ had communion with outsiders. The wedding feast established by Christ was intended for all. We can't blow up that feast by imposing man-made laws.

Church authorities of every generation must not so completely identify the church with Christ. They must not say, "What the church wants is what Christ wants."

I don't think Christ wanted the Crusades, the Inquisition, and the persecution of the Jews. The church wanted those tragedies, Christ didn't. We can't automatically say, then, "Since the church doesn't allow interfaith communion, Christ doesn't allow it!"

Christ's love is larger than our individual churches and their rules. We can't stuff him into our ecclesiastical box, telling him:

> Jesus, forget about your universal love. You have to follow our rules! Forget about your universal acceptance, which is going to wreck our institutions! Jesus, we want our institutions with their rules and punishments. They give us a sense of security and superiority. Your love on the other hand is an all-consuming love, a love too much for us to understand. Your love will destroy us (the false us)—our traditions, ways, customs, habits, and prejudices. Don't love like you do God! You are killing "us."

God answers thusly:

> "My grace is sufficient for you."
> "God is love."
> "He who abides in love abides in God!"

In 1971, a Catholic-Anglican joint statement declared, "There is substantial agreement about the doctrine of the Eucharist."[8] In 1979, they restated their agreement. Officially the Anglican Church accepts the Catholic belief in the real presence. They, however, use the words "spiritual presence" rather than "real presence" and for good reason, as this anecdote shows: A Catholic was disputing an Anglican (Episcopalian), saying, "You believe only in the spiritual presence, but we Romans believe in the real presence." The man answered, "Yes, but we Anglicans believe the spiritual to be real!" The perfect squelch!

In the 1960s, I saw a sign on a London church: "St. Mary's Catholic church, confession times, Mass times." I thought to myself, "This has to be the one, true, apostolic Holy Roman Catholic church." I went in for Mass.

As I knelt, noticing the statues of Mary and others, I felt sure I was in a Roman Catholic Church. Doubts arose when, in his sermon, the priest spoke about his wife. I whispered to the woman next to me, "Is this a Catholic church?" She whispered, "Yes, it's an Anglo-Catholic church."

I thought to myself, "I am in the midst of heretics!" But they seemed like nice heretics. I had just anticipated the 1971 agreement by a few years.

A short time ago, an Anglican priest was visiting the United States. He taught at Cambridge and understood the Mass and Eucharist the same way the Catholic Church does. In England, he said the Anglo-Catholic Mass daily, which essentially is identical to the Roman Catholic Mass.

When he asked the Roman priests to concelebrate Mass with him, some were hesitant to allow it. The fact that Roman Catholic priests would even question an Anglican priest about concelebrating Mass is disquieting. It shows just how far we are "going backwards," to quote the good bishop mentioned in my dedication. Forty years ago, most priests would not have questioned it.

The priests did eventually invite him to concelebrate with them, a victory for common sense and charity. Some "Christians" may have been displeased that two Christian denominations joined in worshiping him, but I doubt Christ was bothered.

Forbidding a person communion may make institutional sense, but it makes no gospel sense. The church acts logically; the gospel is totally

8. Anglican Communion, "Unity, Faith, and Order," sec. 3, para. 12.

illogical. There is innate tension between the church as institution and the church as bearer of the gospel, just as there is tension between religion and spirituality. To recognize that difference is helpful in assigning importance to man-made church laws and to God-made universal laws.

Religion is man-made, it is what we do to relate to God. It is an active experience. Spirituality is "God-made" and, as such, is given to us. It is a contemplative experience! Normally, both are necessary, but religion must be subservient to spirituality.

Spirituality is living in the realization of who we are, that we are children of God. Only when we do that can we act out of that realization. Unless we contemplate and know who we are, and unless our actions flow from that knowledge, they will not be truly life-giving.

Contemplation leads to the freedom of the children of God. To deny people that freedom to contemplate, to communicate with God, is basically to deny who we are: the children of God.

In the matter of who can receive communion and who can't, we always seem to get it backward: "Good Catholics can receive communion, but bad Catholics can't. Sinless people can receive communion, but sinful people can't. Are you a Catholic in good standing?" We say to the spiritual outsider or outcast, "Get yourself in good shape, and then you may join us 'good Catholics' in communion." Christ said just the opposite. He "did not come to call the righteous, but sinners. It is not the healthy who need the physician, but the sick" (Mark 2:17).

He told those who were in need to come to him. He invited the broken, alienated, suffering, and outcast to come to him. We tell that group to "get out, you are not worthy." Who, then, is worthy? Does the church realize that by prohibiting a person from going to Christ in communion, it is prohibiting Christ from coming to that person? Has the church ever considered that Christ wants to come to that person in the sacrament just as he or she is?

We have our priorities about who can and who cannot receive, but we should instead consider Christ's priorities. Christ is always loving and forgiving, whether we are or not. His love is not limited, while ours is, by our pride and stupidity. We should allow people whom we consider unworthy to tangibly receive the love that Christ has for them with this question in mind: Does Christ consider them unworthy?

That question concerns not only non-Catholics receiving communion, but also Catholics who are not in good standing—including those in "bad marriages" receiving communion.

Presently, the German bishops are defending their plans to allow some divorced and remarried Catholics to receive communion. The bishops insist they have the pope's endorsement in this matter, saying that the pope has indicated that in marriage cases "certain issues can be decided locally."

However, a powerful church figure has denied that position. Archbishop Müller, the prefect of the Congregation of the Doctrine of the Faith, said the German bishops' position violates church teaching.[9]

It was the Holy Office that checked the orthodoxy of Catholic scholars. Since the Second Vatican Council, however, their approach has mellowed considerably. They haven't fried a heretic in a long time, much to the disgust of some on the religious Right.

It will be interesting to see how successful the German bishops (with support from the pope?) will be in fighting the Congregation. For pure viciousness, there is no fight like a church fight. Both sides are certain that God is on their team, and so they are fighting for divine truth. In that kind of battle, charity often loses.

Another question concerning Catholics in "bad marriages" is why we deny them communion while they are waiting for annulments of their previous marriage. Some of those seeking annulments have been waiting for years and years! In the meantime, they are denied communion. Why not give them the benefit of the doubt that their first marriage will be declared null? If it turns out otherwise, so what? Who has been hurt? Christ? God?

Again, it is a question of allowing Christ to come to those who are hurting to soothe their anguish. Communion is healing for the brokenhearted. The church seems always to be asking Christians to merit God's love, asking people to work and suffer to earn God's love. That is indeed strange, considering Christ's insistence that God's grace is a free gift, not something we merit.

Humans cannot comprehend God's unrestrictive love. God's love is like that children's chant, "all-y all-y all in free!" We have made the church into an exclusive country club, open to only the spiritual elite who "earn" it. Our love is like baseball: "You're out!" As Pope Francis said, "The thing the church needs most today is the ability to heal wounds and warm hearts"[10] —not to say, "you're out!"

9. Pope Paul III began that Congregation in 1542. Originally, it was named the Supreme Sacred Congregation of the Universal Inquisition, or simply the Roman Inquisition, which was very active in the heretic-burning days. Today, it is commonly known as the Holy Office, and less commonly as "the Hound of Heaven."

10. Francis, *Joy*.

One of the charges brought against Christ by the "religiously proper people" was that he associated with the unworthy. The Pharisees saw this; they asked disciples, "Why does your teacher eat with tax collectors and sinners?" (Matt 9:11). Christ was spiritually free enough to be "religiously wrong," and he expected his followers to likewise be free.

We, however, can't handle God's freedom. We don't want God's love to be a free gift; we want to have to earn it. We want to apply our economics— "we do this to get that"—to our spirituality. There is nothing free in our economic system; it's all *quid pro quo*.

God doesn't love like our economic system, though. In the gospel, the "bad guys" who come late to work receive the same wages as those who worked in the heat of the day. (Not fair!) The "bad son" comes home and gets treated to a banquet instead of the son who stayed home doing all the work. (Not fair!) Martin Luther was right: "If you accept human reason (what is fair and what is not fair) you are forced to say either there is no God, or that God is unjust (unfair)."[11] There is no *quid pro quo* with God. Christ did away with what is fair and what is not fair, and God's free gift of grace makes the problems with interfaith communion irrelevant.

It is fitting that we conclude this chapter on interfaith communion with words from Vatican II: "The Eucharist (communion) expresses and brings about unity among Christians." The council does not say unity among Catholics; it says unity among Christians. Communion is inclusive, not exclusive. Communion is not confined to the visible Roman church; it includes the whole church, the mystical body of Christ.

Is it not time that we start living that reality—that oneness—in our Eucharistic celebrations?

## Community Is Communion

"No man is an island."[12]

"God does not make men holy and save them merely as individuals without bond or link between one another. Rather it has pleased God to bring men together as one people."[13]

11. Dillenberger, *Martin Luther*, 201.
12. John Donne, *Selection of His Poetry.*
13. Paul VI, *Lumen Gentium*, 2:9.

To have a better understanding of the sacrament of communion we must have a better understanding of community. Many people agree with Margaret Thatcher's words, "There is no such thing as society (community), there are just individuals."[14] Whatever she meant by that, it doesn't sound good. That attitude is in direct opposition to the purpose and meaning of the sacraments. The sacraments are "communal symbolic actions (signs) which express the relationship (grace) among Christians."

That definition of a sacrament is merely an existential definition of Peter Lombard's essential definition from the 1100s: "A sacrament is an outward sign which gives grace." The words, "communal symbolic actions," place the sacrament within the context of community. The sacraments are not private affairs between God and me; they are community (church) signs or actions.

It is impossible to be individualistic and partake of the sacraments, especially the sacrament of the Eucharist. In Greek mythology, Plutus, the god of wealth, proclaimed, "What is thine is mine and all mine is thine." Thankfully there are many wealthy people in America who embody that idea. Bill Gates, Warren Buffet, and Michael Bloomberg, to mention just a few, use their wealth for the common welfare.

Most of us, including myself, do not think of our money in terms of the common good. We think of our money in terms of "mine, not thine." Some even put money in foreign banks to avoid paying taxes for the common good. They are not thinking in collective terms. They are not thinking with Plutus, "What is mine is thine." They are thinking, "What is mine is mine!"

Monks follow the Rule of St. Benedict, which was written in the sixth century. Daily, at the noon meal, a few lines of that rule would be read aloud to the monks. Imagine reading a rule of life written fifteen hundred years ago! One sentence from it always struck me: "This vice in particular should be torn out at the roots in the monastery: no one should . . . have any private property, nothing at all."[15]

Individualism is the cornerstone of private property, so when Benedict condemned private property, he was condemning individualism. Monks live in community. They think and breathe community. A novice is told that even the pen with which he is writing does not belong to him; it belongs to the community. A religious community is communism in its absolute and purist form, communism with God. A community, whether it is a religious

14. *London Times*, July 10, 1980, "Atticus" column.
15. Benedict, *Rule of Saint Benedict*, chap. 33.

or marriage community, requires people to leave their individualism. It requires you to "die to yourself" as spiritual gurus say, for the greater good of the community. A religious community requires thinking in terms of us instead of me, we instead of I. Does that sound un-American?

Recently, I recalled the words, "above all, the vice of private property must be rooted out of the monastery," when a fictional character on TV said, "If they pass Medicare, they won't stop until they banish private property." I suspect Benedict would have replied, "Well then, banish private property!" (Very un-American!)

Of course, Benedict was a saint, and for a saint, there is not "me." There is only "we." An economic system based on "me" is, by its very nature, un-Christian because it is based on selfishness and greed.

There are many people living in an un-Christian society who do not succumb to selfishness and greed. Even surrounded by a "me" society, they manage to live in a "we" society.

Unlike monks, however, the average American is not community-minded. Instinctively, Americans are psychologically individualistic. Individualism is the philosophical basis underlying the Protestant Reformation, which greatly influenced our country. Those who founded America were largely the offspring of the reformers.

In general, Protestants are more oriented toward the individual—both religiously and psychologically—than are Catholics. With Catholics, the collective is more important. However, in both groups, their choices are largely unconscious. They are rooted in traditions that go back centuries.

The Anglo-Catholics are similar to the Roman Catholics, in that they have the sacraments as the unifying glue of their spiritual life. The sacraments are community affairs, as a person receiving a sacrament needs people—a person cannot give himself/herself a sacrament.

Our American ancestors came from a more spiritually individualistic background. You can read the Bible by yourself; you don't need others. The Puritans broke away from the Church of England, and the pilgrims came from the spiritual individualism of the reformers, especially the Puritans.

There is another reason that Americans adapted to individualism so readily—America is geographically individualistic. Two large oceans, which once took months to cross, separate us from others. We were, geographically, loners.

Many of the pilgrims felt alienated from their mother countries; they had left because of the dissatisfaction and discord they experienced. These three conditions—religious, geographical, and social isolation—combined to form the rugged individualism so characteristic of American pioneers.

Private interpretation of scripture, a major tenet of the reformers, is just one manifestation of philosophical and psychological individualism inherent in the Reformation. In Protestantism, the individual primarily receives the word of God directly through the Bible.

If an individual believes the Bible tells him to handle deadly snakes, he believes the Bible teaches snake handling. The text means exactly what each individual interprets it to mean. This is known as private interpretation of the Bible, which is a fundamental tenet of Protestantism.

In Catholicism, the individual is important in how he/she understands the word of God, but he/she is not the final interpreter of what the scriptures are teaching. The Christian community, the church, has the role of teacher. In Catholicism, the word of God comes through the church community to the individual, who checks with the community to see if he or she is in line with the community's understanding of that particular text.

Individuals are important in understanding the scriptures, but the people of God, the Christian community, and the church are collectively the final authority, the norm. In Protestantism, the individual is the norm.

By the fourth century, there were numerous "gospels" in existence. It was the church who determined which were authentic and which were not. The Christian Bible, then, came from the church, the people of God, as a whole. It is the community's book, which the individual taps into.

Collectivism is the philosophical and psychological basis of Catholicism. Historically, "the church" was the group, or society, to which all belonged. Unfortunately, until recently, people have thought of "the church" in terms of an institution: the pope, hierarchy, or clergy. The people didn't see themselves as the church. Today's idea of "the church" as "the people of God," or the "Christian community," gives a better understanding of the community aspect inherent in Catholicism. Yes, God does deal with us as individuals, but as individuals living and sharing in community. In Catholicism, a person's spiritual lifeline is attached to God more through community than in Protestantism. At the risk of oversimplification, it may be said that Catholics generally see themselves being saved more as a member of a group. Protestants see themselves being saved more as individuals.

After Protestants and Catholics, the Jewish people make up the third-largest religious group in America. Of the three, the Jews generally have the deepest sense of community, which is embedded in their sense of being called as a people. They felt called as the people of God, not as the person of God. Their entire life was, and is, communal.

It should be noted that philosophical collectivism and individualism do not affect personal generosity. A person who is philosophically individualistic may be much more generous and charitable on a personal level than a person who thinks collectively. Personal charity is not a true gauge of a person's philosophical mindset. No one denomination is more sharing than another. Personal and collective charity cut across denominational lines.

While I was in school, the "common good" was the refrain that echoed the church's social teaching. Many American Catholics, then and now, regard the papal teachings on economic matters as too Far Left. They do not like the collective, community philosophy underlying those teachings affecting economic life. They want to confine religion to Sunday morning and not allow it to affect the marketplace: Sunday-morning pulpits are okay for religion, but Monday-morning Wall Street is not. Sundays, we are one in Christ. Mondays we are individuals stomping each other on the floors of the stock exchange.

I present the following story without comment:

My friend and former abbot, who is now stationed in Rome, had a visitor from another country who became ill. My friend took him to the hospital. After the treatment he asked, "How much do we owe you?" The nurse said: "You owe us nothing, Father. This is not America. Here, we take care of our sick."

The nurse thought my friend was American, and she was getting in "a dig" against Americans. The ironic part? He is Canadian! He delighted in telling me that story and dug into Americans, especially me, right along with that nurse.

Is there a reason the richest country in the world cannot have universal health care? Is there a reason we cannot in the nurse's words, "take care of our sick?" I have no answer.

Five years ago, fifty-eight countries had universal health care. There are thirty-three developed countries, of which thirty-two have universal health care. The lone exception is the United States. Among those who have universal health care are Costa Rica, Iceland, and Kuwait.

Why is it that every advanced country in the world has a transportation system that brings and returns people from work en masse, as a collective? Yet in America, for the most part, each person drives her own car to work and back. Generally, Americans are individuals who see the group as "those others." Though we may offer charity to "those others," we still consider them "others," separate from ourselves.

Individualism sees "me plus you as two." Collectivism sees "me plus you as one." An individualist may be very generous toward others, but the thought behind the generosity is: "I give to you, but we are separate. Me plus you equals two." The thought behind the generosity of a collectivist is: "I give to you because we are one. Me plus you equals one." In individualism, I keep my separate identity. In collectivism, my identity becomes one with the other. In individualism, "I give some of mine to you." In collectivism, "Mine is yours." In the first, I am generous to the other person. In the second, I am the other person. Generous individualism is ethical, which is "humanly good." Collectivism is mystical, which is "Godly good."

The actions are the same, and the generosity is the same. The only difference is the thought behind the actions. One sees the other as a person they want to help, which is good ethical living. The other sees another person as an extension of himself, as one with him, forming the body of Christ. This leads to mystical living.

America was founded on individualism: the Lone Ranger, the "lonesome cowboy," and John Wayne are in our country's collective subconscious. Americans instinctively think in terms of individual rights, not in terms of the common good. For example: My right to own a military attack rifle that shoots 500 bullets a minute supersedes society's need for public safety. (Why shouldn't my right to own an atomic bomb supersede public safety?) Ted Nugent, the pro-gun activist once said he loved Texas because it is "the last bastion of rugged individualism."[16]

The following is an example of how the rugged individual is the American ideal. A woman wrote to her local newspaper to say that she did not go to work during President Barack Obama's inauguration ceremony because she knew they would be watching "that" on the office television. In protest, she stayed home and watched three John Wayne movies. That says it all! John Wayne, the epitome of the rugged individualist, the icon of the American male, was superior in her mind to the community-minded person who was becoming our president.

In America's folklore, the individual, the one acting alone, is the hero. The rugged individualist is regarded as the ideal: Davy Crockett, Daniel Boone. Who is America's greatest hero? Superman! It is not super men; it is Superman. Whether it is the cowboy riding alone into the

16. Bash, "Ted Nugent," para. 12.

sunset or Superman flying over a building, it is the individual who is the savior, not a group.

In the 1800s, Europe was much more densely populated than America. People lived in towns and naturally thought in terms of others and how they related. In our country's beginnings, however, people lived in comparative isolation. In the American frontier, your nearest neighbors might be a mile through the woods, and you didn't have to be concerned with them. You could make all the noise you wanted all night, and no one would be disturbed. You didn't have to think of others' rights or the common good. Our forefathers were, by their very existence, more individualistic than European city-dwellers. As our country grew, our neighbors were no longer miles away. They were on the same block, even in the same building. In a crowded society, rugged individualism is not feasible. A person no longer lives alone and may not act as if he does. You have to take notice of your neighbor, if for no other reason than he or she is right next to you. Unfortunately, in America, many Americans still retain a frontier mentality, where they are not concerned with the common good, but only their own private good. "I want to be the rugged individualist and still live in a big city."

In America, there is, officially at least, an ingrained sense of my private good superseding the community's good. If I want to carry my gun into a bar, or a church, no one should be able to stop me, as a recent Georgia law recently stated. "My individual freedom" is tattooed on the subconscious of most Americans, leaving little to no space for a sense of the common good. Like a two-year-old screaming to his playmates: "My toy! My toy!" Too often in today's society, there is little room for a sense of the common weal. I find it interesting that the oldest, and one of the most-read, Catholic magazines is entitled *Commonweal* or "common good." To get the message of the common good across to Americans, in general, is a difficult task.

In contrast, countries that have a longer history, and that include the idea of the group, the community, the church, have community men as their folk heroes. They are always seen in context of the community; they are working with others, not alone. Robin Hood had his Merry Men of Sherwood Forest, and he worked within that community to better society, though at times perhaps somewhat excessively.

Even King Arthur was no Lone Ranger. He had his community of knights around him—the Knights of the Round Table. The round table itself denotes community. King Arthur instructed his knights, "The greater bounty we may give, the greater our nobility."

Does the past idea of the importance of the community influence the collective unconscious of present-day Europeans, making them more open to seek the good of the community then are Americans?

Do European countries so easily accept universal health care because they are not individualistically inclined? Is their collective subconscious sense of community so powerful that it causes them to think in terms of community rather than the individual? Is universal health care un-American? I don't know.

In America, the individual is given the primary consideration. While I was in the seminary in the late 1950s, a history professor said something I did not understand: "Catholics in this country do not have a Catholic mindset; American Catholics are psychologically Protestant." I knew he was not trying to degrade anyone, nor was he saying that one mindset was better than the other. He was merely stating the difference between individualism and collectivism. At the time, I lacked the historical perspective to understand him. For the first forty years of my life as a Catholic and priest, I was psychologically Protestant. After living in a community as a monk for twenty-eight years, however, I became psychologically Catholic.

My Republican friends say to me, with no small amount of disdain, "You entered the monastery a Republican, and twenty-nine years later you emerge a Democrat! What did they do, fry your brain?"

I answer them, "No, but for the first time in my life I was rendered penniless and had no possessions. I did not have anything about which I could say, 'This is mine.' Everything was ours, and I was totally dependent on others. That gives a person a different perspective. You should try it sometime!" Live with a "we" mentality rather than a "me" mentality.

Dependency is the bedrock of spirituality.

It was not until I entered the monastery and community living that I started to understand my teacher's words about different mindsets. A monk can't be individualistic; he must always think in terms of living in communion with the community while desiring to bring that communion about. Holy Communion is called the "body of Christ." The community is also called the "body of Christ." Communion is the sign of what community is all about—Christ.

The "body of Christ," in Latin, is *corpus Christi*. Yearly, there is a Catholic celebration of Corpus Christi Sunday. What follows is a homily I gave at the monastery in 1978 on Corpus Christi Sunday. Hopefully, it will illuminate the importance of communion with Christ and communion with each other, Christ's body: *corpus Christi.*

> *Because there is one Bread, we who are many, are one Body.*[17]
> *The Eucharist makes the church.*[18]
> *The Eucharist expresses and brings about the unity among*
>  *Christians.*[19]

What is the Eucharist? The body of Christ. What is the Christian community? The body of Christ! The Christian community and the Eucharist are the same, the same body of Christ in different forms.

It is only by having an appreciation of the Christian community, the church, as the body of Christ that we may then progress to an appreciation of the body of Christ in the Eucharist.

If we instead attempt to start by viewing the Eucharist as separate from the community, seeing it in isolation, we will likely end up thinking of the Eucharist apart from, and independent of, the community.

To so isolate the Eucharist is to misunderstand the relationship between receiving communion and the community. For what we say about the Eucharist is always said in context of its relationship to the church, the Christian community.

The Eucharist can be properly understood only when it is seen in its communal aspect. We must understand the mutual dependence between the Eucharist and the Christian community.

When the priest says, "This is my body," all of us are saying, "This is my body." The priest represents the community, the mystical body of Christ. That is why we say the priest represents Christ. What the priest says, we all say; what the priest does, we all do.

This body, this community, this church, is the body of Christ. So when we say, "this is my body," the presence of Christ comes about as the Eucharist, because the presence of Christ is in us, his people.

The movement, or direction, of how the Eucharistic presence comes about, is from the church, the "people of God," (from us) to the bread (the sacrament).

We may picture the Eucharistic presence coming about by an inward motion, from the surrounding Christian community, rather than a

---

17. See 1 Cor 10:17.
18. St. Thomas Aquinas (1250s).
19. Second Vatican Council (1960s).

downward motion, as if Christ is dropping it from the sky. For it is the mystical body of Christ gathered around the altar that brings about the Eucharistic body of Christ for communion on the altar.

Admittedly, words such as "movement," "direction," or "motion" are rather clumsy, when speaking of how the Eucharistic presence comes about. They do aid us, however, in understanding the sacrament in terms of the Christian community. This motion from the community to the bread is the first half of that dynamic.

The second half concerns the "why" of the presence. The Eucharist exists for one reason: to be given back to the community.

The motion or flow of the presence in the Eucharist is, first inward— from the community to the bread—then outward, from the bread back to the community. The community is the cause of, and the reason for, the Eucharistic presence.

The sacrament has, as its beginning and as its end the mystical body of Christ, the church, the community. St. Therese said, "The sacrament is to be received, not put into golden vessels."

It has been said that the place to learn how to love is in communion, that we learn to love Christ in his whole body, the entire and whole Christ. We learn to love Christ as he transcends this community (the transcendent Christ). We also learn to love Christ as he is present within this community (the imminent Christ).

Love for the one Christ, and love for the many who are in that one Christ, is the meaning of communion. Communion can never be a private affair. It always involves the community; it always involves the church.

It may appear when we receive Communion that no one else is there, but in reality, everyone is there. All those with whom we agree or disagree, who we like or dislike. The whole church is there. No one is shut out. No one is excluded. They are all there in that consecrated host—the body of Christ. Corpus Christi. You and me.

In the pre-council days I was saying Mass for a group of nuns. After receiving communion, they would cover their faces with their veils. The idea was they wanted to commune with the transcendent Christ. I hope they realized that they were also communing with the imminent Christ, their surrounding sisters. They were in fact communing with the transcendent Christ through the imminent Christ.

If they covered their faces to keep everyone else out, they were misunderstanding communion and making it easy. They were bothered by their neighbors kneeling next to them, as we all are. We can't keep them, that irritating neighbor, out of our communion. For as Dietrich Bonhoeffer said, there is no such thing as "cheap grace." Receiving communion is very difficult. Like grace, it's not cheap.

The Eucharist is the center of the world, because Christ and his people are centered there: God's misshapen, warped, wounded people, you and me, Christ's body, corpus Christi, is present in that Eucharist.

Receiving communion should be a difficult experience, because learning to love is a difficult experience. Christ doesn't bother me, but my neighbor may. It is easy to love Christ up in the sky somewhere. It is hard to love Christ in my enemy.

Isn't that what the church is all about? Isn't that what the Eucharist is all about—learning to love, love the Body of Christ? We are to love the risen, transcendent Christ and the imminent Christ, as well, in the person we don't like. When receiving communion, we are receiving both, whether we want it that way or not.

If we don't realize how difficult it is to receive communion, we probably have never truly received communion. "If you come to the altar and you remember your brother has anything against you, leave. First be reconciled with your brother and then come to the altar" (Matt 5:23–24). In receiving communion, the sinful, imminent Christ, ourselves, is transferred into the innocent, transcendent Christ. Traditionally, that union of Christ and ourselves has been called the "mystical marriage." This marriage makes us whole, or holy. Accordingly we call it "holy communion."

# 2

# Monastery

## House of Freedom

THE YEARS FOLLOWING THE council were years of spiritual freedom. The spirit of God was free to flow, not hampered by man-made restrictions. Those were lighthearted years.

That atmosphere also was present in the monastery. In that way, my years in the active priesthood and my years in the monastery were similar, and freeing, experiences.

When you enter a monastery, you are a novice for two and half years before you are formally accepted into the religious order. During that time, you are under a monk who is the "novice master." He is in charge of the novices' spiritual formation, and he is their immediate superior. He talks to the group for thirty minutes, twice a week. The novices meet with him individually once a week for about forty-five minutes. For the novice, the novice master is of vital importance to his monk's training—he is his introduction to monastic life.

The conferences cover the history of monasticism, starting with the desert fathers in the early 300s. At that time, they were hermits. Community monasticism as we know it today was begun by St. Benedict in the 500s at the monastery of Monte Cassino in Italy. Americans became familiar with it when we bombed it in World War II because the Germans were using it as a fortification. The monastery was of such historical importance, however, that the Italian government rebuilt it after the war.

In Europe, from 500 to around the 1500s, the monks were the ones who preserved scholarship. The conferences were interesting historically. Of course, the spirituality of St. Bernard, of John of the Cross, of Teresa of Avila, were the meat of the conferences. We were there primarily for spirituality, and history secondarily.

The novice master is a spiritual guide helping the novice through the huge adjustment from life in the world to monastic life. When I entered the monastery in August 1972, there were eleven novices. Educationally we ranged from graduate school—a lawyer, a musician, and two priests—to high school graduates. Intelligence ranged from brilliant to "not too bright." (I tended toward the latter group, not quite to the bottom.)

We had our first conference on one late August evening around seven o'clock. We were sitting in old school desks with open tops. It was very hot and sweaty, and there was no air conditioning. One poor guy had hay fever, and he sneezed constantly. It was not comfortable. As we waited for the novice master, I thought: "What is he going to say to us? With this range of people, how could he hit common ground?" After all of my religious experience and spiritual training, I was not about to be satisfied with spiritual trifles. I remember thinking: "If I have to sit here for two and half years listening to pious prattle about how 'We monks will suffer with Jesus to save the world,' I don't think I am going to make it. That would be even worse than chaperoning high school dances."

When the novice master walked in, I thought, "Well, you wouldn't pick this guy out of a crowd." He was short, and when he sat down I don't think his feet reached the ground. However, he had the walk of a very strong man. I discovered later that he was one of those people who had learned that he was strong enough to be kind and gentle. He was one of the strongest, toughest (in the good sense) men I had ever met. He had the legs of a two-hundred-pound man, which he explained, saying, "I'm from Canada, and I played hockey." I was four inches taller and fifty pounds heavier, but I would be hesitant to get that man's dander up.

Sometimes we had occasion to be side by side, pitching bales of hay into a loft. I would think: "Lord, this is one strong man! When is he ever going to tire?" I sat next to him in the dining hall, and I saw that he ate very little. I knew that he slept very little, five to six hours a night. Our health probably has more to do with our minds than our bodies, and his mind and body were as one—both sound.

On that first day, when he began to speak, I prayed: "Please, Lord, no spiritual nonsense. It's too hot, and I am too old!"

The first words out of his mouth were, "Why does a man come to a monastery?" Not bad for a starter, I thought, but how is he going to answer? Why do you think men join a monastery?

He then answered his question, and I have never forgotten his words: "You come to a monastery to get free for the Lord."

I sighed in relief, and though I wasn't sure I understood what he meant, I had a feeling that "getting free for the Lord" is the reason for monastic life, and indeed for life in general. To get free for the Lord is to free ourselves from the blocks to God's love that we have within ourselves. "If the Son has made you free, you shall be free indeed." (John 8:36)

Within six months, our novice master was elected abbot of the monastery. He was a Canadian from Windsor who had been a monk in the U.S. since 1956. He never took American citizenship or dual citizenship. He would say with an air of puckish defiance, "I'm a Canadian, not an American." He said he did not like Americans because, "Those rich kids came over to Canada in their big cars and stole our girlfriends." Wars, indeed, have been fought over less.

After we became friends, I referred to him as "the Detroit river wetback illegally coming into our country stealing American jobs." He would respond that I was the "typical 'ugly American,' rich, arrogant, and stupid." (We were very good friends.)

When he was abbot, I would talk with him weekly in his office. A monk who had his office nearby said to me, "I can always tell when you are in talking to the abbot. I hear you both laughing all the way down the hall." I took that as a great compliment. Laughter is a sure indicator of a person's soul; beware of a clergyman or preacher who doesn't laugh.

It is a grace to have someone with whom you can speak freely and say what you think, knowing that you are not going to be judged or criticized. That is the way the abbot and I spoke with one another.

A monk really doesn't fit in any group. He doesn't see himself as superior to others; in fact, he sees others as better than himself. However, he is never perfectly settled or at home in any organization. He is always the odd man out. That lack of total commitment or complete identification with a created reality provides the monk with a freedom not felt by those trying to fit into a slot or play a role.

I think this is what my novice master meant when he said, "Get free for the Lord." He was saying: "Get free, in order to find peace and love in yourself. Don't be looking to see if others are as they should be or if the monastery is as it should be. You get free! Find peace and love in the only place they can be found—in yourself, in your Christ-centered self." His words were meant as a challenge to us entering the monastery. They were telling us to get free, to find in ourselves peace and love, and not to look for them in others. Don't try to straighten up others or the world.

We are afraid of peace and love. We are afraid because we intuit that God's love and peace will destroy us. Our fear is that if we live in God's love and peace, there will be a part of us that will die. We sense that peace on one level involves annihilation on another level, the annihilation of our ego, our false self.

Freedom is not in a place or written in a constitution; it has to do with our mind and heart. All those years in prison, Nelson Mandela was a free man. Those practicing apartheid were enslaved, even though they were living in comfort. In a Birmingham, Alabama jail, Martin Luther King Jr. was a free man. Sheriff Eugene "Bull" Connor, the police, and the crowd were the ones who were enslaved. Who is freer than the Dalai Lama? True freedom is an internal matter; it has nothing to do with what is going on outside us. A person could be in Dachau prison camp and still be free. One could be a wealthy American living in the land of the free, yet be totally bound and enslaved by his surroundings. The less we hold on to, the freer we are.

It was forty-one years ago that I heard my novice master's words, and I am still trying to get "free" for the Lord. I suspect the task is never-ending on this side of the grave.

The monastic vows of poverty, chastity, and obedience are ways to get free. Money can enslave us, as can the drive for self-will and sexual pleasure. So a person takes vows of poverty, chastity, and obedience to get free. Food can also enslave us, so at times we fast. Fasting, like all the monastic experiences, is not done to train the will. A person does not take vows to do something difficult for God. One takes vows to get free.

The vows, fasting, and a disciplined life are not ends in themselves. They are merely the means to an end—internal freedom. A person does not have to take vows or enter a monastery to get free. Most people work out their freedom in ordinary life, doing ordinary things.

In fact, in pursuit of religious perfection, religion can enslave a monk or any person. He ends up being just as spiritually crippled, as does the libertarian. Religious nonsense is the most insidious kind, because being religious appears to be so good. Unfortunately, religion can make us less human, which is a negation of "God becoming man, God becoming human."

A monastery reflects its abbot. If he is harsh, the atmosphere of the monastery will be harsh. If he is gentle, there will be a gentle monastery. If the abbot is bound by rules, the monastery will be rule-bound. The atmosphere in the church immediately following Vatican II was one of putting people before rules, and in that sense, our abbot was a Vatican II priest.

In 1998, the monastery celebrated the abbot's twenty-five years in office. I was fortunate enough to give the talk at the Mass celebrating the occasion. At Mass bread, wine, and water are used. They are placed on an altar, or better, a table. A crucifix stands nearby. I used all these to describe our abbot.

*Let us take bread.*
Bread is the simplest, the most unassuming, and the most
    humble of all food. It is so common it neither seeks nor
    attracts attention, yet it is always present, always available.
Bread is humble to the point it is easily taken for granted;
    nevertheless it remains humankind's basic nourishment.
It is used by all, but especially by the world's weak ones—the
    very poor and needy.
Those in need—the truly hungry—don't politely eat bread;
    they pounce on it, they devour it.
What is bread?
Unassuming, humble, available, devoured.
That is bread!

*Let us take wine.*
Wine is healing. It is soothing.
Wine is community-minded. It not only is formed from a
    community of grapes, but it in turn forms community.
People turn to wine in their joys, when they are happy and
    want to share their happiness. They know wine will "rejoice
    with those who rejoice."
People also turn to wine in their sorrow, when their hurt is
    so deep they have to tell someone, so they tell wine. They
    know wine will lend its ear.
Wine is a good listener! It is attentive, taking people where, and
    as, they are.
What is wine?
Healing, unifying, rejoicing, attentive.
That is wine!

*Let us take water.*

Water is life producing, absolutely necessary for growth.

It is clear to the point of being transparent; it has nothing to hide, no deception.

The young at heart can have fun with water; it is fluid, not at all rigid or stiff. It refreshes and relaxes.

Although it has the potential strength of an ocean wave, water's main characteristic is its consideration and sensitivity.

Water is considerate of and sensitive to its surroundings. It doesn't ask that the other adjust itself to it, rather it will adjust itself to the other.

Water will flow into whatever form it meets. It automatically flows to the lowest spot, and there in that lowly posture, it obeys its surrounds.

Water is obedient!

What is water?

Life-producing, transparent, refreshing, considerate, sensitive, obedient.

That is water!

Today, to show our abbot gratitude, we will take these humble, unassuming things and place them on a table.

A table supports and sustains. A table holds things up! It holds people up.

When people are comfortable with and near to each other, they disregard etiquette and put their elbows and arms on the table.

People lean on a table!

After a wedding when most of the guests have left, a few relatives and close friends will gather around the kitchen table.

They are content, leaning on that table in their joy, remembering how the new bride or groom grew up at that table.

And that table is also content and joyful for the sake of its people. For that table knows and understands those people. That table is part of those people.

It is part of those people even to death. After a funeral, the relatives and close friends will again gather around that same table and they will once more lean on it, this time with their full weight.

They will be there speaking in quiet and sad tones now, speaking over and leaning on that table.

And that table bears their weight and their sorrow. And, sometimes, although you don't see it, and although that table is strong and silent, sometimes you know—that table weeps!

Internally and silently—perhaps even unknown to itself—that table weeps!

You see, it has to! Because day after day it not only bears all the sorrows of those who lean on it, but also it compassionates with its suffering people. After a while those people can get up from that table somewhat refreshed. But that—that table—must be willing to allow all their weight, all their sorrow to remain, and more, to seep into its middle—into its guts!

That table is long-suffering!

It takes into itself the burdens, troubles and problems of all who lean on it, and in so doing it relieves their pain.

A table saves. A table redeems!

What is a table?

Supporting, sustaining, long-suffering, redeeming.

That is a table.

In a few minutes we will put our humble bread, wine and water on a special table, special because it is placed in a certain unique position.

This table, and all that is on it, is placed in a shadow. Of all the humble unassuming things we have mentioned, a shadow is the most humble.

A shadow is so humble and unassuming it has no existence of its own. It exists only because of, and for the other.

A shadow is only because it is an image, a representation of another.

And the shadow, which comes across this table, is the special shadow of
the Cross.

Look for yourself; the Cross is standing only a few feet from this table. This table is shadowed by the image, the representation of the Cross.

What is the Cross?

Oil. "Oil poured out."

That is the Cross.

So now let us as brothers and sisters take our bread, wine and water, and put it on this table. This table, which is shadowed by the Cross, shadowed by "oil poured out."

And with these simple, unassuming, humble things; and in this simple unassuming, humble way, we will say "thank you" to God and to our abbot.

What is an Abbot?

Well, a good Abbot is—bread!

A good abbot is—wine!
A good abbot is—water!
A good abbot is—a table!
A good abbot is—this special shadow!
A good abbot is—oil!
A good abbot is oil—poured out!

## My Friend, The Hermit

Another person who provided me with an experience of freedom was my spiritual director and confessor. He had been a monk, living in the monastery, since the mid-1950s. Before entering, however, he taught college science as a priest. In the 1960s, he was given permission to live as a hermit in a very small trailer. It was about a mile from the monastery, but still on monastic grounds. He would come into the monastery for Sunday Mass and then eat the noon meal with the community. After the meal, I would take him and his weekly food and water back to his trailer. Every week we had plenty of time to talk, and sometimes I would go to confession.

I don't know if people associate laughter with going to confession, but we did laugh. If you can't laugh at the foolishness of life and even your own faults and failures, you are in for a difficult time.

He, like my abbot, introduced me to spiritual freedom by his words but especially by his example. One of the principles he taught me was "God never asks us why things are as they are. Rather, God asks us what is our response to the way things are." He often said: "It is senseless to complain about anything, just examine how you are responding to the situation. Your response is what is important."

Once he explained to me, "You can never say something that is, should not be." I asked, "Why?" He answered, "Because it is." He explained this last principle in a most unusual setting, which was even more instructive than his words.

Once a year, we had a picnic-like supper. We always held this in the summer when it was hot. This particular evening, the temperature was in the high 80s. It was a pickup supper in the refectory, and people would eat and leave. As usual, this eating was done in silence. We had picnic food—maybe pizza, pretzels, watermelon or ice cream, and beer. (That was the only "beer meal" we had.) I hadn't had beer since college days, but it was hot and the beer was cold. I was not driving, and I didn't even have to carry on a conversation. What greater excuse does one have to overindulge? We started at about six fifteen, and people came and went. Monks drank from one-quart aluminum cups; they held two beers. This was very helpful, because no one could count the bottles. As I sat there with my pretzels and beer, people came and went and they came and went.

It was a little after seven o'clock, and the last prayer of the day is at seven thirty. The lights were turned off, but there was still enough light to see. I spotted my hermit confessor, who had come into the monastery for the picnic supper, and probably for the beer. The refectory had long, beautiful wooden tables and wooden backless stools. He was sitting at the other end of the refectory. All the others had left, so I picked up my cup and walked to where he was sitting. I sat and asked him about that same principle that we had discussed several times: "You can never say something that is, should not be." I kept protesting, asking about the Holocaust, about Hiroshima, about children being abused. I would say, "That should not be." We went around and around arguing that point, as sweat ran down my arms and it got later and later.

Now it was seven thirty, and the prayer service was beginning. Still we talked. At a quarter to eight, the service ended and the monks filed up to their rooms. Even though grand silence had begun, and would last until morning, we still sat and talked about a half-hour longer, and then we went to our rooms.

All the classes I sat through in my educational experiences never compared to that one hour in a very hot monastic refectory. I learned, not as much from what was said as from the circumstances surrounding what was said. In that one hour, my spiritual director and I broke just about every monastic rule.

Monks are not supposed to talk in the refectory. We talked. Monks are not supposed to miss a prayer service. We missed a prayer service. Monks are not supposed to talk during grand silence. We talked during grand silence. Monks are supposed to go to bed after the night prayer. We didn't. (There is no rule about monks drinking beer.)

Here was my religious superior, who was in charge of guiding me in the ways of monastic living, and he was breaking rules right and left. He never made a move to leave. He never said, "We should go." He never looked anxious. He was completely relaxed and at ease. I am sure if Jesus had walked in, my teacher would have asked him to join us renegade monks with a beer.

With his behavior, he was saying to me: "You are more important than rules. Rules are meant to serve people, not the other way around." He knew I wanted to understand what he was saying, and he did not want to break my concentration. He wanted me to know that he was there for me, that religious life was there for me, and the church was there for me. Rules were only a means to an end. That end is charity.

The abbot was the same in his attitude of service to the monks. Several times, I was speaking with him when the bell rang for vespers at five thirty. We continued to talk; he would not make a move to go to Vespers. And the abbot's not moving also said to me, "You are more important than a prayer service." Wouldn't it be wonderful if the church and clergy dealt with people that way? People would realize that the clergy, the hierarchy, the church are there for the people, not the other way around.

Rules exist for people, not people for rules. We pray so we may live; we do not live to pray. Prayer is a means. Life is the end. If prayer does not lead us to a loving life, it is useless and deceptive.

A few years after I left the monastery, I heard my hermit friend was dying. My wife and I went to see him in the monastic infirmary. He had seen her once before, in fact he had come in from his hermitage specifically to meet her. As far as I know, he never did that for anyone else. He wouldn't leave his hermitage to see the pope, if he even knew who the pope was—he paid scant attention to the clergy or to hierarchy.

My wife is not a Catholic and had never met a priest before she met me. When she first met the hermit, she knew absolutely nothing about the church and the priesthood, not to mention monks and hermits. When I told her my friend was coming in from his hermitage specifically to meet her, I think she envisioned a smelly, gaunt, toothless, longhaired, barefoot creature dressed in a loincloth—a bearded barefoot weirdo. Instead, when he walked in, she saw a clean-shaven man dressed in denim work clothes and work shoes. With a big smile, he hugged her until her back almost broke—she is very tiny. The poor woman was dumbfounded.

My wife has hosted priests as houseguests, and she has stayed in priests' homes. We stayed at two rectories on our honeymoon—I think we were married three times! She has heard "insider priest talk." She knows more about what is going on in the church than most Catholics.

As we drove to the monastic infirmary, though, we were somber. In the monastery, when a monk is dying, another monk sits by his bedside around the clock, twenty-four hours a day. Each monk, including the abbot, takes turns in three-hour shifts. Later, in another visit to the monastery, I spoke to the monk who was with my friend when he died. He described his death as follows: "I was sitting with him during the night, and he seemed to be sleeping well. Suddenly, he sat straight up in the bed, stretched out his arms in a welcoming gesture. His eyes were wide open like he was looking with recognition at something or someone. He smiled slightly, softly said, 'Jesus,' and lay back down. He was dead."

I have seen several people die, though I have never seen a death like that. I hope, even now, he thinks of that hot night and cold beer. I do, and I remember it with gratitude. I remember my good friend, the hermit, and I wonder, did he say, "Jesus," before or after he died?

## Two Old Monks

### Monk on Omaha Beach

One of the most meaningful and grace-filled experiences of my monastic life occurred while I was visiting an elderly monk who was in the infirmary due to illness and dementia. He was one of the many characters who inhabit monasteries and make community life so interesting.

Even when he was young and healthy, he had resembled a weasel that had just crawled out of a hole looking for a fight. He once worked on an oilrig in Argentina; his summary of those days was, "I never ran away from any man or, for that matter, any woman." Enough said!

During the Second World War he drove a landing craft that carried men from the troop ships to the landing beaches. He was at D-Day, and he made repeated trips to Omaha Beach, where Americans suffered their worst causalities of the invasion.

In June 1994, commemorating the fiftieth anniversary of D-Day, *Time* had a picture on its cover of a landing craft unloading men onto the beach. The picture was taken from the rear of the craft, from the driver's point of view, and it showed troops as they descended onto the beach. My friend must have seen and lived that same scene many times on June 6, 1944, fifty years before becoming this old, broken-down man.

The monastery did not get news magazines, but as in prisons, monasteries, seminaries, and Catholic colleges of old, there was always an underground network that beat the system. By stealth, developed through years of such living, I became a master smuggler. I got my hands on the contraband. Under my robes, I slipped the copy of *Time* to the old monk/ ex-soldier in the infirmary. As usual he was sitting in a serene stupor, seemingly oblivious to everything.

I put the picture in front of him. In silence he stared, and stared, and stared, and I felt I was in the presence of an approaching epiphany. Finally he uttered five of the most spiritually meaningful words I have ever heard: "Good men—on both sides." One sentence, then he returned to his inner world of mysterious silence.

The best part of spirituality is that it comes to us when we least expect it. Here was an old man recalling a scene of carnage, where men were killing the enemy and the enemy was killing them. In the midst of that carnage, he utters the words, "Good men—on both sides." On our side, and on the enemy's side: "good men" engaging in bad actions. Did his mystic words, the mystic words of a wild oil rigger, an ex-soldier, and a feisty old monk, spring from the wisdom of old age or from his forty-five years of being a monk?

His one sentence of reality was followed by silence. Though by then he did not know me, and possibly did not know where he was, I now knew him—and where he was—as never before.

In earlier days, he had told me many stories of his service on Omaha Beach, always humorous, sometimes macabre. One I know he would want me to relate is of a time he was taking the wounded back to the troop ship. His was the furthest out to sea, so he would pass ships that were nearer to shore.

Those wounded and dying men wanted to be taken to the nearest ship; they would yell and swear at him to take them to the nearby ships, and he would reply in kind, "No, God damn it, I was told to bring you back to my ship." Once, though the men were verbally assaulting him with special intensity, he again passed a nearby ship. And as he did, it was hit and destroyed.

"If I had listened to them and taken them where they wanted to go, we all would have been killed," he said. "That was my first lesson on the importance of obedience. It was one I never forgot." God forgive us for daily refusing to see good men on both sides.

## Big Mac

Monks are generally not concerned with politics. Not having TV, they are spared the nine months of political torture that precede the elections. This has to be one of the great blessings of monastic life.

Monks are free to vote, though, and some do. There was a monk who was the exception to the monks' general lack of political interest. Born in 1900, he was a delightful character loved by all, a large Irishman from Chicago and a solid Democrat, whom we will call "Mac." The name fits for many reasons.

In the mid-1990s presidential election, some of the younger monks told Mac that the Democratic candidate's personal life was not known for reflecting Christian values. They asked him if he was going to switch his vote to the Republican side.

They knew what his reply would be and joyfully anticipated his reaction. The whole scene was not about politics; it was about making mischief for Mac. They wanted to "get his Irish up."

He responded as expected: "Vote Republican? Never! I have been a Democrat my whole life; even facing death I am not about to change. I do not want to come 'soiled' before my Maker!" Then he would repeat his "Depression years stories" of the inner city Irishman. "The Democrats helped me then, and I am not going to forget them now."

His stories were interesting. I once asked him why he used to jump freight trains. With no small exasperation, he replied: "Why do you think anyone jumps a freight train? To get where they want to go." That is a logical answer to my stupid question.

The best "Mac performance" for the community occurred in the refectory. We had our big meal at noon, although a "big" Trappist meal is somewhat of an oxymoron. We would enter together, eat in silence, and, at the bell, leave together.

A monk read to the community during the meal. The books were of all kinds: histories, biographies, and even some novels.

Mac did not care for any book that leaned Right, whether religiously, socially, or economically. He would become very uncomfortable if a "conservative" book was being read—so much so that if the book got too Far Right, he would pick up his plate and walk out to finish his meal in the kitchen. All could observe his rebellious stomp down the length of the refectory, and it made even eating turnips bearable.

The monks eagerly looked forward to Mac's principled protests. Bets were placed on how long it would take before "that reactionary book" got to him. It was great fun enjoyed by all, including the abbot, another left-leaning Irishman, whom we referred to as our "gentle anarchist." Monks are rebels by nature, or should be. That is why there are so many Irish monks.

Today, if Mac were exposed to Fox News, he would walk out in three seconds. To Mac, no right-winger ever lived in Chicago's inner city, ever experienced the depression, or ever jumped a freight train. "They don't know what they are talking about."

To him, the "Lace Curtain Irish" have forgotten their humble ancestry. Mac's "Shanty Irish" were met with "NO IRISH NEED APPLY" signs and had their heads busted by company goons. To his way of thinking, their present descendants are "spoiled brats who have forgotten, and thus betrayed, their old sod ancestors." It was the old story, repeated throughout history, of the oppressed changing their status and becoming the oppressors.

"O'Reilly and Kelly, Jesus, Mary, and Joseph, Saints above . . . a shillelagh to ye both!"

He is long dead now, and I don't know if anyone has replaced him as the monastic rebel. For the monks' sake, I certainly hope so! As for Mac, I believe he is enjoying the eternal banquet with Tolstoy, Dorothy Day, St. Francis, and Jesus. I doubt he would walk out on that group. They were about as Far Left as you can get!

## A Monk: A Parable

I often remember the words, "you may never say about something which is, that it should not be." These words have challenged me ever since I first heard them. Although I'm convinced of their truth, I daily fail to put them into practice. When something that I dislike happens, the first thing that comes to my mind is "this should not be."

I am forever complaining about the way things are, from religion to stupid drivers, to politics, or young people who talk too fast for this old man to understand. I spend the majority of my day swearing at referees, Tea Party members, and religious fundamentalists. Although in principle I agree with my friend's words, I struggle to put them into practice.

His words are very much like Christ's words, which we all find difficult to put into practice. "Love your enemies, bless them that curse you, do good to them that hate you" (Matt 5:44), or "Resist not evil, and whoever strikes you on the right check, turn to him the other" (Matt 5:39).

Christ's words, like my friend's, are not understandable. They exceed human reason; they go beyond religion, as it is commonly perceived. Christ's wisdom falls within the category of spirituality, even mysticism.

Human wisdom cannot be the judge for understanding God's wisdom. In the Jewish scriptures (our Old Testament) this idea is presented in Isaiah 55:8, where God says, "My thoughts are not your thoughts, nor my ways your ways." Job also wrestled with this problem against his three friends whose arguments were rational, good, and even religious—but wrong! Martin Luther expressed this mystery succinctly: "If you accept human reason you are forced to say that there is either no God, or that God is unjust."[1]

Years ago, there was a popular book entitled, *When Bad Things Happen to Good People*.[2] I find that title troubling, and my question is, "Who says what is happening to us is bad?" From our perspective, things happening to us appear bad, but what about God's perspective? "God's ways are not man's ways, God's thoughts are not man's thoughts."

God deals in the divine realm, we in the human. Are we so arrogant that we suppose both realms are identical? Are we so haughty to presume we think as God thinks? Yes, we are. When something "bad" happens to us, how many times have we said, "This should not be." Later, maybe years later, we realize that what we once thought "should not be" turned out to be a great blessing. Reason and intellect told us one thing, yet just the opposite turned out to be true.

The ability to reason and think is a great gift. It is not, however, our greatest gift. God's greatest gift to us is the ability to see beneath appearances, to see past the visible to the invisible, to see God's activity in what appears to be bad. This is grace, and it trumps reason.

This is not to degrade reason and thinking. On the contrary, we should have more of both. We are saying that, for a believer, reason is not the final word; rather, grace is the final word. What we see, hear, and reason is not life's totality. There are truths that exceed human reason.

1. Dillenberger, *Martin Luther*, 201.
2. Kushner, *When Bad Things Happen*.

Christ taught divine truths not through the medium of human reason but through parables. "To them he spoke only in parables" (Mark 4:34). The wisdom of parables exceeds the limits of the human intellect. In them, divine wisdom oversteps the boundaries of human thought. Today's equivalent of Christ's parables is the eastern koans of the Zen Buddhist masters. "What is the sound of one hand clapping?" Westerners get frustrated when confronted with a koan or parable.

Westerners are logical thinkers. We are the philosophical children of Rene Descartes, "I think, therefore I am," and Immanuel Kant, "Pure reason is the source of morality." We look to our intellects to understand and control reality. Once we leave the area of pure reason, of thinking logically, Westerners often get lost, even frightened. Westerners think; Easterners intuit. This oversimplification is helpful in understanding why Americans have such a difficult time understanding Eastern spirituality, including Christ's. We forget Christ was a Middle Easterner. He was not from Kansas City, nor was he a Greek philosopher who taught in logical syllogisms.

Accordingly, Christ's parables frustrate us to the point of anger, or they would if we properly understood them. To our way of thinking, the parables often have the "bad guys" winning. In the parable of the workers in the vineyard, the late-coming workers, the lazy, indolent ones, get the very same pay as the industrious, responsible workers who worked all day in the "heat of the sun."

Christ's listeners would have known that the late workers had been sitting around drinking wine all day. They would have known that the late workers were the welfare cheats, the freeloaders, those who should not be as they are—lazy, irresponsible.

Not knowing the culture of the times, we miss the point, and thus the "sting." We miss the upsetting message of the parable. The late workers were not your good, industrious, upright citizens. They were the shiftless no-gooders—and they got the same pay? Christ's listeners didn't like the implications, and neither do we. Christ treats them the same way he treats us—with love!

In the parable of the Prodigal Son, the irresponsible, high-living son gets the banquet, instead of the dutiful, responsible, stay-at-home son. That is certainly not fair. But again, Christ is telling us God's love is not limited by our classification of who is deserving and who is not—by what is fair and what is not fair.

In the parable of the Good Samaritan, the pattern continues—the bad guy turns out to be the good guy.[3] To the Jews, all Samaritans were bad guys. They were traitors, unfaithful Jews who were the offspring of those Jews who surrendered to, and became one with, the Babylonians three hundred years before.

A good Jew would not even walk in the land of Samaria, which is just north of Judah, but would go miles out of his way to go around it. And if a Jew happened to walk on Samaria land, he was bound to "shake the dust off his feet." That is the background for our Lord telling the parable of the Good Samaritan.

Who is the good guy in the parable? The Samaritan. The man from Samaria is the one who offers aid to the Jew lying along the roadside. How do you think the Jews listening to that story felt about Jesus telling them that it was their enemy, the person they most hated, who was the charitable person?

In Jewish eyes, it was scandalous to have the people they so hated be more charitable than they. That turned their notion of God, their notion of right and wrong, upside down. The Jewish rabbi walked by the man in need; the respectable Jews left the man in the ditch. The good guys didn't help, but the bad guy, the Samaritan, did. Christ's parables challenge me to see my worst enemy, the person I most disdain, as my brother or sister.

Today, if Christ were telling that parable to us it would go something like this. "There was a man in need, lying in a ditch. People walked by, saw the needy man and walked on, without helping. These people included a clergyman of whatever denomination, a military veteran highly decorated for bravery, the president of the Chamber of Commerce, a member of Mothers Against Drunk Drivers, and the local leader of the Right to Life committee. All saw the man in need, and all walked by.

Then a brown-skinned, heavily bearded member of the Al Qaeda walked by. Or possibly a woman who does abortion counseling. Maybe even a gay person walked by. They saw the man in the ditch and helped him."

How do we feel about that parable, where the "good guys" do not help and the "bad guys" do? Would that scandalous story so upset us that we would want to attack the storyteller? Quite possibly! And that must have been how Christ's listeners felt when they heard the parables.

Our scripture professor told us that one of the reasons Christ was killed was because his parables so angered the people that they wanted to

---

3. See also Luke 10:25–37.

silence his rabble-rousing. One of our greatest illusions is that if we met Jesus today we would agree with him, even like him.

I think Jesus would make me feel very uncomfortable. His acceptance and love of people whom I dislike would upset me greatly. His thinking would be at such odds with mine that it would be difficult for me to be charitable to him—to love him. I think Jesus would anger me.

Christ turns our values—and our world—upside down. Would we not want to silence the teller of today's parable? Are we better than those who wanted to kill Christ? I do not think so. Perhaps we are a little more refined, or a little more civilized than Christ's contemporaries—crucifixions were exceptionally barbaric, after all—but we really are not that much different. Spiritually, we are equally as insecure, frightened, and ready to strike out at our opponents.

Just as at the time of Christ, the Jews didn't want their world, especially their religious world, disturbed—neither do we. We want a world where we can figure things out. We want a "make sense" world and a "make sense" religion, and Christianity teaches neither. Christ didn't make sense. When God loves people I regard as bad, or not as they "should be," that doesn't make any sense at all.

The pope says he knows many Marxists who are very good people, and that he is not at all offended when he is called a Marxist. This doesn't make sense to most American Christians. In fact, it is downright scandalous. The Republican Senator Joseph McCarthy, who was a Catholic, would have attacked Francis with the "wrath of God." Why? Because the pope's words are parabolic, and as such they are disturbing—even angering—to many, as is the following parable.

> A man had an old worthless horse. The horse ran off. His friend said, "Your horse ran off, that's bad." The man said simply, "Maybe it is and maybe it isn't."
>
> The horse returned, followed by another horse. His friend said, "You now have two horses, that's good." The man replied, "Maybe it is and maybe it isn't."
>
> The man's son was riding the new horse, fell off, and broke his leg. His friend said, "Your son broke his leg, that's bad." The man replied, "Maybe it is and maybe it isn't."
>
> *A war broke out and all the young men were taken off to fight, but the son wasn't taken because he had a broken leg. The friend said,*

> *"Your son didn't have to go off to war, that's good." The man said, "Maybe it is and maybe it isn't."*
>
> The son with the broken leg was sitting under a tree. A storm arose, lightning hit the tree, and the son was killed. The friend said, "Your son was killed, that's bad." The man said, "Maybe it is and maybe it isn't."

This parable, like all parables, brings into question whether we humans know what is good and what is bad in the eyes of God. It questions the accuracy of human knowledge about what is ultimately good or bad for us.

If we are honest, we will have to admit that we really don't know, nor should we know, what is good or bad. "And the serpent said to the woman, if you eat the fruit you will not die but your eyes will be opened and you shall be like the gods, knowing what is good and what is evil" (Gen 3:45). Notice that it is the evil spirit who says we will know what is good and what is bad. The liar told us that, not God!

In God's providence do we truly know what is good and what is bad? The hermit's words, "You cannot say something which is, that it should not be," do not make human sense, but they do make "God sense." Hearing Christ's words, we know "God's ways are not man's ways, nor God's thoughts our thoughts." We know that God speaks in parables. Accordingly we Christians are called to live a parable, to live a life that doesn't make complete sense to the world.

Over fifty years ago I read the words of French Cardinal Suhard: "To be a Christian does not mean engaging in propaganda, or stirring people up. It means to live in such a way that your life would not make sense if there were no God." These words are not advocating living a non-sensible life; however, they are saying that there will be times that our faith will demand we do something which in the eyes of the world, even the very Christian world, will seem foolish and make no sense at all. There will be those times when even the good people will say, "You shouldn't do this."

If at times Christian life doesn't make logical sense to the majority of people, monastic life will make even less sense. If the Christian life is often parabolic, it is obvious that monastic life is even more so. To live a monastic life means to live a parable.

As usual, Merton pushed this idea to the extreme—and understandably so, as monks are extreme people. Monks are trying to get at the radical part, the "root" of life. In describing this radical element of monastic life, Merton comes on full force.

"Monastic life is useless, not pragmatic. Our life is not for producing results, even spiritual results. Monastic life has no purpose whatever. It is useless, totally useless. We are not monks in order to save souls; that is not our job, that is God's job. When you enter a monastery you are no longer a factor in the world."[4]

Alan Watts, a spiritual writer of the mid-1900s explained the difference between purpose and meaning in his book *Behold the Spirit*: "Life without purpose is not necessarily life without meaning. A purpose is justified by something beyond itself, but meaning is its own justification . . . it is meaning, rather than purpose, which gives life its justification. Thus the inner life of God and its created reflection is not purposeful; like the greatest achievement of human art, it is meaningful. Insofar as man has not realized union with God he has purpose but no meaning; but insofar as he has realized it, he has meaning and no purpose."[5]

When I was wrestling with the decision of whether to be a monk, I had to face "monastic life as parable." Between God and me, it was a knock-down, drag-out brawl that went on for over a year. At midnight, walking the beaches of Florida and Puerto Rico, it was a slugfest.

Later, in the monastery, I took Jacob as my religious name, the one "who wrestled with God" (Gen 32:24–31). If we have never been in a deep struggle, a crucial questioning with God, have we truly met God? Such a clash will forever affect a person. He/she will arrive at a deeper insight, but like Jacob, they will walk with infirmity the rest of their life. They will know and feel their vulnerability.

I had to ask myself if I was running away from something. Although I was a very poor student, I had turned out, surprisingly, to be a very good teacher. I was totally at ease both in the classroom and pulpit. I enjoyed communicating, and teaching actually gave me a "high." After I taught an adult education class, a fellow teacher, a nun who was herself an excellent teacher, said to me, "You are good, and know you are good. I can tell by the way you enjoy yourself when you are teaching. Your teaching is a performance." I answered, "yes" to both her statements, because truthfulness is not, in itself, boastfulness.

Problems can arise for communicators, however. How do you psychologically unwind after two hours of teaching adults where you were having

4. *Tape* 9.

5. Watts, *Behold the Spirit*, 177.

so much fun they had to tell you the time was up? How do you come down enough to get some sleep before facing 175 high school kids the next day?

A monk, who was formerly a professional organist, once told me that before he was to give a special concert he would always throw up. I could identify with his experience. I had attributed my "highs" to being all ego, but he corrected me. "Sure, ego is involved, but that feeling is not all ego," he said. "That's art." I realized he was right. Teaching is primarily an art. We both ended up being monks, sublimating our natural instincts for something deeper.

A priest friend from another diocese, who, like myself was not a great student but became an outstanding high school teacher, said that while teaching he "loved the center ring." I never saw outstanding teachers who did not have a lot of "ham" in them. Great teachers love the center ring.

When people heard that I was going to enter a monastery where silence was the norm, thus eliminating any teaching or preaching, they objected. They were very logical: "You have been given an exceptional ability, a talent to teach, especially teaching young people. That is God's gift to you, and you can't disregard a talent." A woman said that to me, almost word for word, and she wasn't even my mother. My mother, by the way, repeated the idea like a mantra.

Some even quoted scripture to pressure me to use what I had been given, "You must not hide your light under a basket" (Matt 5:15). I wrestled with that problem. Was monastic life useless? Did it have any purpose? Was I running away from some responsibility?

After all my theological education, I spent years in a monastery looking out the window while wrapping fruitcakes. A trained monkey could have done my job, possibly better than I. In fact, he could have been any ordinary monkey, even one that was a little bit slow.

A person needed absolutely no education or training to wrap fruitcakes. After twenty-eight years of schooling, to spend your life wrapping fruitcakes doesn't make sense. It is not logical, nor reasonable.

My father was a mechanical engineer; he was very reasonable, logical, and smart. He always allowed me to do what I chose to do, from choosing a college to choosing a monastic vocation. He never said anything about my decision. I knew, though, what his engineering, logical, reasonable mind was thinking: "This is foolish, it's not logical, and it makes no sense whatsoever." And he was right. He knew it and I knew it, although those words were never spoken between us.

Monastic life is not logical, it makes no sense, and it's foolish. If a monk tries to have his life make sense so he can be a "spiritual somebody," then he is missing the point of his monastic vocation and falling into spiritual pride. In a monastery, "If you are (trying) to be a somebody, you might as well go outside, where it counts. In a monastery, being a somebody doesn't count."[6] To be authentic, the Christian life itself must be a parable. It doesn't always make complete sense—and that frightens us. We prefer religion to spirituality.

Religion literally means, "to tie together." In religion, we do good actions in order to be tied to God. Religion is strongly ethical. Good behavior is the goal, in order to live a life pleasing to God. Religion has a moral base.

Spirituality is living with the mindfulness that we are already tied with God, that we are one with God. Spirituality is awareness that we are children of God, and our good actions flow from our awareness of that union. Spirituality has a supernatural base.

We prefer actions to the supernatural. We can control ethical behavior; we cannot control God's behavior. Religion (what we do) and the supernatural (what God does within us) go together, but they are not identical. If they are wrongly construed, they can be antithetical.

"My religion tells me to eliminate your religion" may be a religious belief, but it is not a spiritual belief. Did Christ intend to proclaim a religion, to tell us what to do? Or did he want to infuse a spirituality, to tell us who we are? The former makes us good people; the latter gives us a new identity as a child of God. Did Christ come to start a religious organization, or to impart his Spirit of Sonship . . . or both? Are Christians called to be good citizens, or to live the mystery of a parable? They are not automatically the same. Am I called to be a good citizen and participate in an unjust war, or refuse and live a parable of being a traitor? Monks emphatically say we are called to live a parable, as was Christ.

To be authentic, monastic life must be a parable. Indeed, it must be the most radical of parables. This means monasticism must be Christlike, which, from a human perspective, doesn't make a lot of sense.

6. *Tape 9.*

## Monastic Life

I have mentioned that my ten years of active priesthood were fun and we laughed a lot. The same can be said for my twenty-eight years in the monastery. I had fun. That sounds strange doesn't it? A Trappist monastery, one of the strictest orders in the church, is a fun place! Wherever there are people, there are laughable situations.

My room faced west, and in the summer it could be 90 degrees in my room when I went to bed at eight o'clock. There was no air conditioning, but I went to sleep right away. We got up at three in the morning, so by bedtime you were tired enough to sleep in the third layer of hell. We ate all our meals in silence. The first three years I lost fifty pounds and felt great, without spending money going to the YMCA.

Generally, talking was limited and low key. We didn't talk at all from seven thirty at night to seven thirty the next morning—this was called the grand silence. We did talk at work and other times when it was necessary or called for by charity. The silence was not forced or constrained; we wanted quiet surroundings.

The silence was comfortable and relaxing. Sometimes at work we could be completely silent, other times we would talk, sometimes quite a bit. Loud, boisterous talking was out of place, although I did laugh at some jokes a little too energetically.

We played the talking by ear; there was no hard and fast rule. If you felt the person working next to you wanted to talk, you would talk, and vice versa. I never heard anyone tell another that they didn't care to talk. Charity was the rule we tried to follow rather than a rule of silence. "Silence is spoken here" is a slogan that monks appreciate, but they will not impose silence on anyone. They don't impose anything on anyone. If a person wants to talk, the monk will talk.

Since leaving the monastery I have worked at a soup kitchen surrounded by women. How I longed for monks and their silence. (I probably should not have written that line. Believe it or not, there are female "monks" in the Trappist order, called "Trappistines." They keep silence better than the men do.)

Monks sleep on five-inch mattresses laid on boards. We didn't have cushioned chairs. It is Spartan but not harsh; it is a very healthy lifestyle. One of the good results of monastic living is that you quickly learn all the things you do not need—shaving lotion, deodorant, etc. Being stripped of these accessories, you learn you do not need or even want them. You don't spend time deciding what to wear. You have two pairs of shoes, one for inside and one for work outside. It simplifies life.

Many of America's closets hold enough shoes to shod China. I always wonder how long it must take to decide which shoes to wear. If a monk ran the country, the economy would come to a halt within six weeks—can you imagine everyone acquiring only what they need? Now that is out and out subversive! Unpatriotic, even. To make our economy grow, we must buy in excess. That makes life not only complicated, but also wasteful—but it is good business. I have heard of people getting lost in their closets and not finding their way out for days.

The fact that there were no cell phones was a sure sign we were living in the kingdom of God. I picture Hell as masses of people jammed into a small area all talking at once on their cell phones, twenty-four hours a day, for eternity. That should frighten us more than the threat of fire and brimstone. Please God, not that!

We also had no TV or radio. We would not leave the grounds except for doctor visits or other necessary errands. We did have a two-mile-long tract of land to walk or jog, and I jogged daily for twenty-eight years. In the monastery, jogging is called "dynamic yoga." It is great for meditation. There are no basketball hoops or handball courts, as monks are not into competition.

When I entered, we planted a vegetable garden, harvested potatoes, and milked about seventy-five cows. For the first seven years I worked in construction. We did concrete work, used jackhammers, put in water lines. When the sun got hot, we kept our long-sleeved denim shirts on. No T-shirts, no sunscreen—hot but healthy. I loved the work.

During those times, the novices would dig graves for the deceased monks. We would dig the graves the standard six feet deep. We had very talented men, but some didn't know how to shovel dirt. Digging ditches is a given talent, one of the very few I have.

In my novice group we had a graduate (now deceased) of Juilliard School of Music who had made his livelihood as a professional organist. One day, I was in the shop, and in came the organist. He was embarrassed. A monk had asked him to get a pair of pliers, and he sheepishly said to me, "I don't know what a pair of pliers is." He was a Juilliard graduate, an absolute genius, and a great guy, but he did not know what pliers were. So what? I thought a "musical score" was what they played at a baseball game during the seventh-inning stretch.

Different people have different talents, but all are in the body of Christ. That is one of the unexpected blessings of monastic living. You are thrown in with all types of people—people you would ordinarily not have associated with elsewhere. Some monks never finished high school and others had graduate degrees. When a tractor is broken, the smart monk is the one who can fix it, not the one with the college degrees.

Digging graves, besides being great exercise, is a moving experience. The fact that you have lived so closely with the deceased, possibly serving him in the infirmary, makes the experience personal. Being the tallest novice, I was the one throwing out the dirt from the bottom of the grave.

If I wanted to take a rest, instead of climbing out of a six-foot hole I would merely lie down on the bottom of the grave. Lying on the bottom of a grave is a meditative position. Once while I was lying there, an older monk walked by, saw me, and said, "What in God's name are you doing there?"

I opened my eyes and replied, "It's Resurrection Day, and I am the first one up."

"That sounds like something you would say," he answered. "Today's smart-mouth novices—it's not like the good old days when novices knew their place." Remember, "monks speak only when necessary."

Monks are not buried in coffins. Monks hold straps that cradle the body and lower it into the grave. A monk stands in the grave holding the head as the body is lowered. With the body at rest he places a sheet over it. The abbot sprinkles the body with holy water, reminding all of our baptism. He then walks around the grave sprinkling a few hands of dirt into the grave. Then all depart.

The novices change from their robes into their work clothes and fill in the grave. It is very real, very authentic, with no cushioned coffins, no makeup, no artificial grass, no pious empty pronouncements like, "He is in a better place now." It is all done in absolute silence. It is a very dignified and meaningful burial. Relatives and friends in attendance often express their appreciation for the dignity and beauty of the service. We all have our own way of celebrating the rite of passage. I think the monks do it pretty well. There is nothing like the realization of death to focus one's attention and to clarify one's thoughts. The starkness and authenticity of a monk's funeral makes that point.

## Monastic Work

Monastic labor is an essential part of monastic life. Indeed, work is an essential part of everyone's life. Work may well be the most trusted indicator of a person's character. Regarding work, Merton is known to have said, "You can learn more about a man working with him for one week in the fields, than you can by having spiritual talks with him for six months." Talk is cheap and produces little. Most "spiritual talk" is cheaper and produces even less.

The rule for monks that St. Benedict wrote in the 500s emphasizes the place of work in a monk's life. In his rule, work plays an equal part with prayer. Monastic life is described as *ora et labora*, Latin words for "pray and work." Monks have to support themselves by the work of their hands; they are not to live off donations. Every year, the monastery makes a profit from their work in the cheese and fruitcake business. After taking money for expenses, what they have left over, they give away—half to local charities and half to worldwide charities. Those yearly donations totaled a substantial amount of money. You don't find too many religious organizations giving away money.

For work to be truly monastic, it needs to be of a special kind. Repetitious, monotonous work is monks' work. The less thinking required the better. Boxes are needed to ship cheese and fruitcakes. Making up these thousands and thousands of boxes is ideal monastic work. Working in the fields, digging ditches or graves, and harvesting potatoes are ideal monastic jobs. Mindless jobs are contemplative jobs. Working on the floor of the New York stock exchange would not be a good monk's job for more reasons than one.

Gentle bodily motion is an aid in contemplation, it relaxes the body and helps free the mind of thoughts. Contemplative prayer needs silence, and for about fifteen years I had the most contemplative job in the monastery.

For four hours each morning, I stood in a corner by myself, looking out a window, wrapping fruitcakes. I wrapped the cakes (265 cakes a day), put them in cans, and then in boxes, then placed them on a table. There was not another person around, and thus I spoke hardly a word for four hours each morning for about fifteen years.

It takes about thirty seconds to learn how to wrap a fruitcake, and after that half a minute your mind is home free. There is nothing to think about. I could, and in fact did a few times, wrap cakes with my eyes closed. There was some motion in the process; I was not standing still. I would turn left to pick up the cakes off the rack, then turn center to the wrapping table. I would wrap the cake, turn right and place the cake on a hot plate, and then turn to put the cake in a can. Then I would start the process all over. Swaying back and forth, left, center, right in total silence while looking out a window. It was very much like rocking a baby. You can't get more contemplative than that.

If you do a job in silence for fifteen years, you will probably either learn something about yourself or go stark, raving mad. Indeed, some of my friends accused me of the latter. That silence does give you an opportunity to look into yourself. Once we learn what is going on inside ourselves, we begin to learn what is going on inside everyone. Silence gives you some insight into human nature, which may not be pretty or flattering, but it leads to realizing and accepting God's mercy for yourself and everyone else.

The goals of the contemplative life are self-knowledge, compassion toward yourself and others, and gratitude for God's mercy. My fifteen years of wrapping fruitcakes helped me in that process. However, self-knowledge is a job that never ends. It is one area where the older you get, the greater the awareness. Self-knowledge should increase with age.

People ask me what insight I gained during that experience. I had studied theology and spirituality for years, but did I learn anything new at my job? There was one insight that sticks out in my mind because I had never thought about it before nor heard it discussed. It involves the question: Why do we sin? Is there an underlying reason deeper than our instincts of greed, anger, envy, and pride that leads to sin?

I looked at my past life and wondered why I had committed sins. At some time, maybe ten years after I started wrapping the cakes, it dawned on me. I had committed sins because I felt guilty. In other words, I realized that within us, there is a prior sense of guilt, one that exists before the act of sin and is the cause of sin. When you stop to think of it, that makes sense. Why do we always have to feel that we are right? Because unconsciously, we feel we are wrong, or guilty. In any kind of a contest, everyone feels they must win, or they are a failure. Why do we have this drive to win? Because we feel we are losers, that we are guilty.

An adolescent feels worthless: he has failed at everything, not only at school, but also at acquiring friends. He feels a failure and alone, and he feels guilt for his sad situation. In order to "be somebody" he may do destructive things to draw attention to himself, to get the approval of his peers or make himself feel that at least he has done something, even if it is bad.

We see those destructive acts and say that he is bad, but he felt he was bad before he did the destructive acts. Now he is caught in a downward spiral: feelings of guilt, then the destructive act, and more feelings of guilt. The only way out of that damaging cycle is for that kid to realize that he is somebody; that he has worth because he is a child of God. Some adult has to take enough interest in him to lead him to that awareness. That takes time and hard work, with no guarantee of success. It means somebody has to show him love. It is a lot easier just to "put the creep in jail and forget him."

Within each of us, we hold that primordial sense of guilt; it is basic to the human condition. This fundamental, ingrained guilt we feel before we sin is with us from birth. It is associated with what we have traditionally called "original sin," which is a very misleading term. The next question is, "What is always associated with guilt?" The answer is fear. There is never a sense of guilt without an accompanying sense of fear.

The realization that guilt and fear is present within our subconscious before we sin is not easily recognizable. We keep these uncomfortable facts in our subconscious for safety reasons—we want to forget our sense of guilt and fear because they are too painful to accept. We don't totally forget them, though, because they remain in our subconscious. We are merely unaware that we still remember our guilt and fear.

Fear is the most basic instinct. I once saw a rabbit caught in a drain-pipe. I lifted him out, and while I was holding him I noticed his heart was beating so fast and hard that I thought it would burst out of his side. I thought: "Rabbit, you are afraid. Welcome to the crowd. We're all afraid to the point of our hearts bursting out of our sides, we just don't know it." I think that is what God is always saying to us: "Don't be afraid; it is all right. Fear not." These are the most used words in the gospel. Christ repeatedly said, "Fear not."

I felt my insight about subconscious guilt was correct, but I sought some verification. I happened upon a book by Sigmund Freud, in which he told the following story: A few psychiatrists were discussing a group of hardened criminals and how guilty they must now feel sitting in prison remembering their past deeds. And that could be true. Remorse for crimes can be real. But Freud took it a step further and said, "Gentlemen, as paradoxical as it may sound, I must maintain that their sense of guilt was present prior to their offense."[7]

I just about fell out of my chair. I thought, "That fox, he probably came up with that insight over his morning cup of coffee, and it took me ten years standing in front of window wrapping fruitcakes to come to the same conclusion." We feel guilty before we sin. That sense of guilt is in our subconscious. We put it there for our sense of safety, and it is very difficult to pry loose, because it frightens us. That is the reason we hid it away in the first place, because carrying a sense of guilt is frightening and painful.

That is what I learned wrapping fruitcakes. After such a lengthy and complex answer I suspect that the person who asked me "What did you learn?" was sorry he asked. He probably didn't have any interest in Freud.

It would have been better for me, and him, if I had just said, "I learned that Johnny Carson's joke about there being only one fruitcake ever made that we all pass around at Christmas time, is just that, a joke." I wrapped 265 fruitcakes a day, 300 days a year, for fifteen years—that's 1,192,500 fruitcakes—to prove it.

Most monks also had a small, solitary afternoon job requiring about an hour's work. I operated the monastic sewer plant. It had a capacity of 100,000 gallons of sewage, and it was a little less than a mile from the monastery. Sewage plants operate all the time: twenty-four hours a day. They never take a day off. Not Christmas, nor Easter, nor Thanksgiving and Sundays. If it's 105 degrees or -20 degrees, rain or shine, snow or ice, a sewage plant must continue to operate. That means its operator must be there, so there I was. I had that job for about twenty-three years. It was like my fruitcake job—very quiet, very contemplative—besides being very close to nature. When my friends came to the monastery to make a retreat, I would take them down to the plant and we would talk. They had never been to a sewage plant before. They don't know what they are missing.

Sometimes in the summer, when it was hot, I would go down to the plant at 4:30 in the morning, while the moon was still out. The sound of the aerated, bubbling water was like walking on the seashore. With the moon out and the "waves" flopping, I would sit there thinking, "People spend thousands of dollars to go to the ocean to hear the waves and see the moon. I have the same experience for free. It is very contemplative." By the way, a properly operating sewage plant does not smell, and our plant never smelled.

7. Freud, *Character and Culture*, 179.

# Hermitage

I mention the hermit experience for two reasons: first because it is so unknown, misunderstood, and distrusted that it deserves a day in court. Also, because hermits are the fathers of today's monks and have been around for even longer. Most Americans believe the world began in 1492, but hermits remind us of our shortsightedness.

I also mention hermits because of my good friend at the monastery. I owe it to him to show that hermits can be very human, caring people. They are not spiritual egotists or misanthropes.

People today cannot seem to live without noise surrounding them. They can't stand quiet. In public places, restaurants, doctor's offices, and even restrooms there is piped-in noise. Even when they are by themselves, most people want some kind of noise around them.

Ours is the first time in human history that this "surround me with noise" attitude has existed. Before, people had silence built into their lives. Farmers, shepherds, cowboys, seamen, hunters, women in the homes, kids walking to and from school—all were often alone and in comparative quiet.

Now, quiet is purposefully excluded. It will be interesting to see how this generation will develop, these people who have grown up with earphones attached since they were in diapers.

Today, when people hear of hermits it just boggles their minds. They consider a person living in total quiet twenty-four hours a day to be a nut case. I am sure there have been hermits who would fit into that category, just as every profession has its share of strange people. However, you are not necessarily nutty just because you can handle and grow in silence.

In the church today, there are very few religious professed hermits. The hermit life is not encouraged, and rightfully so. It can too easily be an escape from the irritants of community living—the irritants of other monks.

How did hermits come about? In the year 313, the Roman Emperor Constantine wanted a unified empire, so he converted his empire to Christianity. He didn't especially care about religion, but he saw it as a unifying factor. He wanted everyone to be the same.

He was not baptized until he was on his deathbed, and yet he is regarded as one of the champions of Christianity. Constantine's decree, the Edict of Milan, declared that his empire would accept Christianity and that Christianity was the official religion of the empire. He put the cross on his soldiers' shields, with the words, "In this sign we conquer."

Before Constantine, Christians were looked down upon and persecuted. Ironically, that time of persecution was also the time of the greatest growth in the church. Why? Because people said, "Behold these Christians, see how they love one another." Seeing the example of good Christians, others became Christian.

Beginning with Constantine, the Christian situation changed completely. During the 300s, Christianity became the state religion. Christians became "top dog," and with that change in status came a change in attitude. They were now "the establishment," given preference by the civil society. Church laws became civil laws with civil punishments. As time went on, non-Christians were excluded from public life or, in some cases, actively persecuted by Christians.

I heard a history professor and priest say: "Before the Edict of Milan, Christianity was a persecuted church. Since then, Christianity has become a persecuting church." He was generalizing to make the point that power brings evil, that the top dog will always dominate. He was not degrading Christianity; rather, he was telling us how the church must avoid power and its evils—because the church's founder avoided those temptations.

In the same vein, I was talking with a monk who knew some church history, and he expressed a similar idea. "In the fourth century the church was assimilated into the Roman Empire, and, ever since, the church has been preaching the Roman Empire of power and wealth, rather than the gospel of service and love." Again, this is purposeful hyperbole, and it is said not by an enemy of the church but by a loyal son. He was saying that when the church becomes powerful, and the church and state cohabit, the gospel loses.

There is nothing more refreshing and fun than listening to a good Christian who is intelligent, honest, and somewhat of a religious cynic. When Voltaire was on his deathbed, a priest said to him, "It is time to make your peace with God." Voltaire, who was a great cynic, if not a great Christian, responded, "I didn't know we were at odds." God had to love that line, for it is good theology. Yet the church banned his books; the church has a hard time taking a joke.

When the empire became Christian, some Christians didn't feel comfortable in that "Christian Empire." They wanted to get away from "Christian society" because they felt the church had become too friendly with the state. They fled to the Egyptian dessert and lived as hermits. They were the first monks. They also were Christian cynics and rebels.

At the monastery, a monk could go out to a hermitage once a year for a week: Sunday afternoon to Sunday morning. He would take food and water for a week and spend the entire time in solitude. A couple of times, I finagled nine days instead of a week. Once I got to stay four weeks—my reward for being a good monk, or maybe it was for harassing the abbot to let me go. He finally did, I think to get rid of me.

What do hermits and the role they played in the fourth-century church have to do with the reform of Vatican II? In the mid-1960s, young clergy led the way in applying Vatican II spirituality. They played the role that the first hermits played in their efforts to reform the church.

They were the reformers, as were the hermits of old, who left the church society and protested what they saw as the church's becoming worldly and powerful. They rejected the political church. The young clergy of the 1960s didn't flee to the desert, but they did try to reform the church's daily practices, and they did reject the church of power and wealth.

I feel that the church is again in need of reformers like the monks of old and the young priests of the 1960s. We need some new desert fathers and some new young Turks. Who is going to be the loyal opposition? Who is going to be the "hermits" of the 400s? Who is going to be the Vatican II priests of the sixties? Who is going to take up Pope Francis' lead to reform the church? The obvious answer would seem to be the young clergy. However, there is a growing question: Are today's clergy going to be the solution to, or part of, the problem? That problem, to a large degree, is clericalism.

# 3

# Today

## Clericalism

THE MOST OBVIOUS DIFFERENCE I have experienced between the church of
the late 1960s and 1970s and the present-day church is clericalism. While in
the monastery those twenty-eight years, many of my priest friends told me
how clericalism among the younger priests seemed to be growing by the year.

I am no longer a cleric, so I hesitate to mention that negative critique
of the clergy. I do not feel I am in any position to judge the behavior of
priests, or anyone for that matter, nor do I wish to do so. My priesthood was
neither fault-free nor sin-free. After all, "Let him who is without sin cast the
first stone," and I have no right to stone the present-day clergy.

I only mention the topic because it is being discussed by just about
everyone who cares about the church. Those who are the most critical are
the older priests and one other "person of some repute."

Two priests have written books with telling titles: *Clericalism: The
Death of the Priesthood* by a Jesuit, George Wilson; and *Clerical Culture:
Contradiction and Transformation* by Michael Papesh, a diocesan priest.
However, the strongest incentive to mention my observations about clerical
life today is Pope Francis.

When the pope speaks out against clericalism, he makes it fair game
for others to do so. Indeed, Pope Francis said, "I want to get rid of clericalism." How about that? Has a pope ever said anything more radical? Pope
Francis was imitating his namesake St. Francis, who attacked the clerical
culture of his day, though he was not, himself, a priest.

I think they should have the pope's words printed on T-shirts. A priest
saying Mass facing an entire congregation wearing an "I want to get rid

of clericalism" T-shirt would be well grounded, and it would probably shorten his homily.

At "World Youth Day" in Argentina in the spring of 2013, the pope spoke those words and more: "I want to see the church get closer to the people. I want to get rid of clericalism, the mundane, this closing ourselves off within ourselves, in our parishes, schools or structures."[1]

At the beginning of his papacy, Pope Francis said that clericalism was one of the abuses in the church he wanted to correct. "When I meet a clericalist, I become anti-clerical."[2]

That is very radical language. If a person outside the church made such a statement, cries of "Bigot! Anti-Catholic!" would arise from the Catholic Right. Some Catholics carry a martyr complex, always looking for someone to be against them so that they may suffer for a noble cause.

The following is a sad tale of clericalism. While in the monastery, I was told of a bishop who wanted to resume making priests monsignors. The conferring of such "honors" went out of practice in the 1950s, much like the hula-hoop.

No one really knows what monsignors are or do. They are like warts that appear on the clerical skin; no one knows where they come from or what they signify. Actually, "monsignor" is an honorary title that a bishop asks Rome to give to a few selected priests. There are no extra powers bestowed on the recipient, as far I know, as I have looked into the matter very thoroughly in anticipation of a future honor richly deserved.

Most of the monsignors in the past were embarrassed of the absurd outfits they were required to wear—red-trimmed tassels and red birettas. If you saw a bunch of them at a clerical gathering, they looked like a flock of redbirds sunning themselves on telephone lines.

You may be wondering, "What's a biretta?" It is a clerical hat like that worn by Barry Fitzgerald in the 1940s movie *Going My Way*. Bing Crosby was the "new breed priest" and wore a baseball cap, which was rather daring back then. Every Catholic, "under pain of mortal sin," had to see that movie.

As a priest, I lived with two monsignors. They were two of the finest men I have ever been around, and both refused to wear their "Halloween outfits." One refused to even buy the getup; the other kept it in the closet. Monsignors are not intrinsically evil, you see, it is their attire.

---

1. Winfield, et al. "Rebel pope," para. 9.
2. Scalfari, "The Pope."

I like to tell a story about a bishop who wanted to reinstate the practice of making monsignors. The priests had a meeting with the bishop to discuss this weighty matter. The older priests were puzzled by the suggestion but some of the younger priests liked the idea. They had the look of expectancy such as a six-year-old gets on Christmas Eve.

A priest said to the bishop that making monsignors today would send a bad message, that this is the age of the laity and the conferring of clerical honors would be out of place. He then asked the bishop, "What reason would there be for making monsignors?"

The bishop replied with words to the effect of, "I think that if young men who are thinking about the priesthood knew that someday they could become a monsignor, it would provide an incentive for them to be a priest."

If you have any love for the priesthood, which I do, the bishop's words should make you cry. Attaching clerical honors as an incentive to attract vocations to the priesthood is clericalism at its worst. I was delighted when, in December 2013, the pope did away with the title monsignor for parish priests. As a bishop, he had never conferred that title.

It is also obvious that the title "young priests" is not confined to men in their twenties or thirties. There are numerous bishops who have a clerical mentality and who have worked to establish that mentality. Clerically-minded men are attracted to a clerical church.

My closest priest friend told me of an encounter he had with a bishop several years ago. The priest had made no secret he was not overly fond of the bishop, and the bishop asked him, "You don't like me do you?"

"No, I don't," was the reply.

The bishop asked, "Why?"

"Because I think you are superficial," my priest friend replied. "Specifically, I think you are spiritually superficial."

I don't know if I could ever have the courage to be that truthful. Talk about hitting a person where it hurts—telling a bishop that he is spiritually superficial tops the list.

But aren't we all somewhat spiritually superficial? That superficiality within the church results in clericalism, which could very well be the biggest problem the church faces today. The pope seems to think it is. Clericalism is contrary to the spirit of Vatican II.

We have asked, "What happened to Vatican II?" A sizable part of that answer is clericalism. We went from priests wanting to serve people to priests wanting to be served by the people. Since the pope himself has let the genie out of the bottle, let's follow it through to the bitter end.

As a Catholic, and a friend of priests, I don't like talking about that subject any more than you like listening. However, when the pope admits that when he sees clericalism he becomes "anti-clerical," it is sure to be a hot topic of his pontificate, as it has been for older priests for years.

More important than the pope's words are his actions. He lives not in the papal quarters but in the visitors' quarters, and he eats his meal with the guests. He has cut back on the pomp and pageantry of the papacy.

Those ridiculous red shoes were the first things to go; Pope Francis wears a pair of ordinary black shoes. Previous popes looked like somebody you would see in a Mardi Gras parade. When the pope comes out wearing Nikes, though, I know the church will prosper again.

Using the pope's words, the *National Catholic Reporter* had an article on clericalism that is the best I have read, truthful and courageous. Robert McClory wrote how the pope "is building by example, a case against the arrogance and self-satisfaction that provides the foundation for a class-conscious society, those who make the decisions and those who don't . . . The clerical mentality consists of 'those who have given up earthly rewards in favor of honorific titles, fancy liturgical attire and above all—power.'"[3]

Some of those unneeded honorific titles are, to name a few, monsignor, right reverend, very reverend, most reverend, your excellency, your grace, and reverend father (I never did know the difference between a right, very, and most reverend).

I wonder if Pope Francis likes the title "your holiness"? I heard he wanted to drop it. The pope calls himself a sinner, and a person who recognizes his sinfulness does not wish to be addressed as your holiness. In Mark, when a man addresses Jesus as "good," he replies, "Why do you call me good? No man is good" (Mark 10:18).

McClory concludes, "That clericalism is breeding a mentality which breeds ambition, status and power." Clericalism has been around a long time, at least since feudalism with its two-class system of nobility and peasants. The higher clergy were taken from the nobility, and that alone is a class distinction. Added to that was the difference in educational levels, which provided even more distance between the clergy and laity.

I was an active priest for ten years. Was clericalism present in the 1960s and 1970s? Some, but it was nowhere near what it is today. We young

3. McClory, "New Pope."

priests were rebelling against the strong clerical atmosphere that formed our pre-Vatican training. We were the "rebels with a cause"—fighting clericalism. In the seminary, we wore cassocks for six years. You could never walk out of your room without your cassock on. A cassock had 182 snaps down the front, and Lord help you if you had one unsnapped. Military academies have one plebe year, but in the 1950s, seminarians were plebes for seven or eight years. The clerical climate was suffocating. It was a case of clerical inbreeding.

Maybe in the 1960s, in rebelling against our excessive clerical upbringing, we were "unclerical" to the point of being rough around the edges. For sure, we were never accused of being "too clerical."

My first year in the seminary, in the 1950s, I became a close friend to a man who was about to be ordained. I was unfamiliar with just how to address a very close friend who became a priest, so I asked him, "How does your older brother address you now that you are a priest?" He answered: "After one week it was 'Father,' after two weeks it was 'Father Jim,' after three weeks it was 'Jim,' and by the end of the month we were right back to 'old shit for brains.'" That is the best antidote to clericalism I have ever heard—priest or no priest, he was still the kid brother. Priest or no priest, he was still a human being, flawed, as are we all.

A priest gets caught up in clericalism when he sees himself as first a cleric, then a human being. A priest must first accept the fact that, before all else, he is a man (maybe someday a woman) with the faults, failures, mistakes, and even sins that we all have. After first accepting his humanness, he then can recognize that he also happens to be a priest.

If he begins the other way around, thinking, "I am a priest," while forgetting his humanness, he will feel superior to the laity. Even when he is serving others he will have a condescending air about him.

My friends and I, as active priests, never felt superior to lay people. I always felt that lay people, with all the troubles they had with family and finances, were living a better Christian life than was I. I was edified by their courage in facing the challenges of family life and the workplace. I often thought: "That life is too tough for me. I am glad I don't have to work to keep a family together. I hope those good people are praying for me."

Clericalism is the inability to identify with the human condition. Clericalism lacks empathy; it is an inability to realize "I am one with this other person."

Recently, a Catholic newspaper, writing about today's newly ordained priests, said, "Young priests favor a formal liturgy, a more high-church form of worship." Something like the Last Supper, I suppose!

Notice the article didn't say anything about how the young priests see the role of the people for whom and with whom the liturgy is shared. It does not seem that these priests have an appreciation for the people's role in worship. Is it secondary to them that the liturgy be understandable and meaningful to the laity? Do they appreciate that it is the people's liturgy, and the priests are there for the people? If it were not for the people there would be no Mass! It is as if they see the Mass as a grand production of which they are the conductors, and the people's role is to sit back and observe this magnificent orchestration led by the brilliant and talented maestro. That is liturgical clericalism. If people wanted an elegant performance, they would go to a concert hall and listen to Mozart's *Requiem*. Recently, a retired priest told me that a newly ordained priest went to his high school reunion wearing his cassock. Now that is clerical elegance!

My negative remarks about the young clergy are, to some extent, unfair. I am sure that there are young priests who have avoided the arrogant clerical trap, and that there are many good, intelligent young priests serving their people. Indeed, a young priest was very helpful in my transition from priesthood to a layperson. He was not only knowledgeable; he was kind.

Those serving priests will not be offended by my criticism of some of the clergy any more than they are offended by the pope's remarks about some of the clergy. Obviously, the pope's criticism, as is mine, is directed at the abuse of clericalism, not the priesthood itself. Neither the pope nor myself dislike the priesthood! We dislike seeing it misused or used for personal glorification, which is the root of clericalism. I have no problem with sinful priests, being one myself. However, it's sad to see a priest using his priesthood to make himself spiritually better than others. I can handle an alcoholic priest; I can't handle an elitist priest.

I also admit that my contact with the young clergy is very limited. Unfortunately, one experience I have had with a young priest confirmed my worst fears. I was speaking with a newly ordained priest, who was perhaps twenty-six years old. I was eighty years old. As I was leaving he said, "God bless you, my son."

You don't have to know the definition of clericalism to know that is clericalism! A twenty-six-year-old never calls an eighty-year-old "my son." The young priest, of course, would insist that he was speaking in a spiritual sense, but that makes it worse! He thinks his priesthood makes him "spiritually above others."

There is no office or position that makes a person spiritually superior to another. The man carrying out the garbage may be spiritually superior to a priest, to a bishop, even to the pope. There have been some very evil popes and some very good garbage collectors.

Spiritually, a priest is not superior; he is a human being like all other human beings. I never met a priest worth his salt who felt spiritually superior to others. Indeed, that is the worst kind of clericalism.

The John Jay Institute defined clericalism clearly and succinctly: "Clericalism is an over-riding set of beliefs and behaviors in which the clergy view themselves as different, separate and exempt from norms, rules and consequences that apply to everyone else in society."[4]

Every priest should post that on his bathroom mirror so he reads it every morning before he mingles with the people of God—who are his equals, and maybe even his superiors.

## Birth Control? Not Again

Before Vatican II, the major topic of moral matters was birth control. It seemed as though a couple's entire spiritual life was judged on one issue and one issue alone: Did they practice birth control? Their charity or capacity to love was not a consideration. Lately, I had been hearing that message again; accordingly, I was relieved to hear Francis say: "We cannot insist only on issues related to abortion, gay marriage, and contraceptive methods. It is not necessary to talk about these issues all the time." The pope "had been reprimanded for failing to speak often of these things."[5]

After the council, this topic just dropped off the radar; it was a done deal. The Catholic people had decided for themselves, and the priests couldn't have been more pleased. A don't-ask-don't-tell truce had been reached. Everyone was satisfied; or, they had been until now. A priest recently said to me, "The young guys are preaching birth control again." That

4. "Voice of the Faithful," 9.
5. Spadero, "A Big Heart." sec. 10, para. 11.

is the surest sign that we are back to the time before the council. I hadn't heard birth control mentioned in forty years.

The papal encyclical condemning birth control, *Humanae Vitae*, came out in 1968. I remember that well. It was in July, and I was in summer school with about eight hundred priests and 1,300 nuns. When the news hit the campus, you would have thought America had been hit by an atomic bomb. The priests were more bewildered and wondered how this could be? The nuns were just plain angry. In general, they didn't care for celibate males getting too intimately involved with things feminine.

At the time, I thought it was strange that priests and nuns should get so excited about birth control. There are some deeper theological questions involved in that document than just birth control. For many of the priests who were taking theology courses at the time, it was those deeper questions that concerned them. Besides, the priest knew from confessional experience, the papal teaching was going to be largely ignored, which it was.

Today, about sixty-five percent of all Catholics believe that artificial birth control is not sinful.[6] The percentage of sexually active Catholics favoring birth control is even higher. Why is it that the hierarchy, composed of celibate old men, considers birth control a mortal sin while the good Catholic people disagree? Does the voice of God come only through the pope and hierarchy? Is the Holy Spirit not also active in "the people of God?"

Is that expression, "people of God," used by the church merely for effect, like the czars who threw some crumbs to the masses so they wouldn't rebel? Or, are the lay people members of the body of Christ, through whom God also speaks?

After about forty-five years of silence on the subject of birth control, some priests are starting to condemn "that evil practice" again. More and more it is becoming the topic of Sunday sermons: no birth control.

As one who went through all of that birth control controversy in the 1960s, my advice to the present day clergy about getting involved in that is: "Good luck, guys! Have fun!" And also, "Fools rush in where angels fear to tread."

When I hear of priests wanting to return to pre-council birth control days, I think, "They never gave marriage instructions in those days or they would not want to go back to them." The priest gave the marriage instructions, which were embarrassing to him and the engaged couple if they both

6. "Harris Poll."

were Catholic. If it was a mixed marriage, where one was not Catholic, it was not only embarrassing, it was a calamity!

The priest had to explain Catholic marriage laws, which included birth control laws. He first explained the "unacceptable" kind of birth control. Any artificial prevention of pregnancy was not allowed under any circumstances, be they health or financial.

Then the priest had to explain the "acceptable" kind of birth control, called "rhythm." This meant explaining the female fertility cycle, about which, again many of the priests had no idea. Rhythm is refraining from sexual activity during a woman's fertile period. The priest had to speak about sexual intimacies to a woman who possibly had never met a priest— things got more humiliating.

Possibly she did not have regular periods, so rhythm would not be workable. Then she could take a pill to regulate her periods, but she could not take a pill to practice birth control. What if the pill to regulate her periods and the pill to prevent pregnancies were the same pill? Clearly, it got complicated.

The woman had to have a good reason to use rhythm and also have the consent of her husband. Also, it would be wise if the couple talked it over with a priest before. The priest should be the one who could tell them if they had a good reason to limit their number of children. To me, that makes no sense at all. When they taught us that in the seminary, I thought: "How would I know if a couple has a good reason to limit their family? That is absurd."

After those discomfiting discussions about their sex life, the couple had to sign an agreement that they would raise the children Catholic. This included sending them to a Catholic school if one were available. If one member of the couple refused to agree to raise their children Catholic, there could be no marriage.

In the pre-council days I knew a priest who forbad a couple, both public grade school teachers, to go to communion because they did not send their children to a Catholic school. He was a good priest. He was also my pastor for thirty years, but he was trained in the time where policy came before people, the law before the spirit.

Since I worked in the schools, I didn't have many marriages, only a relative or friend of the family. Needless to say, in their instructions, I skipped all the above, insisting that they remember only one obligation—to give the priest a marriage stipend of $25. Some rules I was a stickler on.

I don't have the answer to the birth control question. I do feel that, in justice, the married Catholic people must be heard and trusted. To fail to listen to these people of God, especially in this matter, is an insult. It is saying that the people don't count, that only the clergy count. The classic example of the hierarchy not listening to or trusting the Catholic laity was in the 1960s. In 1966, Pope Paul VI reconvened a commission to discuss and vote on the birth control issue.

The commission had been originally instigated at the request of Pope John XXIII in 1963, just a few months before he died. The new birth control pill had raised questions about birth control: when is birth control artificial, and thus sinful, and when is it natural, and not sinful?

The commission, which met over a period of time in Rome, was expanded to fifty-eight members, theologians, doctors, and members of the hierarchy. Most surprisingly, it included Catholic lay people. At first, all had an equal vote whether to drop or keep the church's ban on artificial birth control. At the end it played out differently, but the result was that all voices were eventually heard.

The most well-known lay couple attending was Pat and Patty Crowley from Chicago. They had started the Christian Family Movement in the late 1940s, and they also were the main speakers in the Pre-Cana (marriage) program. I heard them speak in 1955. They were staunch, faithful Irish-Catholics.

They carried letters with them from Catholic couples asking for a change in the birth control ban. At that time, the only permissible way for Catholics to regulate births was through the rhythm method. The letters said that for the majority of Catholic couples the rhythm method simply did not work. At that time, priests did indeed seem to be baptizing a lot of "rhythm babies." Also, these couples said trying to regulate their lovemaking by the calendar inhibited intimacy and hurt their marriage. "Calendar love" or "clock love" took something away from spontaneity.

The public knew about the commission and that a vote was going to be taken. At the end of the sessions, the great majority of the participants voted to change the past birth control ruling. The great majority of the fifty-five participants voted for the church to end its ban on certain kinds of birth control. That was the first vote, and it was of the entire commission.

However, according to the arrangement, fifteen bishops and cardinals were to have a final and definitive vote. These fifteen went along with the request of the general commission and also voted for a change in the law.

The decision came as a shock to the pope; fifteen members of the hierarchy voting to lift the ban was certainly unexpected. Indeed, the rule giving the fifteen members of the hierarchy the final decision was made at the very end of the sessions—precisely to block the lay people from having the final say. Yet the hierarchy went along with the lay people.

The fifteen votes were hand-delivered to the pope. The details of what happened next are not known, but Cardinal Octoviani, the archconservative who fought Vatican II at every juncture, is known to have influenced the pope to reject both votes of the commission—the vote of the laity and the vote of the hierarchy.

News of the outcome of that vote against birth control had gotten to the public, so people expected that the pope would soon announce the results lifting the ban. No one believed he would not go along with the majority vote. Why would the pope ask for a vote, if he never intended to pay any attention to it? All eagerly awaited the "good news coming from Rome," but it never came.

It seems that two influential bishops on the commission, who voted against the change and lost, went to the pope and said, "We can't change our anti-birth control law because our teaching authority, which prohibited birth control over the years, will be weakened." None of the "non-clerics" on the commission got to talk to the pope, so when all was said and done, the laity really had no voice in the matter.

The pope went against the vote of the commission. In 1968, he came out with the encyclical condemning artificial birth control. The encyclical never mentioned the opinion of the commission or that it recommended for a change.

This was the first time in history that lay people had a voice on a doctrinal issue, and the result was as if the commission never existed. The laity got bushwhacked, and the credibility of the church took a major hit. We are still feeling the effects. Before the vote, the Belgium Cardinal Suenens, in speaking to his fellow bishops, said: "My brothers, let us avoid another Galileo affair. One is enough for the church."[7] It seems we now have two, if not three affairs—Galileo, the *Syllabus of Errors* (which we will discuss later), and *Humanae Vitae*.

7. Maurovich, "Humanae Vitae," para. 2.

Pat and Patty Crowley and the other lay people present were not there as mere individuals, they were representing all lay people, all they who never had a voice in church doctrinal or moral matters, either in the church's present or in its long and storied past. When they were disregarded, all of those they represented were also disregarded.

I don't know if I had then, or have now, a definite opinion on all types of birth control, but I feel the "people of God" have a right to be heard. They were not heard in 1968, and they felt duped and betrayed. They felt some church officials invited them to the commission believing they would simply support the church's traditional teaching. When they did not, they were disregarded and dropped cold. It became evident that the influential members of the church's leadership never really planned to listen to the laypeople's opinions. Their invitation had been merely a public relations gesture, and it was a clerical slap in the face.

Patty Crowley told the story of a cardinal telling her: "The church couldn't change the birth control law. What about all those people who are in hell now because they broke that law?" She asked sadly, "Your excellency, do you really believe that?" Even sadder, he probably really did believe that!

Pat and Patty—and many others—never fully recovered their faith in, or love for, the church. They withdrew from being the recognized lay spokesmen for the church in America. They dropped out of CFM and stopped giving talks to couples preparing for marriage.

As for the general response of the people, they just ignored the encyclical and life went on as usual. Bishops of several countries formally said that Catholic people were allowed to follow their conscience on the matter and still remain Catholics.

In the U.S., nothing formal was proclaimed, but it was just taken for granted. Catholic people were following their conscience and practicing birth control. It was definitely a case of "don't ask, don't tell." The last time a woman asked me about birth control was in 1963.

"The secret" that everyone knew, was that the encyclical was largely ignored. After *Humanae Vitae*, people wondered "Why does the church not listen to her people, we are part of the church also." I didn't know the answer to that question then, nor do I now.

Those who upheld the encyclical did, however, have a definite answer. They said then and still say, "The church is not a democracy, if you don't like what the church says, then leave it." Isn't that a compassionate, charitable answer for troubled souls? Some defenders of true doctrine pride themselves in being harsh and exclusive. They love to say, "If you don't like it, leave it." I suspect it makes them feel "more Catholic" than the rest.

Granted, the church is not a democracy, but does that mean it is a dictatorship? Is the pope, one man totally independent of the body of Christ, the sole and exclusive interpreter of God's will in the church?

I recently heard a harsh critic of the church say: "Catholics believe God speaks into the ear of the pope. Then the pope tells the hierarchy. They tell the priest, and the priest tells the people." The people know for sure, then, what "God said."

I was angry at that description of the church because it is not true. That is not Catholic doctrine, although some misinformed Catholics believe that to be the case. Often, Catholics are our own worst enemies. That description of God speaking into the ear of the pope sees the church as a pyramid with the pope standing alone on top, independent of the rest of the church. That, however, is not the Catholic Church.

The church teaches formally when the pope speaks in union with the bishops. "In union with the whole church" is significant. What does that phrase mean? How does it work out in practice? Those are questions that involve the nature of the church. Also, what do the words "people of God" mean?

Is the pope within the people of God? Is the pope in the church or above the church? Besides that of the pyramid, there is another image of the church: a series of concentric circles. In that image, the pope is the center circle as the final and ultimate authority, but he is not distinct from, or separate from, the church as a whole.

Do we picture the church as a pyramid with the pope above and separated from the body of Christ, or as a series of concentric circles with the pope in the center of body of Christ? The center has authority over, but is not separate from, the whole. The head is not detached from the body.

When Christ said, "Behold I will be with you all days," who is the "you" he is addressing? Is it just the pope? Is it the pope and the hierarchy? Is it the clergy and the lay people? Or is it all combined under the leadership of the pope?

Are the decrees of an ecumenical council infallible? There have been twenty-one such councils, beginning with the Council of Jerusalem in the mid-first century and ending with Vatican II in the early 1960s. It was through the councils that the church experienced its teaching authority, defining the divinity of Christ, the trinity, and the two natures of Christ.

The common teaching of the church on matters of faith came by way of ecumenical councils. Their authority extended even to condemning a pope. In the sixth century, a council condemned Pope Honorius as a heretic. Thirteen years after he died, an ecumenical council declared him a heretic for teaching that Christ had a divine will, but not a human will.

Are the teachings of an ecumenical council infallible independent of the pope, or only when they are in union with the pope? Are papal statements independent of the bishops infallible, or only when they are in union with the bishops?

*Humanae Vitae* is important not for the moral questions it raises but for the dogmatic questions it rises. Who or what is the church? How does the spirit work through the church? Those questions are more important than choosing rhythm over artificial birth control.

A deeper question brought up by the encyclical is whether the Catholic laity will ever be a significant part of the church. Will they ever have a voice in proclaiming Christ's teaching? Is that voice the sole responsibility and privilege of one man, the pope? How ironic it would be if the encyclical that was largely ignored on moral grounds would be the catalyst to renew the study and appreciation of just what, or who, is the church? It would then become one of the most important encyclicals of all time, because it would bring to light the topic of authority in the church. Since the declaration of papal infallibility in 1870, authority may be the most important but least talked about issue in the church. Garry Wills, notable Catholic historian, has maintained that at its base, the *Humanae Vitae* was about church authority and not about sexuality. Since church authority is intimately connected with infallibility, we will devote the following chapters to that hot-button issue.

I will end with a personal note concerning birth control that taught me that human experience is a better teacher than textbooks. In the early 1960s, just a few months after my ordination, I was speaking with a woman who had nine children. We were talking about how things were going for her generally. She said things were tough and added, "Father, I just cannot have any more children!" She then asked about the church's teaching on birth control.

I was aching for her. However, I did feel I had to hold to the church's teaching against artificial birth control. I tried to be gentle and caring, assuring her of God's love and care. Finally she thanked me for the discussion. She said that she had to go because she had things to do, which had to be the understatement of the year. Then she added, "Besides, I have an upset stomach; I am pregnant."

It took me about three minutes to get my breath back. I mumbled the traditional "Go in peace" to her, thinking to myself, "Is that possible? God in heaven, what's going on here?"

I was very uncomfortable. I knew I had no right to alter church teaching, for that would be like a private trying to alter General Dwight Eisenhower's D-Day plans. Privates don't make the rules; they follow them. An individual can't change institutional rules.

I knew I represented the church, and I had been afraid I would misrepresent the church, but I had a suffering person in front of me. As the saying goes, I was caught between a rock and a hard place.

Later, sitting in the comfort of the rectory, watching a color TV that I doubted she could afford, I felt ashamed thinking of that woman. She was likely uncomfortable in many areas—physically, economically, and spiritually—and I felt inadequate to help her. I remember thinking: "I became a priest because I ever wanted to help people. Am I doing that?"

At that time I recalled our Lord's words: "Woe to you scribes and Pharisees, hypocrites! You bind heavy burdens, too grievous to be borne, and lay them on men's (and women's) shoulders. And you will not lift one finger to help them" (Matt 23:4).

That was fifty years ago, and shortly after that conversation I was transferred. I never had contact with her again, nor have I ever mentioned that experience to anyone. Neither, however, have I forgotten it.

It was the first and last time a woman talked to me about birth control. In the sixties, when the people stopped mentioning birth control in confession, I assure you no one was more pleased than the priests. We universally agreed, "Thank God that monkey is off our back." I know that lay people were saying the same. Birth control became a dead issue and everyone was thinking, "May it rest in peace."

Looking back at that incident, I realize I lacked the experience to know how to lift that burden from her. I had been ordained only a few months and was too "green." I didn't have the experience or spiritual finesse to explain to her the role that conscience plays in all moral decisions. It is traditional Catholic teaching that conscience is the final arbiter in making moral decisions. Culpable sin is a violation of a person's conscience!

Individuals are to follow their conscience. They do have an obligation to form a "right conscience," which includes seriously considering church teachings, but the bottom line in all decisions is the individual's conscience. Prayer and consultation must come into play, but no law can replace a person's conscience.

God doesn't force human conscience, so neither must we. That was the principle that some opposing bishops were expressing after *Humanae Vitae* in 1968. In several countries, the bishops explicitly told the faithful to follow their conscience in the birth control matter. That has always been the Catholic teaching but was never stressed to the people. Most Catholics never heard of "conscience." When Pope Francis said, "Conscience is autonomous, and everyone must obey his/her conscience,"[8] it made headlines, when it should have been common knowledge.

No one is more insecure than a newly ordained priest, and it is right that he be so. If he instead feels secure that he has all the answers, he is not going to help anyone. He must always remember that he is a rookie, and the people he is dealing with know more about life than he does. He should also feel that the people he is serving are very likely better Christians than he. In my case, they were for sure.

At that time, my legal rigidity, if faulty, was understandable. I had just completed eleven years of college and seminary training where the emphasis was on enforcing church laws rather than appreciating people's needs and situations. We were taught to be theologically correct rather than Christlike. The textbook overruled people. The letter of the law overruled the spirit of the law.

Objective laws, instead of being seen as an aid to help form conscience, were seen as superseding conscience. Conscience and life's experiences were irrelevant. They counted for nothing. The law counted for everything. If I read the gospels correctly now, that is in direct contradiction to the life of Christ. While not denying the law, Christ always put the spirit of the law over the letter of the law. When God gave humans free will, God took a chance. We are too insecure to be God-like and pass that message onto others. We hold on to law to the exclusion of love, because we want the security that "the law" provides.

I failed my duty fifty years ago when I met with that overburdened woman. Instead of conveying the spirit of the law, I was obedient to the

8. Spadaro, "Big Heart."

letter of the law. I was not free enough to lead others into their God-given freedom. "Too late smart. Too late free."

## Infallibility

### What is it? Who has it?

> The only way to solve the problem of contraception is to solve the problem of papal infallibility.[9]

I doubt there is one Catholic in a hundred who has a correct understanding of church authority, and especially of papal infallibility. Since its declaration, most explanations have been so misunderstood and abused that it is practically impossible to talk to the average Catholic about infallibility.

This is why people were so shocked when Pope Francis recently spoke on the topic, saying: "all the people of God, seen as a whole, are infallible in matters of belief. This is not a form of populism. It is the church as the people of God, pastors and people together."[10]

When Pope Francis speaks, conservative Catholics shut their ears, but not their mouths. They attack. A group of ultra Right Catholics, the "Novus Ordo Watch," said that Pope Francis "does not have a single Catholic bone in his body . . ." and is neither a valid priest nor a valid bishop.[11] Accordingly, they would say, he is not a valid pope. That seems a little strong, to say the least. Admittedly, the average Catholic has never heard infallibility explained in terms of the people of God as Pope Francis did.

It was clearly taught at Vatican II. Infallibility is not about the pope; it is about the church, "all the people of God, seen as a whole." The church is made up of people, clergy, and the pope. The church is not a one-man show.

The image of the pope as a king presiding over his court is the popular image, but it is not the correct image, as Pope Francis so radically stated. The pope is the head, but he cannot separate himself from the body. If he does, he is no longer one with the others. That can't be, because that is not the church. The church is one, one body, the people of God.

Although not officially defined until 1870, the belief in papal infallibility goes back centuries, extending through the Middle Ages—not that

9. Father Hans Küng (1979).
10. Scalfari, "The Pope."
11. "'Pope' Francis," para. 1.

the belief was necessarily universal. As late as 1826, the Irish bishops declared, "The Catholics of Ireland do not believe, neither are they requested to believe that the pope is infallible. It is not an article of faith." The Irish always were a hardheaded lot.

Years ago, a bishop told me a story that highlights the question of papal infallibility and church authority in general. Is infallibility centered just on one man, the pope? Or does it include the people and bishops united, all making up the people of God?

In the early 1960s, the Vatican II document entitled "The Light of the Nations," or *Lumen Gentium*, spoke of the universal teaching of the church, the "universal magisterium," as consisting of "the pope in union with the bishops." That phrase, "in union with the bishops," is the basis for the following story.

The bishop's story took place during the pontificate of Pope John Paul II, when the question of female priests was under discussion. Is the all-male priesthood inherent in Catholic doctrine, or is it merely the result of historical conditions? Is the all-male priesthood an essential teaching of the gospel, therefore eternally valid, or is it merely a practical decision, necessary in an earlier society that could not comprehend it being otherwise? Is the all-male priesthood doctrine or discipline?

In the 1970s, these questions were being seriously discussed. In 1976, in an attempt to answer those questions based on scripture, the Catholic Pontifical Biblical Commission stated that no valid scripture objection could be given to forbid the ordination of women.

It should be noted that the commission did not say scripture teaches that you may, or should, ordain women. It said, simply, that you couldn't *prove* from scripture that women may not be ordained.

The last sentences of the commission's report state: "It does not seem that the New Testament by itself alone will permit us to settle in a clear way and once and for all the problem of the possible accession of women to the priesthood."

In scripture, St. Paul's words limiting women are obviously the result of social customs of the time. "Women are to remain quiet in assemblies. It is a shame for a woman to speak publicly. Let her be silent and ask her husband when they get home." Those words are to be considered on the same level of importance as "women should not pray without a veil, and women should not have short hair" (1 Cor 11:3–10). Obviously, those are not dogmatic teachings; they are societal customs.

They do not have the same authority as Paul's words, "There is no longer Jew or Greek, slave or free, male or female. We are all one in Jesus Christ" (Gal 3:28). Those words comprise divine revelation. Women's hair length or their speaking at assemblies merely reflects common practice.

In light of the biblical commission's statement that there was no scriptural objection to female priests, the bishops actively discussed the possibility of ordaining women. These discussions went on for a period of years, until Pope John Paul told the bishops that they were forbidden to further discuss the matter.

In 1994, the pope issued a pastoral letter stating that the "ordination of women was impossible." On this matter, Pope Francis supports John Paul. Although he has written nothing officially on the subject, Francis has stated, "The door is shut on the ordination of women."

However, those who favor female priests emphasize that Pope John Paul's statements were only made in a pastoral letter, and that Francis' words were not in an official document. Therefore neither pronouncement is an infallible mandate. Neither John Paul II nor Francis' statements were *ex cathedra*, a dogmatic statement, but rather form part of what is called the "common teaching" of the church.

Theologians fight over the difference in binding force between a pastoral letter and an *ex cathedra* or *de fide* ("of the Faith") decree. Until this question over the pastoral letter versus the *de fide* statement is settled, the ordination of women will continue to be discussed, at least unofficially. Both lay people and some clergy continue to discuss this topic. The latter are discreetly asking, "Is that prohibition merely a theological decision, or is it a proclamation of a divine truth?"

I really don't know the answer but, of course, no one is asking me. For many Catholics, however, the papal statements settle the matter. It is as if it has been stated, "There are to be no female priests in the Catholic Church—forever!" What percentage of Catholics feel that way? The polls vary monthly, and the answers depend on whether you ask a conservative or a liberal.

Regardless, forever is a long time. I remember when everyone thought Mass would be in Latin forever. Five years later, we were saying Mass in English, German, Chinese, and Swahili.

Until the mid-1960s it was thought "Catholics would be forbidden to eat meat on Fridays—forever." A few years later, Catholics were inviting pastors to steak cookouts on Fridays. History proves that "forever" might not be as long as we thought.

I know the difference between a church law, which is changeable, and a divine law, which is unchangeable. The problem was, and to a degree still is, that the laity was never properly educated on the difference. Too often, it all got lumped under "God's law," and therefore Catholic law, which was at one time dogmatically expressed as "Sister says."

Until the late 1950s, "Sister says" was the court of last appeal. In a Catholic grade school, which back then nearly every Catholic kid attended, all laws got lumped together under the eternal proclamation, "Sister says."

Why? Our teaching nuns were the last in an unbroken line to God, which went from God to the pope, to the bishop, to the pastor, to the young assistant, to sister, to us—the lay people. That unbroken line was infallible.

That "creeping infallibility" was totally unconscious. It was the common Catholic belief that a person who had any degree of authority in the church somehow mysteriously shared in papal infallibility. All religious authority was painted as "errorless."

The final listeners, the laity, were the only ones in the entire church who were flawed. There was no such thing as degrees of importance; it was all eternally important. All laws, God's laws, church laws, were indistinguishable in gravity, because "Sister said so."

Adding to the confusion, is the fact that violations of God's laws and of church laws carried the same punishments. You could go to hell both for murdering fifty people and for eating a hot dog on Friday. Two different laws—one divine, the other church—carried the same punishment, because both were mortal sins. That leads to confusion about the two types of law and the seriousness of each.

After telling me how the pope shut down the bishops' discussion concerning female priests, the bishop asked me a question: "Can you image the pope telling the body of bishops that they are not allowed to even discuss an issue among themselves?" His question was a theological time bomb that I wasn't going to wade into. In silence, I shook my head and feigned disbelief.

There have been councils held, wars fought, and blood spilled over these questions: Can the pope tell the universal body of bishops what to think or discuss? Can a pope make binding decisions without consulting the bishops?

Today, however, the great majority of lay Catholics would have no problem accepting such a unilateral papal decree over a group of bishops.

Most Catholics would automatically agree that the pope might tell the universal body of bishops what to think and discuss. This shows they have little or no concept of what infallibility means, how it works, or how the doctrine was defined at the first Vatican Council of 1869–70.

Today, the average Catholic knows nothing, or very little, of the workings of Vatican I, where papal infallibility was officially defined. Its persistent and strongest advocate was Pope Pius IX. Out of approximately five hundred bishops present at the council, sixty bishops, mostly European, opposed the doctrine. When they foresaw its passage, they left before the final vote.

The American bishops also left before the final vote because of the impending Franco-Prussian War. In the early balloting, the American bishops voted against the doctrine of infallibility. They were on their way home when they learned it had passed overwhelmingly.

This historical background is necessary to understand the stance taken by the pope and bishops at the council. In the 1800s, a major shift was taking place in society, moving it from autocracy to democracy. The Western world was changing from the rule of kings who were believed to be divinely inspired, to elected officials who were the choice of the people.

The French Revolution had changed the world permanently, and the church was worried and frightened by the change. The Papal States were being dismantled. The last three men executed in the Papal States for revolutionary activity were during the reign of Pius IX. The church was losing ground in more ways than one.

In 1864, a few years before the first Vatican Council, Pius IX issued the much-discredited *Syllabus Errorum* (*Syllabus of Errors*). It was a list of eighty contemporary "errors," including freedom of conscience, of speech, of the press, and of religion. The pope condemned them all, believing he had the authority to do so because he was infallible.

A Franciscan priest first alluded to papal infallibility in the 1200s. Pope Gregory XVI in the 1800s was the first pope to claim infallibility for himself. It remained for Pius IX to make it his mission in life to have "papal infallibility" defined by the church. Not only did the French Revolution frighten him, Pius IX also thought American democracy was a real threat to the authority of the papacy and the church.

The church was at home in society's old order. There were kings, princes, nobility, and peasants—and, in effect, the church ruled them all. There was a direct line of command from the pope to the peasant.

On Christmas Day in 800, Pope Leo III crowned Charlemagne king of the Holy Roman Empire. In the 900s, Pope John XII crowned Otto emperor. In the 1000s, the Emperor Henry IV was forced to walk barefoot in the snow around the pope's castle for three days before Pope Gregory VII allowed him to kneel before him for absolution.

Crowning emperors and demanding public penance from kings are just two examples of how much power the church had over civil society. For centuries, Catholicism was synonymous with Western civilization. You could not speak of one without the other. Civil society was religious society, and the pope headed both.

Under the pope were the bishops, who, besides being the religious authorities, also were civil authorities. The bishops were princes governing territories. Even today, bishops are referred to as "princes of the church."

Everyone in society from the highest to the lowest knew his or her place. Religious sins were also civil crimes punishable by civil authorities with religious backing. The history of the church was rooted comfortable, and many did not want the system changed.

The development of political democracy was seen as a threat. The pope and churchmen did not see how the church could fit into a system where people voted for their leaders. What if a person of different religious beliefs, or even of no beliefs, were elected to be an official? How could Catholic beliefs prosper under a Protestant official? Democracy posed a threat to the church's usual way of governing.

With democracy, the pope feared the loss of Catholic power and influence. To him, democracy would mortally weaken the church, and he saw papal infallibility as a way for the church to remind the world of papal power and influence.

Under the monarchical system, with kings subject to the pope, the pope literally had the last word. Pius IX wanted to make sure everyone knew that word was infallible; he knew if he could get the council to pass the doctrine of papal infallibility, it would enable him and future popes to preserve some of their authority.

Pius IX felt that his power was being eroded by modernity. He was wrong in fearing that modernity threatened his religious power, because democracy doesn't threaten religion. He was right, however, that modernity threatened his temporal power, and he wanted to hold on to both kinds. A German Catholic historian, Franz Kraus, said power was the ultimate issue in 1870. Vatican I was indeed about power: who had it, how did it work, and how far did it extend?

Even a cursory reading of the 1870 Vatican I council reveals the pivotal nature of the question of church authority and power. Vatican I was about church control. In that sense, Vatican II in 1965 was the direct opposite. That council was about the church serving the "people of God." The phrase the "people of God" has far-reaching consequences. The greatest opposition to the 1870 decree on papal infallibility came from England, Germany, and France. In England, the most vocal critic of papal infallibility was Lord John Dalberg-Acton (1834–1902). He was a devout Catholic who remained so his entire life, receiving the sacraments on his deathbed. Acton was a baron, a member of the English parliament, and a renowned historian. He was the most influential English Catholic layman of his time. Acton is best known for his maxim: "Power corrupts, and absolute power corrupts absolutely." He wrote those words in a letter to Bishop Creighton. The "power" that he was referring to as being corrupting was religious power. He specifically mentioned religious power as it was so blatantly misused throughout history, such as in the Inquisition and Calvin's heresy trials. He saw potential for all kinds of abuses stemming from Vatican I and papal infallibility.

## Cardinal Newman

A contemporary of Lord Acton was John Henry Cardinal Newman (1801–1890). Although Newman lived during Vatican I, he had a Vatican II mind. It was the second council that echoed Newman's thoughts and spiritual outlook so completely.

If Fathers Murray, Congar, Chardin, and Rahner are called the fathers of Vatican II, certainly Cardinal Newman deserves to be called its grandfather.

In the history of the Catholic Church, or of any traditional church, I doubt there has ever been a greater defender of the supremacy of conscience than Newman. This posture put him at odds with his contemporary churchmen, and as a result, he drew vitriolic condemnation from church conservatives.

In England, Cardinal Manning was Newman's avowed enemy. Manning refused to refer to Newman as a cardinal at all. Instead, he called him Dr. Newman, referring to his days as an Anglican priest at Oxford.

Manning drew up a list of ten "heresies" that he found in Newman's writings. When anyone mentioned Newman, he would give that person the list of heresies. It is somewhat ironic that Manning and Newman were at such odds. Both served as Anglican priests, both became Catholic priests, and both became cardinals.

Both Manning and Newman were part of the Oxford movement, which received its name from Oxford University when, in the latter part of the nineteenth century and early twentieth century, a large number of Anglicans became Roman Catholics. Generally, they were intellectuals, and some, in addition to Manning and Newman, were quite well known. Gerard Manley Hopkins was one of the leading poets of the Victorian Age. Ronald Knox was a scriptural scholar and translator of the *Knox Bible*. Knox and Hopkins, like Manning and Newman, became Catholic priests, with Hopkins being a Jesuit. Despite Manning's and Newman's common backgrounds and intellectual vigor, their relationship was marked with strife.

Besides Manning, other churchmen attacked Newman. Monsignor Talbot called Newman "the most dangerous man in England."[12] That is quite a statement, considering that Jack the Ripper was alive at that time! Pope Pius IX didn't much care for Newman, either. Pius refused to make Newman a cardinal. His dislike may have had something to do with Newman's criticizing Pius' *Syllabus of Errors* as being an intimidation of every religious man.[13] Newman expressed the idea that those who felt as he did about the syllabus would have to "hold out" for about ten years until its influence subsided.[14] He quotes a friend, Monsignor Dupanloup as saying, "If we can tide over for the next ten years we are safe."[15]

It was Pius IX's successor, the progressive Pope Leo XIII, who made Newman a cardinal. Pius IX was the longest-reigning pope (thirty-two years) when he died in 1878. He was barely even cold before Leo made Newman a cardinal in 1879.

Pius IX was a complex man. He began his pontificate very much a liberal. As he aged, he became more and more conservative—even reactionary. He opened the Jewish ghettos in Rome, which in those times was a radical gesture of tolerance. Later, he closed them. The Jews and Italians saw

---

12. Sartino, *Another Look*, 5.

13. Ward, Life of Newman 1:566–67.

14. Ibid., 1:79–81.

15. Ibid., 1:101.

him as their enemy, and he was the last pope to have temporal power over the Papal States, which at that time included about three million people.

At their height in the 1700s, the Papal States extended from some small sections in southern Italy to practically all of central Italy, and even into France—Avignon. The Papal States began with grants of land given to the church by Pepin the Short,[16] and later by his son Charlemagne in the late 700s.

In return for the land grant, the pope crowned Charlemagne as Holy Roman Emperor on Christmas Day in 800. And we think only today's politicians and rich people engage in "pork barrel" politics!

Immediately before the Protestant Reformation in 1515, the Papal States were still significant enough to have Pope Julius, the "warrior pope," wage three wars in their defense.

I think the church losing the Papal States, with their temporal power, terrified Pius IX. He feared the whole ship was about to sink, and he became defensive to the point of paranoia. In the 1870s, he excommunicated the king of Italy, saying that the kingdom of Italy was illegitimate. He declared himself to be a "prisoner" of the Vatican and refused to leave, even to go into Rome. His successors also took on the label of "prisoner" of the Vatican. It was not until 1929 that the Vatican recognized the kingdom of Italy again. From 1870 to 1929, no pope ever left Vatican City—an area of one-sixth square mile. They developed a martyr complex. Despite portraying themselves as wronged prisoners, the popes were, in fact, free to leave anytime they wished. No one was stopping them.

Some historians have suggested that in his later life Pius IX may have suffered mental deterioration. He was a lifelong epileptic. In old age, his frequent emotional outbursts and rages may have been the result of mental imbalance. Mental imbalance, fortunately, does not prohibit a person from being a saint. A number of saints showed signs of neuroses. The process for the canonization of Pius IX was begun in 1907, but it was dropped because of many objections. Several years later, his cause was opened again but, again, dropped soon after.

Despite the objections of many, especially Jews and Italians, Popes Benedict XVI and John Paul II again pushed Pius IX's cause for sainthood. John Paul II declared Pius "blessed" in 1985. Swiss priest and theologian

---

16. Charlemagne had a son, also named Pepin. He was tall, thus history awarded his grandfather his nickname to distinguish between the two.

Hans Küng, however, felt that the beatification process for Pius IX had become over-politicized.

To put Küng's words in context, Pope John Paul II and Küng rarely saw eye to eye. In the 1960s, Pope John XXIII appointed Küng as a *peritus*, or "theological expert," at Vatican II. In 1979, the newly elected Pope John Paul II banned Küng from teaching as a Catholic theologian. Küng's words about John Paul II's many canonizations being politically influenced have to be seen in the light of the John Paul versus Hans Küng duel.

It is true that Pope John Paul II has been called the "saint-making" pope; he declared 483 saints and had another 1,340 people beatified. That is more than all the popes together have canonized in the past 500 years. In all the years of canonizations before John Paul II, there were ninety-eight people canonized.

Both John Paul II's admirers and critics admit that he was an astute politician. That is a gift that any leader, civil or religious, can use. In the 1300s, St. Catherine of Siena used her political skills to persuade Pope Gregory XI to move back to Rome from Avignon, France. Catherine was always interesting to me because her mother bore twenty-five children. I always felt her mother was the one in the family who should have been called saint—or maybe even martyr.

Every human relationship is political; to say Pope John Paul II was political is saying he was skilled in human relations. A priest I have known since 1961 coordinated John Paul II's first trip to the United States in 1979. He told me, "Watch the papal caravan, I will be in the second car." I asked, "Who's going to be in the first car?" He answered, "I forget his name, but he will be in white, and can he work a crowd!"

Before that papal visit, many meetings were held in Rome to make arrangements. The priest frequently had lunch with the pope and one of the pope's travel advisors. During the luncheon conversations, it was always very apparent who was running the show and whose ideas would ultimately be accepted. Everyone knew it was the pope's way or the highway.

John Paul II never doubted the doctrine of papal infallibility, thus the joke: "Who does he think he is? He thinks he's the pope!" However, and this was the pope's genius, he would make you feel that whatever it was, it was your idea in the first place, even if you really didn't care for the idea. Now that's a good politician!

My friend, now deceased, became an archbishop. He was a holy and extremely intelligent man, and everyone who knew him felt he would be a cardinal someday. He was repeatedly passed over for that position. I asked him: "Why are you not getting the red hat? While eating with the pope, what did you do? Slurp your soup?"

Popes John Paul II, Benedict XVI, and Pius IX had a common denominator—all three favored a strong, centralized church. The cornerstone and linchpin of a centralized church is papal infallibility; collegiality of the pope united with the bishop is seen as secondary. What is important in the doctrine of papal infallibility is to keep the power centralized. This may be correct and necessary. I don't have the competence to speak on the merits of a strongly centralized church versus a more diversified source of authority. Regardless, it is obvious that infallibility is at the heart of the question, "Who or what is the church?"

In 1870, when papal infallibility was declared a Catholic doctrine, Newman said, "I never expected to see such a scandal in the church."[17] Less than two months after the beginning of Vatican I and the decree of infallibility, Newman described it as "a great calamity. Many minds are presently disturbed when they look toward Rome, infusing in us . . . little less than fear and dismay. . . . What have we done to be treated as the faithful were never treated before? . . . All I do is pray to the early doctors of the church, Augustine and the rest, to avert so great a calamity."[18]

Being the faithful Catholic that he was, Newman eventually reconciled himself with the doctrine: "As for the infallibility of the pope, I see nothing against it, or to dread in it. It must be so limited in practice that practically it will leave things as they are."[19] In today's language, "No big deal." Although this was a softening somewhat from his initial negative response to the decree, he also predicted the day would come "when the whole church would be heard" and Catholic instincts and ideas would "assimilate into the living tradition of the faithful."[20]

Aren't his words predictive of Pope Francis' speaking of infallibility in terms of "the faithful" and the "people of God," the whole church? Although Newman eventually accepted papal infallibility, he was against it being defined as a doctrine of the church. He felt "it would raise more questions than it would solve."[21]

17. Sartino, *Another Look*, 36.
18. Ward, *Life of Newman*, 2:287–89.
19. Ibid., 1:101.
20. Sartino, *Another Look*, 36.
21. Newman, *Letters and Diaries*, 24:334.

In this, Newman was a prophet. Since its declaration, papal infallibility has indeed raised more questions and problems than it solved. The reaction was swift and lasting. One of the more tragic effects was the breakaway of a large number of Catholics, who, at that time, broke from Rome and formed the Old Catholic Church.

The Old Catholic Church still functions today. I have attended their Mass. They have red-trimmed monsignors and biretta-bearing priests, plus lots of incense. Today, they truly are the Old Catholic Church. Upon the decree on infallibility, some thirty Catholic historians in Germany protested and resigned their teaching positions at Catholic universities.

The church has always taught that infallibility only concerns matters pertaining to "faith and morals," which theoretically limits the scope of the decree. Those who object to papal infallibility respond that the clause "only in faith and morals" does not, in fact, limit infallibility. Every facet of human life involves morality, from having your tonsils removed to watching TV. Saying the church is infallible in morals is like saying the church is infallible in every aspect of human behavior, from how to vote to which sports teams to support. They both involve moral judgments. Everything a person does involves moral judgments. As a result, many felt that the decree was too broad, and theoretically there would be nothing on which the church could not make an infallible statement.

During the time of open rebellion against papal infallibility, Newman's password was "Patience!" He even spoke of there being a new council and a new pope in the future who may "turn the tide." And so there were—Vatican II and Pope Francis.

Time marches on. There is an ironic postscript to the Newman, Manning, and Talbot drama, which occurred after all three were dead. In the church's process of declaring a person to be a saint, there are three stages. The first stage is to be declared "venerable," which Newman was in 1991. The second stage is to be declared "blessed," which Newman was in 2010. The third stage is to be declared a saint. Newman? Not yet.

He is on the runway, though, getting ready to take off into stage three—sainthood.

Where are Cardinal Manning and Monsignor Talbot? They haven't gotten to the airport yet. Very few have even heard of them.

We will conclude this section on Newman with his words, noble and brave: "I shall drink to the pope, but, if you please, conscience first, and to the pope afterwards."[22] We should all be able to toast with Newman.

## A Source of Division (Just Whose Chair is It?)

We tend to think the decree on infallibility is a topic that concerns only Roman Catholics. Other Christian denominations, Orthodox and Protestant, are also involved in a correct understanding of infallibility. We have been discussing infallibility, yet we have not mentioned a Scripture text that is often used, mistakenly, to support papal infallibility. The text is from Matt 16:18: "You are Peter and upon this rock I will build my church," words spoken to Peter by our Lord. Matthew's text refers to Peter and his successors, the popes, as being first in the order of importance and respect. The text is about Peter's primacy, not about Peter and his successors' infallibility. St. Paul's refutation of Peter concerning observance of the Mosaic Law is evidence that Paul did not consider Peter infallible. Obviously Paul did recognize Peter as having a position of primacy and leadership. However, Paul did not regard Peter as being free from error.

Primacy involves the structures and functions in the church. Infallibility concerns God's revelation. Primacy is not infallibility. The President of the United States has primacy, yet he does not have infallibility. The professor has primacy, yet he does not have infallibility. Here we will not be speaking about the pope's primacy in jurisdictional matters. However, we will be speaking about the pope's infallibility in doctrinal matters.

The 1870 decree on papal infallibility had negative effects on the relationship among Christian churches. It intensified (if that was possible) the hostility that existed at that time between the Roman, Western, or Latin Church and the Orthodox, Eastern, or Greek Church. The Eastern Church has a long history of outstanding patriarchs, scholars, and saints. They have contributed much to the mystical component of Christianity. The West was influenced greatly by the Roman Empire. Thus, the rule of law became very important in the Western church. In the Eastern Church, the emphasis was more on spirituality. The Orthodox Church felt that by centering all the authority in one person, the Western pope, the Latin Church had insulted and demeaned half of the church, the Easterners' heritage. They felt that such a unilateral emphasis on one person was a misreading of Christian

22. Newman, "Letter to the Duke."

history. To them, it seemed to be a power grab by the Western Christians over the Eastern Christians.

The doctrine of papal infallibility further opened the wounds that had been festering between the Western Catholic church and the Eastern Orthodox Church for centuries.

The great Christian schism between Constantinople and Rome occurred in 1054. The hostility was so intense that each side excommunicated the other. The West moved first, excommunicating the Eastern Church leaders. The Eastern Church returned the favor. This 1054 mutual excommunication and resulting schism between Western and Eastern Christianity was further intensified by the crusades. In the early 1200s, on their way to the Holy Land to "kill infidels for the glory of God," the crusaders in their fourth campaign passed through Constantinople. There they went on a killing and pillaging rampage. The medieval historian Steven Runciman wrote: "There was no greater crime against humanity than the crime of the crusaders against Constantinople."[23] In his meeting with the Patriarch of Constantinople Athanasius, Pope John Paul II said that the massacre was a "source of profound regret for Roman Catholics," and he asked for forgiveness.

The Eastern patriarch literally applauded the pope and said that his apology was the first to come from Rome since the tragedy, eight hundred years before. Despite that effort at reconciliation, the divide between the Greek and Roman Christians still exists.

The Greek dislike of the Roman church is surpassed by the Russian Orthodox church's dislike for Rome. The Russian Orthodox Church has given no indication that they desire to heal the rift of 1054. President Mikhail Gorbachev invited Pope John Paul II to visit the Soviet Union, and there was a certain rapport between the two men. Gorbachev referred to the pope as "an example for all of us." The pope replied to the invitation, saying, "it was one of his greatest dreams to visit Russia." But he never did. Why?

The Patriarch Alexis II of Moscow let it be known that such a visit would merely bring up "unresolved problems" of the past. Personally, the Patriarch was "not enthused" about a papal visit. He made it very clear that the pope was not welcome in Moscow.

The Patriarch did, however, thank the pope for returning an icon, the "Virgin of Kazan," or "Mary, the Protector of Russia." He could not resist adding, "The icon was stolen from Moscow in 1918." The Patriarch seemed to have carried a grudge for a long time. I find it telling that a Christian and

23. Runciman, *Crusades*, 3:130.

a communist—Pope John Paul II and Gorbachev—could get along where two Christians could not; perhaps it accurately illustrates the entrenched nature of bitter family feuds. All the historical differences between the East and West make any attempt to heal the break of 1054 extremely difficult. Papal infallibility merely added to the death knell of any reunion.

The split between Roman Catholics and Orthodox Catholics has effects even today. The Russian President Vladimir Putin is a very conservative, devout member of the Russian Orthodox Church. As we have seen, the Orthodox Church's hatred of the West runs much deeper and longer than does the Communist hatred. Putin's conviction that the West is decadent has its roots in the 1054 schism and the crusades of the 1200s. Putin's idol is Vladimir the Great, the tenth-century saint who converted the Slavs, Czechs, Poles, Ukrainians, and others.

Putin said of him: "His spiritual feat of adapting Christian Orthodoxy . . . united the people of Russia, Ukraine, and Belarus."[24] We can see where Putin is coming from in the present crisis in the Ukraine. Frankly, I'd feel more comfortable if he was a Communist. Vladimir the Great is a saint in Western and Eastern Christianity. His feast day in both churches is July 15. It is said that, at one time, Vladimir had more than eight hundred concubines, numerous wives, and now he is a saint! Who says you can't have it all?

In Western Christianity, the divide resulting from the Protestant Reformation in the early to mid-1500s still exists. Thankfully, Vatican II has done much to reduce the hostility between the two groups. There are no longer Christian armies fighting each other.

The Christian denomination closest and most favorable to Roman Catholicism is the Anglican Church. In America, it is the Episcopal Church. Pope John Paul II referred to the Anglo-Catholic church as "our beloved Sister church." That is a far cry from the Thomas Cranmer and Thomas More divide of the 1500s. Today, there are Anglican theologians who look forward to a possible reunion with Rome. They even go so far as to be willing to accept the pope as the head of the church. However, they clarify this by saying they accept the pope's leadership as being "first among equals."

I do not have enough knowledge of the Anglican position to explain what it means in practice to say that the pope is first among the bishops, yet equal to them. It does, however, show a willingness to talk on the subject and to discuss the meaning of words.

24. Buchanan, "Vladamir Putin," para. 2.

There is no doubt that the decree on papal infallibility has been a major stumbling block to Christian ecumenism. In both Orthodox and Protestant churches, it is an ever-present thorn in their side.

The doctrine of papal infallibility conveys the idea of "one man rule," and the idea that one man alone holds all the power in the church is prevalent among Catholics. That is why so many Catholics were confused by the words of Pope Francis: "All the people of God are infallible." Catholics have never heard the "people of God" mentioned when speaking about infallibility.

In the Vatican II document, *Lumen Gentium*, the church is referred to as the "people of God." Simply those words signify a breakthrough. Before that time, people thought of the church as being the pope, the hierarchy, and the clergy. The laity was of little or no significance. The document went shockingly further—it connected the people of God with infallibility.

> The holy people of God share also in Christ's prophetic office. . . .
> The entire body of the faithful, anointed as they are by the Holy
> One, cannot err in matters of belief. They manifest this special
> property by means of the whole people's supernatural discernment
> in matters of faith. . . . From bishops down to the last of the lay
> faithful they show universal agreement in faith and morals.[25]

That startling statement never worked its way down to the laity. When ordinary Catholics heard the word "infallibility," they did not think of themselves. They thought of the pope. Francis has changed that idea. He has taken the notion of papal infallibility and enlarged it beyond just the person of the pope. He has connected infallibility with the people of God.

The subtitle of this book is *Pope Francis Revives Vatican II*. There is no place where this revival is more evident than in the understanding of papal infallibility in Vatican II. Until 1972, when I was a priest in the active ministry, the phrase "people of God" was in common use. Catholics repeatedly heard that the church comprised the people of God.

The laity also was told that they formed a royal priesthood. They offered Mass, along with the ordained priests, as co-offerers. When I returned to parish life in 2000, I seldom, if ever, heard about "the people of God," and I never heard that phrase connected with infallibility, as Vatican II explicitly taught. I don't recall the popes before Francis linking infallibility with the people. Not surprisingly, then, when Francis joined infallibility with the people of God, it was thought to be something new and different. He was simply retrieving a truth that had been neglected, if not outright

25. Paul VI, *Lumen Gentium*, 2:12.

lost, since the council. Pope Francis is not an innovator; rather, he is restating a neglected teaching of Vatican II. The ideals and spiritual regeneration of Vatican II had been entering their death throes. Thankfully, Francis is reviving them.

In terms of historical significance, Francis has never spoken more radically then when he connected the idea of the people of God with infallibility. My bishop friend was making that very point when he told me the story of how Pope John Paul II intervened in discussion concerning the possibility of female priests.

He asked me, "Can you imagine the pope telling the body of bishops that they are not allowed to even discuss an issue among themselves?" That question, asked of me by the bishop, touches on fundamental ecclesiology. What is the nature of the church? Who or what is the church? Who are the people of God? What is the relationship between the pope, bishops, clergy, and the people of God, or are they all one?

What did Francis mean when he said, "All the people of God, seen as a whole, are infallible in the matters of belief?"

In the future, the church's central question will not be about homosexuality, birth control, or even female priests. It will be about how the church understands infallibility, how authority works, and who shares in church authority. These will be the meaningful questions. In fact, they are already upon us. Unfortunately there are some in the church leadership who don't seem to realize that.

I readily admit, I am not qualified to give answers to those questions. I am not a historian. My critics, whom I suspect are many, say, "If you are not an historian, why do you comment on church history so readily, sometimes even critically? Leave those questions to the experts."

I am not a historian, but I have lived church history imminently for more than eighty years. Christians live in history and have been formed by history. Catholics, especially, are living the results of church history. To be ignorant of, or worse, detached from history is a recipe for disaster. We have an obligation to learn the history of why we twenty-first-century Catholics are as we are and behave as we do.

Present-day Catholics have been formed to a large degree by the 1870 decree on papal infallibility. Asking about infallibility and how it works is the pertinent question of today. We should not feel we are disloyal Catholics because we ask questions. Vatican II gave us permission to ask questions.

Vatican II was a corrective to Vatican I, and also to the *Syllabus of Errors*. We can't understand the extent of that corrective until we understand what they were trying to correct. Knowledge of the "what and the how" of Vatican I and the *Syllabus of Errors* will aid us in understanding what Vatican II was trying to accomplish.

Unfortunately, until Pope Francis, too few church leaders had the courage and honesty to try to understand what Vatican II was trying to say. Far too many of them, while paying lip service to the accomplishments of Vatican II, were subtly and at times not so subtly, sweeping the council under the carpet. Pope Francis, on the other hand, seems intent on reviving Vatican II. He will be met with opposition, perhaps even from those in high places.

Any reform will have to examine the doctrine of infallibility. When it was declared, it was a source of discord between Rome and the other churches. Today, it continues to be a barrier between the Orthodox and Protestant churches and Rome. However, in the Roman church, there now is a new interest in learning the true meaning of papal infallibility. A new look is required, and Pope Francis' words will provide the impetus for that examination.

Our discussion on infallibility has been largely theoretical, but the following is a quaint little story about how papal authority and the bishop's authority work in practice. It speaks volumes about the collegiality of the bishops, and therefore papal infallibility. It is an illustration that papal infallibility is not the absolute autonomous power that many assume it to be:

A few years ago, my wife and I visited the cathedral in St. Louis. The interior of the church is adorned with mosaics that took more than seventy years to complete. Tours are conducted to explain and admire its magnificence and minute workmanship.

Every Catholic diocese worldwide, from New York to Uganda, has a cathedral, because every diocese is headed by a bishop. The bishop's chair, the cathedra, is placed in a cathedral, "the place of the chair." The chair is referred to as the bishop's throne. It is the visible sign of the bishop's authority in that diocese. Every diocese has one—and only one—such chair, in its one—and only one—cathedral because there is one—and only one—bishop who has the authority in a diocese.

During the tour, it was pointed out that there were two thrones in the cathedral. The guide explained that Pope John Paul II had visited St. Louis and came to the cathedral to say Mass. Since he could not sit on the bishop of St. Louis' throne, they built a second throne for the pope.

That brought a naughty giggle from the crowd who obviously felt that they had been made privy to a slightly off-color Catholic joke. Everyone was thinking: "The pope can't sit in another bishop's chair, are you kidding me? Isn't the pope like the elephant who sits anywhere he wants?" I suspect my wife—who is Protestant—and I were the only two people present who knew why the pope could not sit in the bishop's chair. It was simply because the pope is not the Bishop of St. Louis.

This seemingly insignificant antidote about the two chairs has far-reaching ramifications concerning church authority and the role of bishops vis-à-vis the pope.

The first and official title of the pope is the Bishop of Rome. The Bishop of Rome may not sit in another bishop's chair in a cathedral that is not his own. St. Louis is a diocese in the United States that has its own cathedral. Rome is a diocese in Italy that has its own cathedral.

Geographically, Vatican City is surrounded by Rome, but civically and politically it is not in Rome, or even in Italy. Vatican City, the home of St. Peter's Basilica, is an independent country. It was made so in 1929 by a treaty between Italy and the church, signed by the Italian dictator Benito Mussolini, who was a buddy of Adolph Hitler during World War II. The treaty is intact to this day.

Vatican City is a separate country; St. Peter's Basilica is not in Rome. Obviously, you cannot have the Bishop of Rome's chair in another country, be that in America or in Vatican City. The chair for the Bishop of Rome must be in Rome's cathedral. The cathedral for the diocese of Rome is St. John Lateran located in the heart of ancient Rome. It ranks above all the churches in Catholicism because it is the home church of the Bishop of Rome. Emperor Constantine gave the Lateran to the church in the 300s.

The Bishop of Rome may not sit on the Bishop of St. Louis's throne because St. Louis is not his diocese. We find that confusing because we don't understand or even know the pope's proper title. The more historical and traditional title of the head of the Catholic Church is not pope; it is Bishop of Rome.

In the church's early centuries, the title *pope* (Greek for "father") was applied to all bishops. It was not until the eleventh century that the title "pope" was officially reserved to the Bishop of Rome.

Pope Francis is said to prefer the title of Bishop of Rome to that of pope. By that choice, he not only has humility on his side, he has history. The story of the "two chairs" in the one cathedral seems incidental. The story is not incidental, however; it is filled with history and theology, and it should lead to all kinds of questions about church authority.

Now that Francis has opened Pandora's box, saying, "Infallibility is the people of God," questions will be asked more boldly. Is there a similarity between Pandora's box and a can of worms? Is infallibility an absolute power reserved to one man, the pope, or is it a shared power? If it is shared, shared by whom? Infallibility: What is it, and who has it? These are tomorrow's questions being asked today.

It may be fitting to conclude these pages on infallibility with Pope John XXIII's words: "I am only infallible when I speak infallibly, but I never do that, so I am not infallible." Leave it to Pope John XXIII to ease the tension a bit.

While I was in seminary studying infallibility, I sometimes wondered what would happen if the pope said, "I hereby infallibly declare that I am not infallible." I didn't ask that question, of course, because I wanted to be ordained. We will let the Opus Dei Catholics untangle that theological conundrum.

Some Catholics take pride in saying "the church never changes." That probably gives them a sense of security, a nice nest or womb to rest in. It is not true, however, as we have seen in the doctrine of infallibility. In 1870, infallibility was seen as being present in one man—the pope. Now we see infallibility as being more a shared gift of the church. Thanks to Vatican II's *Lumen Gentium* and Pope Francis, we have broadened our horizons. That is change; we shouldn't be frightened. As cardinal, blessed Newman said: "To live is to change, and to be perfect is to change often."

## Oh, Foolish Galatians, Who Bewitched You?

The church undoubtedly has a long history. The questions we presume to be raised only recently are, in fact, questions that the church has been dealing with from the beginning. This is especially true in the area of church authority.

The question of church authority was raised during the church's infancy. The person who raised it at one time persecuted Christians—the swashbuckling, take-no-prisoners Saul of Tarsus (later the Apostle Paul).

Later, in his letter to the Galatians, Paul "the apostle to the Gentiles," took on the question of authority in the person of St. Peter. The letter was pivotal, not only in enabling Gentiles to become Christians, but also for understanding authority in the church: who has authority, how does authority work, and how binding is the church's authority? All of the questions are contained, however latently, in Paul's letter to the Galatians.

This letter is significant for many reasons. It was the very first New Testament writing, probably around the year 48. Paul was the actual author of the letter. In some other New Testament writings, a disciple of the named author probably wrote the text; but this letter was from the pen of Paul himself.

Paul was angry with the Galatians. He had visited Galatia and made a number of converts among the Gentiles. Being Gentiles, he did not think it necessary that they be held to Jewish observances. Many, if not all of the early preachers of the gospel, believed that you were bound, even as a Gentile, to follow the Mosaic Law.

All of the early converts were Jews being introduced into Christianity by Jews. The more ardent, hardline Christian preachers were called "Judaizers." They were Jewish Christians who observed the entire Jewish law along with their Christian beliefs. They upheld circumcision and dietary laws. Peter and James believed that Jewish converts should continue to practice Jewish laws. They believed that Gentiles were also bound to practice Jewish laws.

To understand the significance of Paul's anger toward the Galatians, we have to understand the tension, if not outright hostility, that existed between the Jewish Christians and the new Gentile Christians. That tension is emphasized in the second chapter of Paul's letter to the Galatians.

The second chapter of Galatians says much about the church and the authority of the leaders of the church. It speaks of freedom in the church and, most of all, the courage of Christians to demand that church authorities follow the message of Christ. Paul insisted that the truth of the gospel had a higher claim than the authority of church officials. There was conflict between Paul and the other church leaders, and Paul was willing to confront Peter and the other disciples in order to defend the gospel.

This was a brave gesture when you realize that Paul was, at that time, insignificant in the order of church leadership. After his conversion on the road to Damascus, he went to Arabia, Damascus, and Syria to preach the gospel. He did not meet any Christians in his travels.

He had never met the apostles, nor befriended any Christians before he began preaching. After preaching for three years, he went to Jerusalem. He stayed fifteen days, meeting only Peter and James. Paul was definitely the outsider and the new kid on the block.

After their meeting, he started preaching and writing follow-up letters to various Christians he had converted. The New Testament has about a dozen of these letters, or epistles, including Corinthians, Galatians, Romans, and Ephesians. Along with the gospels, they form the heart of the Christian message.

Fourteen years after his first and only meeting with Peter and James, Paul returned to Jerusalem. There, he met with the rest of the apostles in what is known as the Jerusalem Council. It is considered the first council of the church, whose twenty-one ecumenical councils extend through the ages down to the Second Vatican Council of 1962–65.

Like every other council, sparks flew. The big question of that time was whether or not new Gentile converts could be fully accepted as Christians without observing Jewish laws. At the beginning, all Christians were Jewish and they continued to adhere to their Jewish rules on circumcision and diet alongside their new Christian faith.

Paul began converting Gentiles to Christianity. Thus arose the problem of what to do with Gentile Christians. The question was whether or not Gentile Christians could be fully accepted as Christians without observing Jewish laws. Paul had been converting Gentiles to Christianity without demanding that they follow those laws. His practice was crucial to the spread of the Christian faith to the Gentile world. Had Paul not prevailed, the question could well be asked if there ever would have been a Gentile Christian world.

At the Jerusalem Council, James (the first Bishop of Jerusalem), Peter, and the rest of the apostles were on the side of the Judaizers, demanding Jewish observances from those Gentiles who accepted Christianity. Paul, the outsider and total stranger to everyone except James and Peter, took on the Judiazers.

That, in itself, is amazing. Paul, who at one time persecuted Christians, had the audacity to contradict church leaders. For the early Jerusalem Christians, Paul was suspect. Chapter two of Galatians tells about that first council of the church and the debates that took place.

Paul had brought Titus, one of his Gentile converts, with him. The question arose: must Titus be circumcised, if he were to be a Christian? Paul was not pleased. He thought they were the "false brethren who spied out our liberty which we have in Christ Jesus, to bring us into bondage" (Gal 2:4). Paul definitely did not like the idea that Titus had to be circumcised. I imagine Titus was not too keen on the idea, either.

After no small debate, the apostles and Paul reached an agreement. In practical terms, it came down to "You (Peter and James) do your thing, and I (Paul) will do mine." Finally, they agreed that Gentiles did not have to become Jews; Paul won that battle. The rest of the apostles tentatively agreed, but they were not completely sold on the idea. Indeed, some backtracked later.

Those Jewish Christians did not much care for the Gentiles "getting in free." Through the ages, how often has nationalism triumphed over the gospel of Christ? Even today, our country or our nationality, right or wrong, take precedence over the gospel. Few Christians accept that their first obligation is to their God, not to their country. Or worse, they try to play it both ways, insisting that God and country are the same.

The Jerusalem Council concluded peacefully, and "after extending the right hand of fellowship they departed." The last words of that first council are the most significant. They agreed, "We (both Paul and the opposition) should remember the poor." The most meaningful, unifying idea that sprang from this first church council was, "We should remember the poor." That shows that remembering the poor is the essence of the gospel. Every other theological dispute should be secondary to that basic message.

The plot thickened, though. The question was not totally settled at the Jerusalem Council. Sometime later, Peter and Paul had an encounter at Antioch. In every generation, church authorities, bishops, popes, and others should memorize this meeting. Here, they discussed the question of who, or what, is the ultimate authority in the church: Christ and his good news, his gospel, or church authority? That question is at the bottom of every theological and church dispute that has occurred throughout the centuries. Can, or does, the church ever limit the spirit of Christ? If so, who is to call the church to accountability—a St. Paul? A St. Francis? A Pope Francis?

At Antioch, Peter was eating with the Gentile Christians. He was eating non-kosher food. A group of Jewish Christians came from Jerusalem. Did James, the Bishop of Jerusalem, send them? As bishop, he would have, at the very least, known they were going to Antioch. Paul indicates that James did send them. While this isn't provable and doesn't affect the encounter that ensued, it does show that Paul was suspicious of the apostles at Jerusalem.

Those who went to Antioch were Judaizers. They would have had nothing to do with Jews eating non-kosher food with Gentiles. When Peter saw the Jerusalem group come in, he left his Gentile friends and their food and went to eat the kosher meal with the Jewish Christians. Paul says that Peter so acted because he was afraid of the "circumcision party." Paul, on the other hand, thought that group "didn't walk upright according to the gospel" (Gal 2:14).

We must remember this was Peter, the first pope, and Paul, who was practically unknown by other church leaders. Yet this nobody, renegade Paul, went after Peter like a hound dog after a rabbit.

He confronted Peter: "I withstood him to his face because he was wrong" (Gal 2:11). Then Paul adds, "I said before them all." Not only did Paul rebut Peter, but he also chastised the group that came from Jerusalem. He accused "the rest of the Jews who joined Peter in his hypocrisy."

The Judaizers had even swayed Barnabus, Paul's traveling partner and the pastor of the church at Antioch, to join them. What did Paul say about this group? "When I saw they were not acting in line with the gospel, I said to Peter in front of them all, 'Peter, how is it you force Gentiles to follow Jewish customs?'" (Gal 2:14).

After the confrontation at Antioch, Paul moved on, convinced he was preaching the gospel of Christ, which he saw as superior to every doctrinal decree of the church. He converted many Gentiles at Galatia and then left to preach at other places.

While away in Rome, Paul learned that some Judiazers had come to Galatia after he left and convinced his new Gentile Christians that they must accept Jewish laws along with their Christian faith. So now you have Christians whom Paul converted, who were "bewitched" into taking upon themselves Jewish laws.

Paul was angry at their behavior and wrote from Rome telling them so. He thought they were either out of their minds or under an evil spell. He had good reason to so believe. How else can we explain those who have been introduced into the spirit of Christ's freedom who then forfeit that freedom for the security of feeling right with the law? They preferred the bondage of rules to Christ's emancipation.

That is a temptation we all succumb to more often than we should—we want to feel saved rather than live in Christ's love. In the life of the spirit, feelings can be very misleading, and we all want to feel safe.

What saves us—the observance of laws or the spirit of Christ? Essentially, Paul told the Galatians, "You have been given the freedom of living in Christ, and now you turn around and gladly enslave yourself with religious laws. Who tricked you, fooled you, and bewitched you, foolish Galatians?

You do not earn salvation by keeping the law." Following laws is a sign that you are living in Christ, not that you are earning Christ. Following laws is the result of living in grace, not the means of achieving grace.

As with human love, do you do kind and good acts for your beloved, to earn his or her love? Or do you do these as a sign of the love that already exists between you? Laws are only a sign of love; they are not a cause of love.

Too often, the church is interpreted as saying: "Do this. Follow these rules, and you will be a good Christian." By belonging to the church, a person does not merit salvation. The word "merit" is totally out of place when speaking of the Christian life. In this world, everything is based on merit and demerit, rewards and punishment, but it is not so in God's world.

God's freedom, his love, his life, everything divine is really ours as a gift. However, we may not want freedom, or that free gift, because we cannot control a relationship with God that is based on his free gift. We can control a relationship that is built on the following of laws and rules: "I do this, and God does that." I obey the laws, and God gives me a reward. Love as a gift is beyond our puny minds. We tend to think in terms of "this for that," reward and punishment.

Humans cannot comprehend a relationship with God that doesn't match our human relationships. We really cannot comprehend God's granting us freedom. As Fyodor Dostoyevsky wrote in *The Brothers Karamazov*: "Nothing ever has been more unsupportable for a man and human society than freedom . . . which men (and women) fear and dread."[26] We want to make ourselves worthy of God. As Merton says:

> A popular misunderstanding of merit presupposes that God's love can be gained by what we do; so merit divides everything into meritorious or unmeritorious, worthy of God's love, or unworthy of God's love. And that, besides being blasphemous, is just laughable. In the true Christian version of God's love, the idea of worthiness loses its significance . . . the mercy of God makes the whole problem of worthiness laughable: the discovery that worthiness is of no special consequence is a true Liberation.[27]

We are tempted to think that Paul's rebuke of the Galatians concerned only their following of Jewish laws. We think it was merely a case of Paul telling the Gentile converts that as Gentiles they need not follow Jewish laws of circumcision and diet. But Paul's condemnation of law goes further

26. Dostoevsky, *Brothers*, 130.
27. Merton, *New Seeds*, 75.

than condemning only the Mosaic Law. Paul was condemning all law. He is saying that, as Christians, they were not so bound.

For Paul, the law can no longer accuse and trouble our hearts, for as he tells the Galatians in his letter, "I no longer live, but Christ lives in me." And, "I am dead to the law so that I may be alive to God." He reminds the Galatians that, "He who is led by the Spirit is not under the law" (Rom 7:6). Finally, "For no one is justified by the law, in the sight of God."

Paul's idea that we are free from the law is based on the salvation that Christ won for us. It is not a sociological freedom, it is a theological or spiritual freedom based on Christ's death and resurrection. By his redemption, Christ overcame not only sin and death, with which we are familiar, but he also overcame the law. Most of us are not that familiar with that aspect of our salvation.

For St. Paul, our hearts are troubled because of three adversaries—law, sin, and death. Paul brings all three together and considers them as "the enemy" to that peace and freedom won for us by Christ.

We easily see why sin and death are in opposition to the peace of Christ, but we may be puzzled as to why Paul includes law. He is speaking here from his personal experience, and to understand him we have to enter into that same experience. Experience—above reason and logic—opens us to Paul's understanding of the law as leading to sin and death. When Paul speaks of the law, he is speaking not only about the Mosaic Law. In response to Paul's word that "The written law brings death, but the Spirit gives life,"[28] Saint Thomas Aquinas maintains that Paul means any law, imposed from the outside, even the moral precepts of the gospels.[29]

Paul sees law as the harbinger of sin and death; it spawns sin and death. He laments, "When the law came, sin sprang up, and I died, killed by the law itself" (Rom 7:9). What does Paul mean "killed by the law?" Why does he see law as leading to death?

It is difficult to intellectualize an intuitive experience or awareness. We have to try—try to see how Paul would, in today's language, explain his experience of law as leading to death.

The idea of law is very close to all those "shoulds" and "should not's" that we carry around in our head. The law symbolizes perfection, and if we are driven by the ego's idea of perfection we will die. Regardless of how we

---

28. See 2 Cor 3:6
29. Aquinas, *Summa Theologica*, 108:2.

regard perfection, compulsion toward achieving perfection will ultimately destroy us because it does not originate in God.

As St. Thomas said, law is basically external, "imposed from the outside." Our word "law" means, "laid on" or "fixed to." So even though we internalize it, "law" still remains an alien, a foreigner, something imposed from the outside. This is why law is destructive. It is a foreign body, which, for our own sense of well-being and security, we impose upon, lay on, or fix to our true Christ-centered self. This relentless, unforgiving law is made up of all the commands and prohibitions we have ever encountered—all the way from "Thou shall not kill" to "Thou shall eat thy spinach."

The law, the foreign intruder, then becomes our enemy, our personalized "Jew" and "Greek" who regard the cross of Christ, and the freedom it won for us, as a stumbling block. As a result, the law continually attacks and accuses our true selves. Night and day, the law attacks and accuses our Christ-centered selves.

The law attacked Christ with all the hate and fury of the crucifixion. The biblical law clearly states, "Cursed is anyone who hangs on a tree" (Deut 21:23). Since Christ was hung on a tree, the law with all of its haughty self-righteousness proclaimed, "Jesus, you are cursed!" Jesus "became a curse for us." The law, both civil and religious, accused Christ, "Jesus, you are a law-breaker, therefore guilty." The law always accuses; our word Satan means "one who accuses." There is, therefore, a connection between Satan and the law, as there is between Christ and freedom. Satan and law versus Christ and freedom form the spiritual battleground.

The law, being alien, did to Christ what it does to everyone: it attacked him, and it accused him, but he refused to be defeated. Law did not inwardly crush Christ because he did not internalize law and its accusations. Christ denied law's entrance into the realm of his spirit. He repudiated its intrusion into the area where it had no right to be.

Instead, Christ countered law: "Law, even though you accuse me, even though you say I am guilty, I refuse to accept your sentence! For I am the Son of God, loved by my father, who will save me from your (laws) death." Paul describes this battle—Jesus versus Law—in these words: "Jesus made prayers and requests, with loud cries and tears to God, who was able to save him out of death and he was heard" (Heb 5:7). The law attacked and accused Christ. It laid its sin and death on him, the law said Christ was cursed because he was hung on a tree, but it could not defeat him—not ultimately, not finally.

Why? Because even in the face of being hung on a tree, and thus wrong before the law, Christ was sure of his father's love for him and therefore would not accuse himself. He did not move against himself—as we do. He did not oppose himself—as we do. He did not internalize law—as we do. Christ did not derive security from, or seek to be saved by, the law—as we do!

For our own sense of security, we appoint law to be our judge. Christ refused to do so. Instead he trusted, as the first letter of Peter tells us, "He trusted in the righteous judge" (1 Pet 2:23). Jesus, the "pioneer of our faith" (Heb 12:2), trusted in the father's love for him to save him out of the death imposed by law, "and he was heard" (Heb 5:7).

Even though the law, and the religious people who interpreted the law said, "Jesus, you are guilty, you are a sinner, you are going to die," Jesus refused to set himself against himself. Even though the law told him to do so, he refused to move against himself, to oppose himself; that is, he refused to sin. For sin is moving against oneself; sin is opposing oneself; sin is inner alienation. Christ did not move against himself, did not oppose or alienate himself, and since he would not allow law to force him into such self-destructiveness, sin and death had no claim on him.

Jesus Christ lives! Despite what the law said, on the cross, Christ took the law, sin, and death onto him and overcame them, so that now they can no longer accuse us and take away our peace of heart. The crucified Jesus, by taking the law upon himself, has taken the power out of law. If we are willing to be on the cross with Christ and say, "I no longer live, but Christ (the one who vanquished law) lives in me," the law can no longer accuse and trouble our hearts. To be crucified with Christ—what freedom!

In Paul's mind, the cross is the instrument of freedom from the law. On the cross, Christ was the law-breaker, yet the father saved him. On the cross Christ abolished law, condemned sin, and destroyed death.

Paul knew that it was the crucified Christ who freed us from the accusing law. "Christ redeemed us from the curse of the law" (Gal 3:13). And in that freedom, Paul proclaimed, "I am dead to law, so I might be alive to God" (Rom 6:11). The law, perfection, the one that troubles our hearts night and day, has been cast down.

We often hear sermons on how Christ saves us from sin and death, usually at funerals. We don't hear sermons on how Christ saves us from the law. That is because religious leaders too often see themselves as enforcers of the law instead of liberators of the law. I have been blessed to be around three "religious liberators." If you have had the good fortune of encountering one, you have been blessed.

As a final word, we must add something, which at first may seem to contradict Paul's insight that "he who is led by the spirit is not under the law" (Rom 7:6). Paul does go on to say that specific, concrete laws may be good and should be followed. Even though laws are to be followed, they are to be followed not in the perfection of the law, but in the spirit of Christ. We can and we must follow laws, but we cannot follow laws as "the law."

"The law" is a mentality, a mindset derived externally, by which we strive for divinity, for perfection, for that illusory "should be." Laws are rules of behavior, or ways of acting, that are necessary to live within human limitations. Laws are to be observed, but we must not permit laws to become "the law" for us. This impulse is deadly; for then, we are under compulsion, enslaved by a foreigner. However, when we follow laws in the spirit of Christ, we are free persons whom the law has no jurisdiction over. The person of the law is moved from the outside in, and dies. The person of the spirit moves from the inside out, and lives.

Persons of the law follow laws to gain a sense of security; they feel it is the following of laws that makes them good that makes them like they "should be," that makes them perfect. They transfer laws into the saving "law," seeing their observance as their justification before God, their observance making them like the gods. This is humanity's first, middle and last temptation: "Eat the fruit and you shall be like the gods" (Gen 3:5).

They overlook Paul's declaration that "the law will not justify anyone in the sight of God" (Gal 3:11), and so, "I am no longer trying for that perfection which comes from the law" (Phil 3:9). Those of the spirit, even though they, too, follow laws, do not internalize them. They do not impose that foreign body—the law, perfection—into themselves; they do not lay it on themselves.

Instead, they live in the freedom of Christ's spirit welling up within them. They are under no compulsion to see themselves as good, or to be as they "should," or to be "perfect," and nor do they expect that of others.

What freedom! To be, by our ego's standards, what we "should not be!" To allow others to be what they "should not be!" We must be in that freedom to experience the crucified Christ as Paul did, and thereby understand his approach to law. For on the cross, Christ was opposed to the law. He was what he should not have been; yet he was in the freedom of the Son of God.

Certainly we must follow laws that dictate what we should or should not do. But like Christ, we must not allow the law of what we should or should not be control us. We must not permit the law to invade our inner self, to intrude against our Christ-centered self.

We must not enthrone the law in our hearts. If we allow our hearts to become so troubled, sin and death will inevitably follow. It is our Christian obligation to not let our hearts be troubled. Christ said so just before he departed: "Let not your hearts be troubled" (John 14:1). Death has been conquered. Sin has been conquered. Law has been conquered.

No explanation of St. Paul's teaching on faith would be complete without mentioning Martin Luther and the Protestant Reformation. Paul taught that faith is the source of salvation, not the keeping of the law, even the Christian law.

For Paul, anyone who depended on the law was denying the salvation won for us by Christ's death and resurrection. They were denying the free gift of God's grace. Are we saved by our good works or by our faith in God's love? That is the faith versus works debate. We have seen that was the point of division between Paul and the Judaizers, and it became the point of division during the Reformation between Luther and the Catholic Church.

Unfortunately, that point in Luther's time was based more on a misunderstanding of what is meant by faith. That misunderstanding was not corrected until the Catholic-Lutheran dialogue began in 1964. There were a lot of good things happening in the 1960s in ecumenism. There was an effort on each side to understand the other's position.

In 1994, the Catholic and Lutheran churches made a joint declaration stating a consensus between the Catholic and Lutheran communions: "Justification always remains the unmerited gift of faith." That statement asserted that the major theological difference of the past between Lutherans and Catholics no longer existed. More importantly, it asserted that it hadn't really existed at the time of Luther in the 1500s. How did that disastrous misunderstanding of faith and good works happen?

It happened largely because of semantics. Luther was speaking in terms of his understanding of faith, and the Catholics were speaking in terms of their understanding of faith. They weren't the same. In Luther's mind he was reacting to the church in the very same way Paul had reacted to the Galatians.

Luther was saying: "Oh, foolish Christians, who bewitched you? Are you saved by faith or by observing laws?" Luther was using the very same argument and the very same words as Paul to the Galatians. A person is "saved by faith and not by works."

On the other side, the Catholic position was that our good works must be added to faith. This is where the different understandings of the meaning of faith come into play. At that time, scholasticism was the philosophical language employed by the church to explain religious truth. In the mid-1200s, a Dominican priest, St. Thomas Aquinas, championed scholasticism.

My theological training was in scholastic terminology, and I assume Catholic priestly education is still based largely on scholastic terminology. Transubstantiation, substance, accidents, matter, form—are all scholastic terms.

Luther never cared for scholasticism. He felt it relied too heavily on rational explanation rather than on scripture. Admittedly, scholastic philosophy did go to extremes at times. "How many angels could dance on the head of a pin?" was the taunt of the anti-scholastics. In its attempt to harmonize theology and philosophy, scholasticism became very speculative.

Luther was an Augustinian monk. Augustinians trace their order back to St. Augustine in the fourth century. There was intellectual rivalry between the Augustinians and Dominicans, and Luther naturally leaned more toward Augustinian terminology than the Thomistic terminology derived from St. Thomas Aquinas.

In Thomistic theology, "Faith was the assent of the intellect to the truths of faith." For Luther, though, faith was a total commitment of a person's whole being to God. It was not solely an act of the intellect. In Luther's mind, faith did involve works—it did involve how you act—but those works and actions did not save you. What saved you was the faith in Christ, which included a person's whole life: how he lives, behaves, thinks, and acts. Those were all included in Luther's idea of faith.

If you took Luther's idea of faith, he was right. If you took the Catholic idea of faith as solely an assent of the intellect and applied it to Luther, he was wrong. On the theological level, at least, the Reformation was based on a misunderstanding of terminology. They were fighting over words, and that misunderstanding was not officially clarified until the late 1900s.

Besides his being at the center of the faith versus works debate, I have a personal reason for inserting Luther into this discussion. It gives me a chance to mention two nuns who were helpful to me when I was struggling in grade school. It is puzzling to me why and how it happened, but early on, I became attracted to Luther's teachings.

I was in the fourth grade. I can remember where I was sitting, facing north in the middle of the room. The teacher, a nun, was talking about Luther, and I am sure she was not presenting him in the best light. This was in 1944, twenty years before it became fashionable to speak about Protestants as our "separated brethren." Sister was speaking, very likely trying to persuade us to see the devil in Luther. She was speaking about indulgences and Martin Luther's opinion of them, which was not very high. I remember thinking: "I think Luther is right. Sister is not making any sense." I specifically recall saying to myself, "I would have gone with him." Those were my exact thoughts. I can't explain to you why I thought that. I can't even explain it to myself. "I would have gone with him." I was ten years old, and young children don't usually object to religious "truths" presented to them by their teachers. In this case, I did.

The most obvious reason for a student to go directly against a teacher is that he does not like her, and therefore rejects anything she says—the student is rebelling against the teacher more than the subject matter. Not liking the teacher was not the problem between this sister and me. I liked my fourth-grade teacher, Sister Irma. She was honest. She was a straight shooter, and she was very helpful to me. I was a poor student; I couldn't read. I had dyslexia, but back then no one had ever heard of learning disabilities.

I still mix up letters and words. Recently, I was with my sister and saw a sign. I said, "They have a warehouse over there." She said, "My dear well-educated, learned brother, that sign does not say 'warehouse,' it says 'housewares,' you lummox!" We were always close.

She may have been right. While in college a very old English professor returned my writing assignment with these encouraging words: "In all my years of teaching, this is the worst paper I have ever seen." I was tempted to reply, "At least you know I didn't cheat."

I had, indeed, failed the third grade, the year before. Was it because I had dyslexia or because I was, indeed, a lummox? I always say the former. My family insists the latter, saying I am just using dyslexia as an excuse, but that I was just plumb dumb.

Sister Irma took an interest in me, though, and talked the principal into allowing me to come into her fourth-grade class, conditionally. If I didn't improve in six weeks, I would go back to the third grade. She didn't send me back.

Sister Irma was my friend; there was nothing personal in my not accepting her presentation of Luther. I was just convinced that Luther was right on the indulgence question. The subject was poorly explained and sinfully misused.

Today, you don't see hordes of people doing ridiculous things to gain indulgences. As an example, on "All Souls Day," when the church prays for the dead, you could get an indulgence applicable to a departed soul if you visited a church and said the required prayers for the departed.

In the seminary after night prayers, more than three hundred seminarians would walk out of the chapel, turn around and walk back in to say another prayer for a deceased loved one. You had to go out and come back in to make it a separate visit, and you had to make a separate visit—out and in, out and in—for it to count. There would be some 300 men trying to get out and in through the same door at the same time to get that indulgence for a deceased loved one.

It was like going through the gate of an Ohio State/Michigan football game, only worse. In an effort to pray, you could get trampled. After a few years of that hassle, I quit going in and out. I still said the prayers; I just dropped the gymnastics. I am sure today's seminarians do not do that revolving door routine. Thankfully, Vatican II did clean up some of the spiritual nonsense.

Praying for the dead is a charitable act, and it is our obligation and privilege to do so. But turning sacredness into foolishness is sacrilegious; religion is not well served by ridiculous behavior. On the contrary, such foolishness invites ridicule of the sacred. Some people make fun of religion, and it is often we believers who give them cause.

As it turns out, both Luther and I won the battle on indulgences—Luther against the church, and I against Sister Irma. God bless her kind soul. She was wrong on indulgences but right on kindness, and kindness is where it counts.

Right after the council, when Catholics understood their Catholicism in a new way, some looked back at their pre-Vatican II school education with displeasure. They blamed the sisters for teaching us "all that nonsense." That is giving the sisters a bad rap; it is not fair. The sisters were teaching only what the clergy told them to teach. It was the clergy who wrote the religious textbooks, not the nuns.

For years, the nuns became the whipping boys for everything that Catholics didn't like in their pre-council training. As a student I had some great teachers. As a principal of a high school I worked with twenty or thirty nuns, each well qualified and dedicated to the extreme. Let us not blame the sisters for the 1940s and 1950s in the church. I also want to mention my fifth-grade teacher, Sister Eugenia. We became lifelong friends and, fifty years after she taught me, she visited me for a couple of days at the monastery. Most of my teachers hadn't seen any academic promise in me, but Sister Eugenia didn't quit trying to encourage me. In fact, she often pulled my ears for fooling around (of course, I was innocent and wrongly accused).

In high school a priest, in seeing my report card, said, "You will never get into college with these grades." I didn't pay any attention to him. I remember Sister Irma and Sister Eugenia daily in prayer, but I have mostly forgotten about the priest.

## Oh, Foolish Christians, Who Bewitched You?

After preaching to the Galatians, Paul left feeling good, grateful for the church he had established there. Later, he heard that things were not going well in Galatia. The church there was no longer living in Christian freedom, the way Paul had instructed them. He was saddened by that change because he knew the spirit had been dampened. He asked, "Who bewitched you?"

I left the active ministry in 1972 and lived in the monastery for twenty-eight years. When I left in 1972, the church was enjoying the spirit of Vatican II. While in the monastery, I heard from priests in parish work that things were changing. They told me that the climate had started to shift in the 1980s, and gradually the spirit of freedom begun by the council was slowly, but surely, being extinguished. When I returned to parish life in 2000, I saw evidence of this change. I then asked, "Who bewitched you?"

Right after the council, in the mid-1960s, the emphasis of the church was on the spirit of the law. We had laws, but they were seen only as a means to enable people to grow. After I returned, I noticed that the letter of the law had replaced the spirit. The emphasis seemed to be on making sure everyone followed the law, so that law and order became the core of the church's teaching.

What happened to Vatican II? The spirit of the law, which was evident immediately after the council, says that people are more important than law or policy. Yet the letter of law says the law is more important than people. And policy before people had once again became the guiding principle for the church.

I say this once again because for years before the council, the emphasis was totally on the law before spirit, policy before people. That attitude was so complete that it is totally incomprehensible to present-day Catholics. It is only the very aged Catholic who can say with a tone of regret, "I have been there, done that, and I don't want to go back to the 'good old days,'" back to policy before people, back to pre-Vatican II.

The following are a few examples of how entrenched was the idea that policy came before people, and those examples can be multiplied. It was the way the institutional church dealt with people; it was accepted policy, and nobody questioned it.

In the pre-council days, "Mother Church" was often a harsh step-mother instead of a tender nurturer. This harshness was no more evident than in the case of Catholic suicides. For a Catholic, to be buried in the church, in the community, is very important. Not to be allowed to have a Catholic funeral Mass was tantamount to saying that the deceased was damned to hell.

Until comparatively recent times, if Catholics committed suicide they could not have a funeral Mass or have a Catholic burial—policy came before people, law came before the spirit. The church regarded suicide as a mortal sin and refused burial. Can you imagine how that affected the Catholic family of the deceased? A member of a family, that for generations has been Catholic, commits suicide and is denied a Catholic burial: how cruel for the family to suffer that indignation. Now the church recognizes that we may never judge a person's soul, nor know the state of a person's mind at the time of suicide. The church now allows a Catholic funeral for a victim of suicide.

When I was a young priest in 1963, a slightly older friend of mine related an experience he had a few years before. At that time, he was a young priest, and his pastor was much older. A seven-year-old, in the excitement of his first communion, threw up after receiving communion. I will not tell you what the pastor made that child do to retrieve the regurgitated host, but the letter of the law was followed.

Do you see why we needed the reformed council to start to put people before policies, the spirit before the letter? My friend, who witnessed that scene, was an ex-serviceman and my handball opponent. He was a big, hot-headed Irishman, and I was surprised he didn't give the pastor what-for. In those days, however, the assistant didn't tell the pastor what to do or not do. In those days, the letter of the law prevailed.

In 1941, I made my first communion at the age of seven, when the law was in full force. In those days, if you were going to communion, you could not eat or drink anything after midnight before you received. If you forgot and drank some water during the night, you could not receive communion the next day.

After the council, those pre-communion laws were relaxed. As a priest, one Sunday morning, before I was to have Mass, I had breakfast at home. My mother sat and watched me gorge myself on a breakfast she had prepared. This was just a few hours before I was to have Mass.

She said, "Times have surely changed." She then told me about my first communion. "The night before you made your first communion, I slept hardly at all. I purposefully kept awake. I feared you would get up in the middle of the night and take a drink of water. Then you couldn't make your first communion."

She was right. If I had drunk water I could not have received. I also doubt that if she had told a priest what I had done that the priest would have changed church policy—thou shalt not eat or drink before communion. Forget about charity toward people; forget about the young child who had been preparing in school for three months for this day; forget about the money spent on the white suit, the white knee socks, and white shoes; forget about the coming of grandparents, uncles, aunts, and cousins; forget about the house the mother had been cleaning, the food she had been preparing; forget all that. Forget about the people; follow the law.

The rule had to be followed; no communion for this little law breaker. That is putting the letter of the law before the spirit of the law, putting policy before people. When you do, you become uncharitable for the sake of the law. You become unchristian for the sake of Christianity.

Up until the council, the hierarchy held sway over the laity, not only religiously, but also politically and socially. The 1950s were the time of the Red Scare and overall political anxiety. Catholics, because of their manic hatred of Communism, were very much caught up in the holy crusade against anything considered too Far Left.

Cardinal Spellman was the spokesman in this battle. He was continually fighting Dorothy Day, the founder and leader of the Catholic Worker House, a famous shelter for the homeless, destitute, and outcast of New York. She was also a Christian socialist and pacifist who often was jailed for her protests against war.

Today, it is impossible for us to appreciate the power of the Cardinal of New York. No Catholic priest ever got a traffic ticket or was arrested for DUI in New York City. No newspaper ever printed a story that the cardinal did not want printed. A powerful politician or an ambassador would make a phone call to the paper's editor, and the story that might have displeased His Excellency never saw the light of day. Clericalism is using the clerical office as a source of power, and Cardinal Spellman wrote the book on clericalism. He was one of the most powerful men in the country.

Spellman, who was also a rabid capitalist and the chief military chaplain, didn't much care for Dorothy Day's socialist and pacifist views. He would go ballistic when she would get publicity, usually by being put in jail for her anti-war protests. She would be pictured in jail, and he would be shown in the cardinal's mansion—both Catholics! It made for great copy. People could choose sides, the poor pacifist or the clerical warrior. At the time, I considered Dorothy Day un-American, which shows you where my values were! In my youthfulness, I assumed that spirituality had to include blind, unquestioning patriotism. Unfortunately, my stupidity was not uncommon at the time, and it still isn't.

Ironically, the Archdiocese of New York has recently introduced Dorothy Day's cause for sainthood, while Cardinal Spellman has not been so introduced.

The Cardinal made it very clear where he stood politically, way out in right field, and that he expected all good Catholics to follow his example. In the 1950s and 1960s, the cardinal was completely identified with the political Right. He was a vocal supporter of Senator Joe McCarthy and publicly supported Richard Nixon over John Kennedy in the 1960 presidential elections. He had urged American intervention in Vietnam as early as 1954 and was such an outspoken supporter of the war that it came to be known as "Spelly's War."

Surprisingly, however, in the 1940s he befriended Franklin D. Roosevelt—but not Eleanor, whom he called anti-Catholic. The political Right was always suspicious that Eleanor had communist leanings. After all, she was very supportive of black people and the poor.

The Irish Catholic Senator Joseph McCarthy was the lay counterpart of Cardinal Spellman. He led the battle against anything Left. At Senate hearings in the mid-1950s, his attacks became so vicious that Army Counsel Joseph Welch angrily asked, "Senator, have you no sense of decency?" The Senate later censured McCarthy, indeed, for having no sense of decency.

This senator from Wisconsin and far too many Catholics saw communists everywhere: Water fluoridation was a plot to poison Americans, *The Wizard of Oz* promoted socialist ideas. He unmercifully persecuted the movie industry. Some lost their jobs because of false accusations. Charlie Chaplin pleaded, "I am not a communist! . . . I want nothing more for humanity than a roof over every man's head." Talk about subversive!

In the late 1950s through the 1960s, the extreme Right John Birch Society had a substantial following among Catholics. While working in Catholic high schools, I had the misfortune of seeing just how destructive that group could be. Even the archconservative William Buckley was worried that the Birch Society could slide into fascism.

Our high school would have an "all-school Mass" for the entire student body and faculty on church holy days and on special occasions. If a public figure died, anyone from President Kennedy to a state senator, we would have a Mass for him or her. Politics were not involved. The Mass was a gesture showing we prayed for our country's leaders.

After Martin Luther King Jr. was killed, we scheduled an all-school Mass. Before Mass, two students came to me and said their parents had told them if we had Mass for Dr. King they should not go, because he was a communist. We never forced a student to attend Mass, so I had no choice but to allow them to sit in the office. I felt sorry for the kids; they were good kids. I knew they felt awkward and, I suspect, a little ashamed.

Today, the religious political atmosphere seems to be mirroring that of those years, and people are getting caught up in the rabidity of it, as they did back in the witch-hunt days. I have never heard such hateful, contemptible words directed against a president as I have heard against President Obama, and I date back to Roosevelt and the caustic anti-New Dealers. Someone recently sent me an article about the president, saying: "What a low-life, lying racist, Muslim, Marxist, Manchurian coward we have running our government. It is a disgrace to the office." The person, a Catholic, who sent the article, added his own thoughts about the president, calling him "that spineless, phony usurper at 1600 Pennsylvania Avenue." The sender was a Catholic—"in good standing," no doubt!

Just as during the days of the Red Scare, when many Christians were attracted to zealotry of Senator McCarthy, many Christians today either silently or actively contribute to the venom of the anti-Obama people. Ted Nugent, while campaigning for Texas Republican gubernatorial candidate Greg Abbot, referred to the president as a "sub-human chimpanzee." Abbot did not object to Nugent's words.

I have heard the president referred to as "that black thing in Washington." It is no crime to kill a "sub-human" or mongrel. We daily kill cows, pigs, chickens, and fish. We also destroy "things"—wrecked cars, old houses—with no thought. When we apply the terms "sub-human" and "thing" to a person, we are in dangerous territory. To the Nazis, the Jews were sub-human things who, accordingly, could be destroyed.

Those who use inflammatory language against the president may not themselves commit acts of violence. However, a person who is mentally unstable or full of hate may act out the verbal violence he hears from others. Those who use such hateful language cannot excuse themselves of the crime. They fuel the twisted minds, and by their words they are creating a deadly climate that influences not only the morally weak, but also the mentally weak.

When President Kennedy was shot, some Dallas school children clapped with approval. The perpetuators of hate had influenced their young minds. Words have effect. Language incites people to action. I am not at all suggesting that the Catholic Church or the hierarchy is promoting such hate and dangerous language; but neither did I hear from the church a persuasive call for civility during the last elections. On the contrary, I heard that directives were given from some pulpits on the way a "good Catholic" should vote. In one Catholic paper, a priest responded to the fact that Obama carried the Catholic vote by saying, "Those aren't the votes of good Catholics."

Once again, we are seeing the hierarchy giving very strong clerical "advice" on how to vote. This paternal guidance, where the wise father leads the uneducated and uninformed child to correct political decisions, seemed to be in vogue again in the 2000s as it was in the 1950s.

Recently, in the midst of a political gathering, a bishop publicly declared that he is now an officially registered Republican. He held up his baptismal certificate and his newly acquired registration certificate. Was he trying to persuade Catholics of the supposed innate connection between Republicans and Catholics? I don't know.

In the 1940s and 1950s, in addition to its political involvement, the church was the guardian of social life. The hierarchy was much involved in censorship, especially movie censorship. It got so absurd that Catholic censorship was the butt of jokes. In fact, *Time* entitled an article "Religion: To See is To Sin."

Again, it was Cardinal Spellman who was the crusader for "the custody of the eyes." In the 1950s, he labeled *Two-Faced Women* as "an occasion of sin ... dangerous to public morals." He called *The Miracle* "a vile and harmful picture, a despicable affront to every Christian." *Forever Amber* also came under condemnation, but far and away his most notorious venture into movie censorship was his tackling of the movie *Baby Doll* in 1956. He ascended to the pulpit of St. Patrick's Cathedral in all of his Episcopal glory and announced, "Catholics are forbidden to see the movie *Baby Doll* under the pain of mortal sin." Hell is a long time to burn for the sake of a movie. The cardinal must have spent a good deal of his time going to movies to sort out all the bad stuff. I wonder if he enjoyed his job?

Everyone got into the *Baby Doll* fight, including the Archbishop of Paris and Norman Vincent Peale, who both disagreed with the cardinal. I had just graduated from college. I enjoyed the excitement of the fracas, but as an obedient Catholic I would never have gone to see the film.[30]

Since my return to parish life in 2000, I see a return to the 1950s church. The hierarchy has been "Spellman-like"; it seems once again to be cuddling up with the political Right. Even Cardinal Spellman's censorship seems to be making a comeback, although in a much softer manner and without mortal sin and the accompanying threat of hell.

A few years ago, the bishops had scheduled a seminar to be held at Notre Dame, and the bishops were to stay on campus. During that time, a class was putting on a production. It was intended to be an academic exercise, not for public entertainment. It was not held in the university's theater but in a classroom. It was primarily for the students and school officials.

There were to be discussion panels afterwards, where the differences between the play's theme and Catholic moral teachings were to be discussed. However, there was a problem. The production was not along the lines of *Lassie, Come Home*; it was *The Vagina Monologues*.

When the bishops heard that the play was to be held during their planned stay on campus, they fled the "pit of sin" to the safety of Mishawaka, Indiana. There is no more "safe place" than Mishawaka, Indiana. Even if you wanted to change your Fundamental Option, you couldn't do it in Mishawaka. Even college kids can't get into trouble in Mishawaka. I know! I tried, unsuccessfully, from 1952 to 1956! There, in the secure shelter of a convent, the bishops had their meeting. I don't know what topics were on the bishops' agenda. Hopefully, it was of something of more importance than college theatrical productions.

---

30. I can't resist quoting Adlai Stevenson, who spoke about Norman Vincent Peale's statement that no American should vote for John Kennedy because of his Catholicism. Stevenson commented, "I find (St.) Paul appealing and Peale appalling."

In the 1950s, you had a cardinal telling people they would go to hell for seeing a movie, today you have bishops escaping from a "sinful" campus with their virtue intact, singing "Good Ship Lollipop." For the bishops, Shirley Temple is "safe." God must have a sense of humor to put up with us religious people.

Matthew devotes an entire chapter of his gospel—the "woe" chapter—to castigating the clergy for being overly concerned with trivia. "Woe to you scribes and Pharisees, you strain out a gnat and swallow a camel" (Matt 23:24). Getting involved with the insignificant is the professional hazard of all leaders, especially religious leaders. It also weakens God's message of love and opens it to ridicule.

The bishops' actions harkens to Cardinal Spellman and *Baby Doll*. Surely there must be bigger problems in Catholicism and the world in general than having students discuss the moral pros and cons of *The Vagina Monologues*. A university is supposed to be a place where ideas are exchanged and their merits evaluated.

The bishops evidently knew it was a "bad play." That would have been a good reason for them to go see the production when it was being presented as an academic setting. They would then have been in a much better position to criticize. That would have given them a chance to listen to what the students thought about such topics. What did Pope Francis say? We don't come "to proselytize, but to listen." Do we really want to go back to the patronizing church of the pre-council days, when the hierarchy felt no obligation to listen?

It may seem as if I am against American bishops. In fact, I am pleased and feel blessed to have been around three bishops, whom I counted as friends. We played together and went to ball games together, and I worked with two of them. Also, two of my classmates were appointed bishops; one became the top Catholic military chaplain. Both were good friends. I refer to them as "the appointed." They refer to me as "the disappointed."

The history of the American hierarchy has been praiseworthy. I don't think that any other Catholic religious body has spoken out for social justice and pleaded the plight of the poor. Generally, the American church has been blessed with courageous leaders.

Cardinal Gibbons of Baltimore saved the American labor class for the church. In the early 1900s, he battled Rome on the question of labor unions. Rome was about to condemn the U.S. Knights of Labor, forbidding

Catholics to join them. Rome looked upon all unions with suspicion, based on their experience with the radical European labor unions.

Cardinal Gibbons had a way of getting around Rome's directives, sometimes even ignoring them outright. He fought Rome on the church's condemnation of the Knights of Labor, and for many years, the U.S. church was known as a "friend of labor." It took courage for the cardinal to go against Rome's suspicious attitude.

The American hierarchy has had a glorious history of getting a feel of what the Catholic people want, such as labor unions and religious freedom. They fought Rome to get these ideas accepted in the church.

Today, many bishops have bravely spoken out for reforming immigration policy, raising the minimum wage, and abolishing the death penalty. In May 2014, the bishops called for a reduction of carbon pollution to mitigate climate change. Some "good Catholics," however, oppose some, if not all of those positions. When you take on the coal industry, you are taking on an opponent with huge political and financial clout. The bishops have shown courage; however, these positive signs on the national level have not been mirrored in the average parish. Since my return to parish life in 2000, I have seen a return to the more conservative atmosphere that existed during the pre-council days.

When I stepped out of the monastery in late December of 1999, I felt as if I had stepped back to the 1950s. I felt, in the words of the bishop, that "we are going backwards." Thankfully, Pope Francis is reversing that backward movement. It is as if the he is saying with St. Paul: "Oh, foolish Christians. Who bewitched you?"

## Religious Liberty

The most well known instance of the American hierarchy leading both the American and the universal church happened in 1965 with the church's proclamation of religious liberty. The first time religious freedom was declared by the church was at the Vatican II Council. The U.S. bishops led the way against a powerful group of bishops in Catholic countries that opposed the idea of religious liberty. They felt non-Catholic religions had to be suppressed, or at least limited, as they always had been in their countries.

The American bishops came to the council, led by a bright and brave Jesuit priest, *Father* John Courtney Murray. His views on religious liberty were the ones expressed in the American Constitution and accepted by

American Catholics as a fact of life. Americans, Catholics among them, grew up with a belief in religious freedom.

For the past 30 years, many Catholics have felt the church was limiting the freedom won for them by Christ. "For freedom, Christ has set us free. Stand firm then and not submit to the yoke of slavery" (Gal 5:1). Pope Francis seems to be offering to us the freedom that was instigated by Vatican II and then slowly withdrawn. May we have the courage to embrace it, so that Paul may not say to us: "Oh, foolish Christians. Who bewitched you?"

Not many Catholics are aware that the church officially condemned religious freedom until 1965. They condemned the idea that people should be allowed to practice the religions of their choice. Americans accepted religious freedom, so they assumed that the church also accepted it. That is not so. In accepting religious liberty, the church is a Johnny-come-lately.

Through the centuries, the official church teaching on religious freedom was summarized and proclaimed in the church's document of 1861, the *Syllabus of Errors*. In that decree, the idea that "every man is free to embrace that religion . . . which he shall consider true" was declared to be heretical.[31] By the nineteenth century, it was still heresy to believe in religious freedom. The *Syllabus* condemned just about everything that today we accept as basic human rights.

The *Syllabus* has been a source of embarrassment for the church from its conception. It is considered the low point in the church's denial of human freedoms. It was overturned completely at Vatican II. In the late 1950s we seminarians were shocked to read in our theology textbook that the church's condemnation of religious freedom was still in effect. The logical syllogism in our textbook proving that religious freedom was not permissible was as follows: "Error has no rights. Non-Catholic religions are in error. Therefore, non-Catholic religions have no rights."

As Americans, we were caught in a conundrum. Our church forbade religious freedom, while our country promoted it. Personally we all believed in religious freedom, but the church was telling us not to accept that freedom for others.

If you accepted the major and minor statements of that syllogism, you had to accept the conclusion, that "non-Catholic religions have no rights." Our logic course taught us so. The professor tried to soften the impact by telling us that there were some American theologians who were studying

---

31. Pious IX, "Syllabus Errorum," 3:15.

the problem of religious freedom. Father Murray was the "some American theologians."

We then quickly turned the page, chalking it up to just one more of those "unsolvable" questions in church history. Why did they condemn Galileo? Why did they burn heretics at the stake? The condemnation of religious liberty was just one more "why" in the long list of whys that was quickly glossed over in the seminary. We moved on to more pressing problems, such as the morality of poaching. There were many, many pages on that important subject: "If my cow was grazing on your land, eating your grass for many years, whose cow is it now?" Our textbooks were rather dated.

Religious liberty took a long time to be accepted in the Catholic Church. Even at the council, the acceptance of religious liberty did not come easily. The conservative bishops, especially those from Catholic countries in South America and the Mediterranean, fought against what to them was a new and dangerous doctrine—freedom of religion.

The council's declaration on religious freedom, "The Dignity of the Human Person," was the American hierarchy's finest hour in the universal church. These bishops, as in the case of protecting labor unions sixty years before, were leaders pushing the church to realize that conditions change in the world. To preach the gospel effectively to all people at all times, the church can't put its head in the sand and pretend it is still in the 1400s.

When the Vatican decree was published in 1965, a group of ultra Right bishops and priests broke away from the church and formed the Society of St. Pius X. They said that the church had fallen into heresy, and they considered the decree on religious liberty the most horrendous of its heresies. The society had priests widely spread, including my home diocese, and it was a force to be taken seriously. They retained the church exactly as it had been before the council, especially the church's condemnation of religious liberty. They were not a fun group to be around. Through the entire previous history of the church, their position had been considered right, but after the council, they were wrong. Vatican II was the first time the church officially declared religious freedom, and the Pius X society would not accept it.

In case you are wondering how John Courtney Murray beat that syllogism, he pointed out that the statement "error has no rights" is incorrect. "Error" is an abstraction. An abstraction, such as "whiteness," does not have anything because it doesn't exist in itself. Whiteness must exist in another reality to have existence. A white house has size, shape, and strength; however, the abstraction "whiteness" has nothing. It does not exist independently. To say error has no rights is as meaningless as saying whiteness has no rights. They are both abstractions.

It is people who err, and people have the right to be wrong. Human beings are fallible; it is in our nature. To say a human being who errs has no rights is a denial of our humanness. If that were true, no one would have any rights.

Father Murray had an interesting career as a theologian. Several years before the council, Rome censured him for expressing his views on religious freedom. Rome said that by so doing he was denying Catholic doctrine, which at that time denied religious liberty. Father Murray was later exonerated and was invited by the American bishops to be a theologian at the council. The bishops brought theologians as advisors. The church at one time censored his thoughts, and then later vindicated and honored him. That practice happened to several theologians and writers who were first censured by the church and then later absolved. Today's heretics are tomorrow's saints.

Recently the American hierarchy has pushed to protect religious liberties. The present emphasis is the result of tension between the government's medical insurance policies and Catholic hospitals. When I hear priests today championing religious freedom in this context, I wonder, "Do they know the church's history regarding religious freedom?"

Paul Claudel the twentieth-century French dramatist said, "The Christian alone has liberty."[32] Recently, a member of the U.S. hierarchy approvingly quoted those words, which surely oppose the American understanding of religious freedom. Generally, Americans do not believe that "The Christian alone has liberty," but after his quoting Claudel, I don't know where that bishop stands on the issue of freedom for all Americans.

The present freedom of religion debate is a very complex problem for a pluralistic society to solve peacefully, and those who have dogmatic and easy answers to the problem very likely don't understand all of its implications.

A past example of the religious freedom debate surrounds Prohibition. In the 1920s, many Protestant churches taught that drinking alcohol was sinful. They felt that not only they, but also others, should not drink. They worked to get a law passed that declared it a crime to sell alcoholic beverages. Prohibition was passed largely because many Protestants demanded a law that supported their religious beliefs.

32. DeCosse, "Imbalance," para. 8.

Thus, Americans who did not regard drinking as sinful were not free to buy alcohol. It was against the law. The prohibitionists said, "My religion teaches that it is a sin to drink; so the state must forbid it because religion trumps conscience." Opposing groups said: "My religion says that drinking is not a sin. I have a right to follow my conscience, even if it differs from your religion. Your religion does not have the right to tell my conscience what is right and wrong."

Substitute birth control and abortion for alcohol, and you have today's version of the dilemma of one group's religion superseding all others' conscience. Does my religious belief that birth control and abortion are sinful have a right to overrule your conscience, which says they're not?

The concept of freedom of conscience means not denying the rights of those who believe differently. If a young wife, the mother of six young children is told that in her present pregnancy she will die unless she aborts the fetus, she and her husband would have an excruciating decision to make. Possibly and hopefully they would follow God's law as they see it and not directly kill an innocent life.

Can they demand that another couple faced with the same decision follow their religious belief? Can they make a law forcing the other couple to follow what they believe? Is a person who does not believe the way I do a hardened sinner, having no rights?

These are difficult questions. They are at the root of the freedom of conscience versus freedom of religion debate that is raging today, unfortunately with hateful words and actions on both sides. I have more questions than answers.

Is it true that a conscience, which is in error, has no rights and therefore no freedom? Is it true that others are not free to break God's law *as I see it*, be it about alcohol, birth control, or abortion?

Is a dialogue possible with those whose consciences differ from our religious beliefs? Is it true that freedom of conscience is the cornerstone of freedom of religion? Does my freedom of religion permit my denying your freedom of religion? Does my freedom of conscience restrict your freedom of conscience? Getting through those thorny questions requires much honesty and even more charity.

It is not the present-day health insurance issue that concerns me as much as the way some of the clergy are presenting the church's position about it. Too many are presenting the church and themselves as the champions of religious liberty and painting the U.S. government as the enemy of such liberty. Historically, the Catholic Church has not been the champion of religious freedoms in America—the government has.

In 1776, about two hundred years before Vatican II and the church's first official declaration on religious freedom, our founding fathers declared for religious liberty. It was a motley group of deists, agnostics, and skeptics about organized religion that had the insight, the grace, to realize that religious freedom is a basic human right.

It was the secular state, not the religious establishment, which first proclaimed that principle. The first amendment to the U.S. Constitution has two parts. First, it prohibits the government from having an established religion, though "established" religions had been the norm throughout world history—where the king was Catholic, his state was Catholic; where the king was Protestant his state was Protestant. Usually, dissent was not tolerated.

It is the second part of the first amendment that so opposes traditional Catholic and, in most cases, Protestant teachings as well. It prohibits the government from making a law against the free exercise of religion. That was considered heresy in the Catholic Church all the way up until 1965. Catholic (and some Protestant) countries felt they not only had the right, but the obligation, to prohibit "false religion," and they made laws accordingly.

In mainline churches, freedom of religion was considered a novel and dangerous idea, sponsored by "faithless" people. Generally, men who were not strong churchgoers promoted religious freedom. Most were believers of some sort, but they were not active in churches.

Thomas Jefferson, who deserves to be given the title "the Saint of Religious Freedom," was considered, at one time, unfit for public office because he did not have "orthodox" beliefs. Thank God for that, too; he didn't want to burn people at the stake. The New England Congregationalists warned that people should hide their Bibles if the Jeffersonians seize power. Jefferson didn't dislike spirituality or people relating to God; he disliked organized religion.

A monk told me a humorous story about "organized religion." Someone said to him, "I have three fears—death, venereal disease, and organized religion." That does have a certain Jeffersonian ring to it.

Jefferson wrote, "There never would have been an infidel, if there had never been a priest."[33] He wanted people to be free to accept religion, and

33. Jefferson, "Letter," lines 33–34.

also free to reject it. "It does me no injury for my neighbor to say there are twenty gods, or no god. It neither picks my pocket nor breaks my leg."[34]

When church leaders today give the impression that the church, and not the government, is the true advocate of religious freedom, they are misrepresenting not only American history but also the church's history. Our government has always been more diligent in respecting religious freedom than has been the church. To gloss over that fact in today's discussion is misleading, to say the least.

The church works very hard to protect the Catholic church's freedom, but it is rather weak in protecting the freedoms of others. From our pulpits comes the message, "We Catholics must protect our rights against the godless state that is trying to take away our freedom." Throughout American history, this "godless state" has been more protective of the religious rights of all people than the church has been.

Our government must also protect others' rights, including those of non-believers. Our government's protection of all people's rights drives some "good Christians" crazy. We want the government to protect Christian rights. Freedom that only benefits some is no freedom at all—it is merely self-centeredness on the part of the chosen few. Truth, not self-interest, should be the main concern. Searching for truth, individually and collectively, is a difficult task.

Thomas Jefferson said, "Truth is great and will prevail if left to herself."[35] Today's Catholic clergy should consider his words; they may be pushing too hard and with a touch of arrogance in proclaiming that the church has been shamefully mistreated in the health insurance/Catholic hospital problem. Shouting "religious liberty, religious liberty" is not charitable and may be counter-productive. It is simply hypocritical for officials of the Catholic Church to paint themselves as the champions of religious liberty when, historically, this just isn't the case.

## Four for Freedom

The concept of religious freedom or religious liberty is comparatively recent and had its roots in American soil, beginning with the Constitution. American priest John Courtney Murray was in the vanguard of having the church accept of the "modern idea" of religious freedom.

34. Bowman, "Jefferson's Religious Beliefs," para. 1.
35. Jefferson, "Virginia Act," para. 1.

Fathers Yves Congar, Thomas Merton, and Pierre Teilhard de Chardin, along with Murray, are of importance in any discussion of the church freedom. All were living in 1950 and were harassed by the church for their advanced thinking. These four were loyal and obedient to the church, yet the church tried to intimidate them for their scholarship and spirituality.

These four Catholic priests and scholars were denied their religious liberties by the church, not in the usual sense, but in a very real sense nevertheless.[36]

The greatest gifts we have been given by God are our ability to think and choose. Intellect and will, two attributes of God, are the roots of our freedom. People's freedom is restricted when they are told they are not to think in a certain way, as if thoughts, in themselves, are wrong. How many "wrong thoughts" in one generation became "right thoughts" in a later generation: once condemned, later exalted? As the council said, religious freedom is a natural right. It can't be taken from us. For many years, these four were harassed for the way they thought!

The fact that all four were exonerated speaks well for the church. Also, by inviting Fathers Congar and Murray to be experts at the council, the church showed an exemplary search for truth. Those four men, and the church's reconciliation with them, are important for us today. We can learn from their experience and their loyalty to the church.

Before Vatican II, under the façade of a very successful, contented church, there were some very unchristian strong-arm tactics. The average Catholic had no idea what was happening, but the church was treating some of the finest Catholic scholars uncharitably.

One of the most censured theologians of the twentieth century was Father Yves Congar, a Domican priest ordained in 1930. For five years, 1940–45, he was in a German prisoner of war camp. Father Congar was ahead of his time in promoting the church's obligation to encourage Christian unity. The impetus for Christian unity was forged in the Nazi prison camps during the Second World War. In those camps, people of all faiths were reduced to essentials. They saw the need to forget denominational differences and strive to be united in their common faith in God. It was Father Congar's experience in these camps that gave him the desire to work for Christian unity after the war. It was this desire of like-minded people that led to the ecumenical council Vatican II.

36. For a more detailed explanation of the four, see Father Robert Nugent's book, *Silence Speaks*.

Prior to the council, no one talked about Christian unity. The attitude of the church was: "Protestants are in heresy. If we can no longer persecute them, we at least have an obligation not to talk to them." Because Father Congar talked to Protestants in an attempt to reduce the hostility between the two groups, he also was considered a heretic. Under Pope Pius XII he was banned from teaching. He was also forbidden to preach, lecture, or even meet with his students. He had to have his writings submitted for Rome's permission before they could be published.

Around 1959, his fortunes changed. Pope John XXIII lifted the church's ban on him and then invited him to be an advising theologian (*peritus*) at the council to aid the bishops. That invitation was the most visible proof of Father Congar's justification as a theologian.

In 1994, Pope John Paul II made Congar a cardinal. It was mostly symbolic because Father Congar was ninety years old and unable to travel to Rome to receive the honor, but it was a charitable gesture on the part of the pope. It was a way of saying, "We are sorry for the way the church has treated you." Congar died shortly thereafter; he had been a priest for sixty-three years.

Here was a man who, in 1955, church officials placed under house arrest at the Dominican House of Studies at Oxford University. "He was forbidden to have public talks, writings or contacts with Protestants."[37] Seven years later, he was an "expert" at the council on Catholic-Protestant relations. Father Thomas Merton also was having troubles with the church over his talks with Protestants. He invited some pastors and scholars to visit him at the monastery for discussions and soon thereafter received a communication from church officials urging him "to diminish contacts with Protestant scholars."[38]

Doesn't that tell us about the significance of the council, and especially about Pope John XXIII? I don't know if he was the most important pope we ever had, but he may have been the bravest since Peter was crucified upside down. No doubt, in 1962, some of the church fathers wanted to do the same to this lovable "fat, homely peasant." He was shrewder and stronger than anyone suspected. As Merton expressed it, "The Council was tremendous. Pope John has been a great gift of God to all of us. What a superb pope, and what a heart."[39]

37. Nugent, *Silence Speaks*, 44.
38. Nugent, *Thomas Merton*, 132.
39. Ibid., 117.

I recently heard an interesting story about Pope John XXIII. Though the point of the story is true, the details remain an open question. When Pope John was a bishop, he was under "suspicion." This son of an Italian tenant farmer had "heretical leanings" and felt the heavy hand of censorship. After he was elected pope, he went over to the Holy Office, which is a department in the Vatican that keeps an eye on orthodoxy and punishes transgressors. In Congar's words, "the Holy Office, in practice, rules the church and makes everyone bow down to it through fear—it is the supreme Gestapo, unyielding, whose decisions cannot be discussed."[40] I find the use of the word "Gestapo" interesting when used by someone who spent five years as a German prisoner of war.

In the Holy Office, Pope John XXIII found his folder that recorded his activities as a bishop. He wrote on the front of the folder, "I am not a heretic." He signed it Pope John XXIII and put it back in the file along with those of Congar, Chardin, Murray, and Merton. Heretics are not dull, that is for sure!

Jesuit priest and paleontologist Pierre Teilhard de Chardin was severely censured between the two World Wars for his work on prehistoric life and evolution. He had received his doctorate in science from the Sorbonne in 1922 and was ordained in 1930. He spent many years in China working in archeology and was recognized as one of the world's top paleontologists.

The monk Thomas Merton was censured for writing about the immorality of war, especially regarding atomic warfare. He said that the censors permitted him to write about war, but they did not allow him to mention the bomb. He joked that that was like telling someone they can write about marriage but are not allowed to mention sex.

In the years following the council in the 1960s and 1970s, censorship lessened, and an era of tolerance ensued. In the 1970s, Father Robert Nugent and Sister Jeannine Gramick co-founded the New Ways Ministry. Their ministry's purpose was to serve and care for homosexuals and their families. This was at the time when homosexuals were harassed by civil and religious society. The organization had the support of several bishops, including Francis Mugavero of Brooklyn, Thomas Gumbleton of Detroit, and Matthew Clark of Rochester.

Their support embodied the atmosphere of Vatican II. As time went on, however, the climate of openness and acceptance began to change. By the mid-1980s, the conservative reaction against the council was in full

40. Nugent, *Silence Speaks*, 43.

force. Repression was back in style, and the champions of orthodoxy were on the alert.

In 1999, the Congregation for the Doctrine of the Faith condemned New Ways Ministry and ordered Father Nugent and Sister Gramick to discontinue their work with homosexuals. This was the same congregation that silenced Fathers Congar, Murray, and Chardin in the 1950s. It was formally named the Holy Office, which Father Congar referred to as the "supreme Gestapo."

The congregation imposed an order of silence on Nugent and Gramick. They could not write, speak, teach, or counsel in the area of homosexuality, nor could they speak, write, or discuss the process that led up to those orders.

Whatever the differences involved, I think Pope Francis would not have handled it in such a heavy-handed manner. Francis' style seems to be "meet and discuss." In the pre-Francis church, the style seemed to be "separate and destroy!"

Another example of how the openness immediately following the council later changed to condemnation is the case of Father Hans Küng, the highly respected Swiss theologian. While visiting the U.S. in 1962, he spoke at our seminary. His book *The Council and Reunion* was written about the council. He, like Fathers Congar and Murray, was a *peritus* at Vatican II.

After the council, he taught Catholic theology at Tubingen University in Germany, where he also was the head of the theology department. In that capacity, he hired Carl Ratzinger as professor of theology. Gradually Küng fell in disfavor, and Ratzinger fell in favor with church authorities. Ratzinger became a cardinal and headed the Holy Office for twenty years. He then became Pope Benedict XVI. In 1979, Hans Küng was censored by Rome and could no longer officially teach as a Catholic theologian. He remains a priest in good standing and can preach at Mass.

Again, I doubt that Francis would have handled the Küng situation in such a manner. In both the Nugent-Gramick case and the Hans Küng case one could ask, "What happened to the spirit of Vatican II?" In 2005, shortly after he was elected, Pope Benedict and Küng met and had supper. To the credit of both, the meeting was cordial and respectful.

No one today remembers the people who were making condemnations from the Holy Office. But Murray, Congar, Chardin, and Merton have influenced practically every Catholic. Chardin and Merton were, and continue to be, my inspirations; Chardin more while teaching, Merton while in the monastery. In the seminary, I read Chardin's *The Divine Milieu* while hiding in a closet. A classmate had whispered to me, "I found a book I think you would like." He then passed it to me wrapped in a brown paper bag. (Chardin was suspect at that time.) I consider it one of the most deeply spiritual books I have ever read, and it influenced me greatly.

While teaching, from 1962 to 1972, I wrote a textbook that combined the teaching of Vatican II's decree entitled "The Church in the Modern World" with Chardin's *The Divine Milieu*. The two texts fit perfectly together, so much so that I don't see how a person can understand "The Church in the Modern World," with its evolutionary thrust, without understanding the *The Divine Milieu*.

"The Church in the Modern World" specifically speaks of how a positive appreciation of evolution is necessary to understand and benefit from contemporary Christian spirituality. The document states, "The destiny of the human community has come all of a piece . . . Thus, the human race has passed from a rather static concept of reality to a more dynamic, evolutionary one."[41] That was the very point that Chardin was trying to make. Maybe the Vatican II bishops had read him, for in that decree they added, "Historical studies make it much easier to see things in their mutable and evolutionary aspects."[42] I find it ironic that the church would officially express Chardin's ideas.

Apparently, during a meeting before the council, Chardin was called to Rome to explain his ideas to church officials. He came out of the meeting with tears in his eyes, saying, "They wouldn't even listen to me." Here was a man who was recognized as one of the world's most outstanding thinkers and scientists, and some prelates in Rome—who probably could not even spell evolution—crushed him like a bug. Some things never change. "Blessed are you when they persecute you falsely. So did they persecute the prophets who came before you" (Matt 5:11). Prophets make any institution uncomfortable; prophets always are first disbelieved, and later honored.

Some consider Galileo's case unique in the history of the church, but it was not. A monsignor in New York censored Thomas Merton's books. Chardin was "martyred" by those officials in Rome—all in the name of religious orthodoxy. Interestingly, however, just like Dorothy Day under Cardinal Spellman, Congar, Chardin, Murray, and Merton were obedient. They sometimes complained in the name of truth, but they were obedient.

41. Paul VI, "Modern World," para. 5.
42. Paul VI, "Modern World," para. 54.

Unfortunately the church's suspicions of Chardin have not been completely erased, even today. People don't understand his terminology and are frightened by his language. Mystics are never easy to understand, for they speak outside the box. Chardin was both a mystic and a top-rated scientist, and that combination of mystical and scientific language is too much for many to comprehend.

However, in 2009 Pope John Paul II, who was not known as one of Chardin's great supporters, paid him a surprisingly high compliment. John Paul equated Chardin's vision of the church with that of St. Paul's vision, "At the end (of time) we will have a true cosmic liturgy where the cosmos becomes a living host."[43] That is as close to Chardin as you can get; I hadn't realized that it was also Pauline.

Chardin returned to New York in 1950 an aging and beaten man. Legends always grow up around great people. The one about Chardin concerns his death. It is said that he prayed to God that "if he had been right in his teachings and insights concerning creation and its relationship to God, that God would give him the grace to die on Easter Sunday." He died Easter Sunday, 1955.

Is the legend true? Who knows? Like all legends, it really doesn't make any difference. It is the point that counts, not the story. Because of my fondness for him, I like to believe it is true. Whether or not he actually made that prayer to God, the point is Father Teilhard de Chardin was one of the most "Easter Christians" who ever lived. His life was dedicated to life, so it would be fitting for him to die on Easter Sunday—"the feast of Life."

> I have come that you may have life and have it more abundantly.
> (John 10:10)

---

43. Nugent, *Silence Speaks*, 32.

# 4

# Tomorrow's Challenges

IMMEDIATELY AFTER VATICAN II, the church addressed the problems of the time—not with negativity, but with openness to develop positive solutions. What will be tomorrow's problems that will demand a creative Christian response? Will the church respond with the openness of Vatican II?

One of the new situations is the debate over the acceptance of homosexuality. What will be the church's response to gay people going forward? Throughout church history, the response has been negative, to the point of sin. Certainly churches cannot merely repeat the anti-gay hostility of the past. The first part of this epilogue, therefore, concerns the question of homosexuality and the church's response.

The second section concerns religion and its contribution to intolerance and violence. In the centuries prior to Vatican II, religious intolerance and violence was the norm. In the mid-1500s, the church adopted a defensive attitude in reaction to the Protestant Reformation. This fortress mentality permeated the Council of Trent in the 1560s. The church took on a combative attitude toward the reformers and toward all non-Christian faiths. Most of the mainstream Protestant churches responded in kind and, thus, religious intolerance and violence became the accepted practice.

On the Catholic Church's side, Vatican II changed the church's defensive attitude toward other religions. For the first time in church history, the era of Ecumenism was introduced. Today's average Christian does not realize the historical significance and novelty of that change. It was unique in inter-church relations. As the years passed, this arena of respect and acceptance began to fade. Ecumenism was no longer in the forefront. Hostilities between religions reappeared. At Vatican II, believers in non-Christian religions were described with respect, based on the fact that Muslim, Jewish, and Christian religions all share the same father (Abraham) and worship the same God. Even atheists were spoken of positively.

Today, the spirit of acceptance is dwindling, and hostility is on the rise—not only among Christians, Muslims, and Jews, but also among Christians themselves. The conservative Christian churches think the more liberal churches are betraying the gospel, and the liberal churches see conservative churches as unthinking reactionaries. Both groups generally act as though atheists have no right to exist in this "Christian country." Hopefully, this second section, entitled "Religion and Violence," will remind us of our bloody past and its interfaith bitterness. When we lose the openness of Vatican II, bad things happen. When religious fundamentalists, be they Muslim or Christian, gain control, bad things happen.

## Religion and Homosexuality

In every age, the church is called to be present to the world with a message of love and peace. New situations arise that demand a Christian response, and the church and civil society must meet these new situations with charity. Unfortunately, in many situations the civil response has been more advanced and more tolerant than the church's response. In civil rights and women's rights, the church lagged behind civil authorities in offering understanding to those oppressed.

One of tomorrow's compelling questions will be, "How does the church relate to homosexuals?" Will a gay person feel accepted by the church—officially and individually? Will he/she feel at home in the church? These and similar questions already are being asked. How does the church plan to adjust to a society where gays and lesbians are becoming more acceptable every day? How does the church plan to address the homophobia present in society, especially among church authorities and churchgoers?

Historically, churches and religious people have been among the cruelest in their treatment of gays and lesbians. At one time, the church sentenced gay individuals to the death penalty, though both Da Vinci and Michelangelo—both thought to have been homosexual—escaped the religious net. "Death penalties" are still being passed today, only in more subtle forms. Indeed, the church has quite a bit of work to do to reduce prejudice in both its own ranks and in society at large.

We will center on the recent decision concerning the Boy Scouts of America allowing gay members in their organization, in which the unchristian attitudes and ugliness of the past surfaced again. Unfortunately, in this case, "good Christians" often were the ones leading the hostile attacks.

To keep our topic from being lost in abstractions, we will give examples where both religion and God have been misused in attempts to make the world "better" (in our "image and likeness") by eliminating undesirables. These examples should make us uncomfortable. They show how we misuse God to achieve our selfish ends and hurt others.

To talk about gay people in general is one thing; to talk about a friend who is gay is entirely different. We won't talk about the abstraction of gay people; we will talk about a person who happens to be gay. There is no better way to shed our negative predispositions than to see a gay person not as a bad thing, but as a good person.

I doubt there is a profession that does not include gay members. There are gay doctors, lawyers, teachers, athletes, clergy, and military. Many gay people have given their lives in service of their country. This being so, I was surprised when I learned of the Boy Scouts of America's rule that banned young gay boys from membership.

Recently, Tammy Smith became the first high-ranking female military officer to openly come out as a lesbian; it seems that either the Boy Scouts or the military is amiss.[1]

I think the Boy Scouts of America's policy was neither Christian nor just. How can we exclude young boys from belonging to any group based on their sexual orientation? Where does such a prohibition stop? Are we to forbid them from playing Little League baseball because some parents don't want their sons to be around "those kinds of kids?" Are we to stop them from joining the YMCA for the same reason, prohibit them from attending "our" schools?

If we can make such prohibitions against gay people, why can't we apply the same to other "undesirable" kids (i.e., blacks, Hispanics, Muslims, and maybe Catholics)? Who gets to decide who is acceptable and who is not?

How could a parent tell their son that he may not join the Boy Scouts because of his sexual orientation? What message does such discrimination send to our children—that some people are unacceptable? Recall the words from the *South Pacific* song, "You've Got to be Carefully Taught." Are we teaching our children to hate? We must avoid passing on our prejudices.

---

1. Wald, "First Openly Gay."

When the Boy Scouts were rethinking their anti-gay policy, a spokesman for the Catholic bishops said that the bishops wanted to ensure that organizations "model core values and integrity." That is self-evident and to be expected. It is unfortunate, however, that the statement was made as the Boy Scouts were discussing gay boys. The inference was all too obvious: if the Scouts chose to, they could exclude gay youngsters because they are lacking in "core values and integrity," and the bishops would not object.

That is slanderous against gay boys. What about all the other organizations that include gays—the military and others—do they also lack core values and integrity? How about the Daughters of the American Revolution? Is participation by gay people going to be the criterion by which the bishops approve or disapprove of a particular group?

We are continually tempted to use God as a defense. Father Thomas Merton once said: "Most people use religion to try to get God to do what they want, to get God to come through with something, to get God on their side. This is paganism, tabooism."[2]

One of the characters in Dan Brown's novel *The Last Symbol* says it best: "From the Crusades, to the Inquisition, to American politics—the name of Jesus had been hijacked as an ally in all kinds of power struggles. Since the beginning of time, the ignorant had always screamed the loudest, herding the unsuspecting masses and forcing them to do their bidding. They defended their worldly desires by citing Scripture they did not understand. They celebrated their intolerance as proof of their convictions. Now, after all these years, mankind had finally managed to utterly erode everything that had once been so beautiful about Jesus."[3] I would like to see that statement posted in every church where all could see it, every Sunday. There could be no better homily. Why is it that the clergy generally cannot speak as nobly as a secular author? There are exceptions, when clergymen have spoken out about religion's misuse. Reinhold Niebuhr, the Protestant theologian of the last century is one exception. He stated, "The tendency to claim God as an ally for our partisan values and ends is the source of all religious fanaticism."

It's not surprising that churchgoers justify their hate of gay people by claiming God is on their side. People have been using God to justify their hate and the killing of others since the beginning of time. Today, such "compassionate" groups as the Ku Klux Klan, the White Supremacists, and

2. *Tape 5.*
3. Brown, *Lost Symbol*, 327.

the neo-Nazis offer their support to those "good" Christians trying to marginalize gay people. We would do well to look at the person with whom we are sleeping because that person tells us a lot about ourselves. Anti-gay Christians have very strange bedfellows.

In the 1930s, the church was declared guilty by association for having signed a Concordat with Fascists, Hitler, Mussolini, and Franco—leaders of Christian countries, mostly Catholic countries. Today, in our efforts to exclude the gay community, we would do well to look at our allies, our partners in crime.

Recently, a young man was dismissed from a college fraternity when he admitted he was gay. The university had a nondiscrimination policy that requires all student groups to accept any student regardless of their beliefs. Some churches, including the Catholic Church, refused to accept the university's anti-discriminatory policy against gay people; so they now meet off campus.

There is irony in the fact that the Newman Club moved off campus rather than accept the university's anti-discrimination policies. Newman was very effeminate in his manner, and it is generally accepted that he was gay. If this were so, then today Newman would not belong to the Newman Club at that university.

As Newman already is "blessed," is it possible that soon we will have a canonized gay saint? What is the world coming to? What kind of people is God accepting into heaven? Who wants to associate with "those kind of people"—for eternity, no less?

The saintly, scholarly, and liberal Cardinal Newman must be turning over in his grave at the behavior of his namesake campus clubs. Years ago, there were fraternities and sororities that refused to accept Jewish, Catholic, and black students. We look back on those times with incredulity and disgust, and yet, today, we often tolerate bigotry against gay people.

Thankfully, in contrast to the church's discrimination, Notre Dame has created a student organization to make students from all walks of life feel more welcome. This university initiative expands services to gay students. There is an organized group of gay and lesbian Notre Dame alumni. They held a gay film festival on campus that was well received. After the event, the sponsors met with ninety-six-year-old Father Hesburgh, the retired president of the university who held that office for thirty-five years.

Father Hesburgh gave them his blessing, thanked them for their hard work, and told them God loved them.[4]

Of course, that charitable policy has been met with some opposition from "good Christians." As a general rule, if you have the courage to be radically Christian, many Christians will be frightened, and they will fight you viciously and cruelly. Hell knows no ruthlessness as that of the self-righteous. With the support of the school's board of directors, Notre Dame's current president, Father John Jenkins, invited President Obama to give the commencement address. The reaction and hostility directed toward him by "good Christians" was nothing short of sinful. The "saints," figuratively anyhow, martyred that good priest.

The homophobia toward the gay community is alarming. Throughout history, gay people have been persecuted, including the church burning them at the stake. Under Nazis rule, the Jews, gypsies, and homosexuals were ordered to be exterminated. However, in the concentration camps, it was gay people who were subjected to the most humiliating and degrading jobs. Jews wrote of special humiliations that were imposed on gay prisoners; they were often assigned to clean the latrines and garbage pits. Gay prisoners often were the first made to carry bodies from the gas chambers to the furnaces.

During the 1930s in Germany, Jewish children were prohibited from joining the nation's youth groups, which were Hitler's version of the Boy Scouts. They were not permitted to attend school or even play with non-Jewish children. Christians accepted that policy, and we know the tragic end resulting from that bigotry—the Nazis' eventual reign of terror!

Could that happen here? Could Americans turn on and eliminate our "undesirables"? As the story goes, in the 1960s, speaking to a small group of monks at Gethsemani, Thomas Merton is reported to have said, "Don't be surprised if someday you see Americans goose-stepping down Fifth Avenue." Hopefully his invoking the specter of American Nazis was hyperbole; but perhaps it is not.

In the past few years, the number of hate groups in this country has skyrocketed. There are more than 1,000 officially recognized hate groups in the United States, as compared with 600 in 2002. Was Merton's insight on target?

Recently, a gay candidate for the office of mayor in Clarksdale, Mississippi, was brutally killed. His death is being investigated as a hate

---

4. Dacey, "Inspires," 9.

crime. I suggest that the FBI, in their search for suspects, start with the local churches.

Not too many years ago, those who were lynching black people on Saturday nights were reading the Bible or attending Mass on Sunday mornings. Now it is the homosexuals' time to feel the wrath of the "good Christian folk."

Thank God there have been some churchgoers fighting the trend toward gay bashing. There also are some churches that have supported the gay community, and even have openly gay ministers. When we speak of the "church's anti-gay agenda," these more liberal churches (more Christian churches) are not to be included in our condemnation of "churches."

In 1973, UpStairs, a gay bar in New Orleans was the target of arson, and thirty-two people were burned to death. Before that fire, the city had two unrelated and accidental fires, killing eight and six people. The response to those two fires was widespread sympathy: the mayor and governor issued statements of condolences, the city's churches had memorial services, and the Catholic bishop offered his support and that of the church.

What was the community's response to the thirty-two people who died in the 1973 UpStairs fire? Almost total indifference. The head of the Detective Bureau said, "You knew that was a queer bar," as if to say those people don't count. The city joke was, "What do you bury thirty-two queers in?" The answer, "A fruit jar." With one exception—the United Methodists—no churches had a memorial service. At that time, New Orleans was about fifty percent Catholic, but the church was silent on the tragedy. There were no statements concerning what one paper called "the Nazi Incinerators." Recently, New Orleans' archbishop apologized for the "churches past silence and not offering care and concern."

I find it sad that Catholics can be insensitive to present-day bigotry against gay people because they once were the objects of hate and discrimination in this country. The "oppressed become the oppressors" is a recurring theme throughout history. Now that Catholics have been accepted and successful (in the last election, both vice presidential nominees were Catholic), they have forgotten their humiliating past and in some cases are joining the oppressors.

The message of the gospel is, "Don't get on top, don't get power. . . . Blessed are the poor, those that mourn, the meek, the merciful." The message of the crucifixion is the same. Christ's crucifixion was a repudiation of power, the repudiation of oppressors.

What does getting on top mean? It does not mean being socially and financially well off; it does not mean being successful. Position and wealth may lead to a mentality of thinking that one is on top, better than others, but in themselves those accomplishments are indifferent.

Being "on top" is a mentality of how we see ourselves in relation to others. If I see myself as superior to others because of money, social position, knowledge, education, talents, race, or even spirituality, then I see myself as one of those who are "on top." If I see myself as being better than another because of my sexual orientation, I am seeing myself as someone who is "on top." The gospel says that is a dangerous place to be.

The desire to be on top leads those who have little or no social prestige to seek out others to look down upon. A member of the white underclass may look down on all black people, even black college professors. A criminal heterosexual may still feel superior to a law-abiding homosexual. No matter how low we are on the social and economic ladder, we will seek someone, or some group, before whom we may feel superior.

That desire to be on top so contradicts Christ's message of love. Through his actions and by his words, Christ repeatedly said: "Don't get on top. Don't feel that you are superior to others. Instead, love one another."

Another reason it is so disturbing that Catholics are not in the forefront of defending gay rights is the accepted fact that the church has gay people in leadership roles. For anyone to deny that the church has gay people in the priesthood, hierarchy, and religious orders, both male and female, would be either naïve or dishonest.

I spent forty-four years in religious life—about forty of them in the priesthood—and I know several gay people in the ministry. They are good men and women who are doing the work of the gospel. These gay religious leaders and clergy are carrying out their responsibilities with integrity and love. That being the case, it is sad and hypocritical that the church should be remiss in protecting them.

All people can be hypocritical, but institutions carry our personal sins to a new level. It is in the nature of all institutions to take on lives of their own, beyond the dispositions of their members. This predisposition is seen in group behavior, where the mob's viciousness far exceeds that of any one individual. The official institutional position may often exceed in harshness what individuals in the institution feel.

What makes that even more interesting is that at Vatican II, the church was defined as "the people of God." These people of God don't seem to carry much weight with the hierarchy, which does not have a history of listening to what the people are saying.

It might do us well to examine ourselves, as well as our feelings toward gay people. In the church's long history, it seems that there almost certainly has been a gay pope. Have there been gay saints? Does that strike us as impossible? Recently, some scholars have pointed to indications that St. Paul may have been homosexual. There may be some basis for that supposition because of Paul's lifestyle. At that time, a Jewish father had three obligations toward his son: Teach him the Torah, teach him a trade, and find him a wife. The Jews were looking for the Messiah, so fatherhood was a sacred obligation to increase the chances of the Messiah being born. Paul's father would have properly instructed his son on the Jewish obligation of marriage.

In Paul's own words, he was a "Pharisee, a Hebrew, born of Hebrews" (Phil 3:5). For such a Jew, it was nearly unheard of not to be married; in addition he was of marriageable age long before his conversion. Being unmarried was not a Christian decision for Paul; he had chosen the single state before he became a Christian. Was Paul gay? Who cares? Paul's contribution to Christianity is unequaled. His discourse on Christian freedom superseding law is unique in religious literature. The Gentile world owes its hearing of Christianity to Paul of Tarsus. Did Gentiles hear of Christ from a gay man? Again, who cares? It's the message that is important, not the messenger. God chooses whom God will to lead. God's ways are not our ways, and God doesn't have to ask our permission to choose whom he will.

If Paul were gay, it fits a pattern throughout salvation history. For messengers, God has chosen the most unlikely people: as David, the adulterer-murderer and the most prodigious womanizer of all time; the stuttering Moses ("heavy of tongue") to speak to Pharaoh; Jacob the thief and liar to be the father of the chosen people—those are God's bizarre choices. The pattern of the unlikely being chosen continues into Christianity, where the improbable ones are the chosen ones. The apostles would not make anyone's "Who's Who" list—they denied Christ and, at times, seemed downright stupid.

St. Paul rejoices in the fact that the early Christians were not the elite of society. "Where is the wise man? Has God not made foolish the wisdom of this world? God has chosen the foolish things of the world to confront the wise." (1 Cor 1:20) We always look at others through human eyes, instead of allowing God to look through us with divine eyes. In our arrogance and conceit, we try to pass judgment on who is worthy and who is not worthy of God's love. Some think that the whole idea of gay saints is blasphemy, as if God couldn't love a gay person and be so loved in return. How quick we are to say that God couldn't love certain people, just because we don't. How slow we are to admit our own prejudices.

It is timely here to relate a true story about a well-known person—Vince Lombardi, the 1960s legendary football coach of the Green Bay Packers. In his first meeting with his assistant coaches, he told them that if any coach harassed a gay player, that coach would be fired immediately. This story seems miraculous for at least three reasons:

First, this was in the early 1960s, when gay people were hardly ever talked about. I was in my 30s and vaguely knew about "queers," as they were frequently then called. I was certain I had never met one, and I presumed they were probably from Mars and had infiltrated the U.S. by some commie trick (in the 1950s, everything was a "commie trick").

Second, this was the National Football League! This was the epitome of manliness. Everyone knew that queers did not play football on any level, let alone professional football. The NFL is the home of guys so tough that no one, not even their mothers, ever saw them smile. Just watching those guys on TV frightened me.

Third, this was Vince Lombardi, the most macho man God ever created. His 275-pound players were afraid of him. His family was afraid of him. When he and his wife would eat out with the team, he would not allow his wife to eat ice cream, because the team was not allowed to eat ice cream. His wife was afraid of him. The whole world was afraid of Vincent Lombardi, this Catholic Italian from New York City. Yet this man, who looked like he mixed nails with his cereal every morning, decreed that everyone in the Green Bay Packers organization would treat homosexuals with dignity and respect. Whence cometh such a miracle of kindness? Vince Lombardi's brother was a homosexual.

Michael Goodell, the brother of NFL commissioner Roger Goodell, told a similar story of how Roger would protect him from bullies when they were kids. "I am gay, and I needed help."

University of Missouri linebacker, Michael Sam, who came out before the NFL draft, was picked up by the St. Louis Rams, became the first openly gay player in the NFL. Could the NFL be more Christian than the churches?

In 2013, NBA player Jason Collins—a center for the Brooklyn Nets—came out as gay. Could the NBA be more Christian than the churches?

In fact, it seems that just about anyone, including the American Civil Liberties Union, can be more Christian than the churches. It seems, shamefully, that at times the most unchristian people are the Christian people.

The Boy Scouts have reviewed their position and now allow gay youngsters to be members. In general, the church has been positive in its response, and that is something for which to be grateful. The bishops have stated basic Catholic moral teaching, affirming "the dignity of all persons" and have said "homosexuals must be treated with respect accorded to all." Accordingly, having gay members in the Boy Scouts is not opposed to Catholic teaching.

It seems, however, that each bishop may decide how his diocese will respond to the Scouts' decision. What if a bishop decides not to allow his diocese to have a Scout program? Does that not violate the church's moral principle of affirming the dignity of all persons?

Some individual clergymen, bishops, and priests are resisting the acceptance of gays members. The cardinal in the Dominican Republic publicly calling the U.S. ambassador nominee a "faggot" didn't help the situation. One bishop stated that his diocese would "prayerfully consider whether our continual partnership with the Boy Scouts of America will be possible." My reaction that statement is, "Aren't you praying for an answer you should already know? That is like praying for God to give you an answer to the question, 'Should I be loving toward others?'"

The National Catholic Committee on Scouting made two statements, which seem to be contradictory. One said that they affirmed the Scouts' decision and that it did not contradict Catholic teaching. However, another statement said, "Since the new Scout policy will not go into effect until January, we will have time to study its effects."

My question is, "Aren't you saying that you are committed to studying a problem where the church has said there is no problem?" It is like Christ saying to those who were about to stone the woman taken in adultery, "Give me a few months to study its effects and think how to answer this problem."

The answer is evident from the start: homosexuality is not a problem. You don't condemn people; you accept them. In the case of the Scouts, the answer is evident from the start. You don't condemn young boys; you accept them. You do not need time to study a nonexistent problem.

Elsewhere, a pastor, while calling gays "lesser men," closed the parish Scouting program because of the Scouts' admission of gay members. If I were his bishop, I would suggest that he get a job as a greeter at Wal-Mart and learn to greet all who come in with kindness. Would Wal-Mart hire him if they knew about his anti-gay remarks? Probably not. Does that mean Wal-Mart has higher ethical standards than some churches? I wonder.

Pope Francis raised some eyebrows when he spoke about "gays," which is the word he used. His tone was different from that of his predecessors who expressed the teachings of the church in much different language than did Francis: "Who am I to judge?"

The Catholic catechism describes a "homosexual inclination" as "objectively disordered." I think the phrase "the homosexual inclination is objectively disordered" needs further clarification. I assume the word "inclination" means something natural to a person, an inborn trait. Some people have athletic ability, and some people don't, the same with musical and artistic ability. They have those traits for the same reason we have red or black hair, that we are tall or short.

A person with a musical, athletic, or artistic inclination does not ask for it; he or she is born with it. They are predisposed to be a musician, athlete, or artist. LeBron James surely has an "inclination" to be athletic. He didn't ask to be athletic. He just *is*.

It is an established psychological fact that homosexuality is an inborn trait. It is not something a person chooses, either for or against. Some Far Right Christians say that homosexuality is learned throughout life, that it is willed and therefore can be "unwilled." That false position has caused much pain. Recently, a leader in such a church retracted his former position of trying to change people's sexual orientation. He admitted that he hurt people psychologically and apologized for his damaging treatment, for trying to "straighten them out."

There also are spiritual people who maintain that you can change your basic sexual orientation. They claim success in changing gay people into straight people through vigorous spiritual discipline and will proudly recount their "success stories." The question is, were those who "changed" really gay? It's more likely that they only believed that they were, so there was no real change in their sexuality after all—just a change in their sexual self-understanding. Is misunderstanding one's sexuality possible? The following illustrates that it is.

A psychiatrist, while speaking to a group of monks, talked about a man who came to him saying, "I am gay and want to change." This doctor did not fit the stereotype of the passive, gentle, all-pleasing psychiatrist. He was known for being about as indirect as a punch in the stomach, and his colleagues called him "razor lips."

After listening to the man the doctor told him: "I have some good news and some bad news. The good news is that you are not gay. The bad news is that you are as crazy as hell." He worked with the man for a period of time, and the man is now happy with a wife and several children. I am leery of those who claim success in changing their sexual orientation. They just might be "crazy as hell," and the people trying to change them may be crazier yet.

My question is, if God created people gay, how can we say that inclination is "objectively disordered"? How can God create something that is innately bad or evil? That old saying that "God doesn't create junk" applies here. How can we tell people to change the way God created them? Gay people I have known say their sexual orientation has been with them from the beginning, and that they never have experienced heterosexual desires. They did not ask for or do anything to bring about their homosexual orientation—it just was.

A young man once came to visit the monastery for spiritual guidance. He said he was gay and was greatly ashamed of that fact. He was not talking about repenting of gay actions, as he had performed none. He was talking only about his "inclination," about his orientation. He started to cry, saying: "I don't want to be gay. Why did God make me this way?" My reply was: "God knows what God is about. Mistakes were not made in the general creation, nor were they made in your creation. Remember, 'God saw everything that he had made and, behold, it was very good.' And God made you."

I know a gay couple, both professional people. They are very caring. They raised two children, sending them to Catholic schools through college. When I am with them, I don't sit and judge, for it is very likely that they are better than I am. Besides, as Francis said, "Who am I to judge?" I certainly don't think they are evil or "intrinsically disordered." I enjoy their company. Maybe keeping company with gay people is the solution to gay bashing. Get to know a gay person, a gay couple; see them as people rather than as a category, or worse, as an "inclination."

I know very little about the psychology of homosexuality. Indeed, I once erroneously assumed that gay people are more likely than heterosexuals to be pedophiles. This is a common misconception, but study after study has shown that gay men are not more likely than straight men to be attracted to children. Pope Benedict XVI, en route to America, was questioned about sexual abuse among the clergy, and he answered, "I do not wish to talk about homosexuality, but about pedophilia, which is different."

The medical community agrees with the pope. Dr. Thomas Plante, a professor of psychology, states, "Homosexuals are not more likely to commit sexual crimes against minors than are heterosexuals."[5] This is in direct contrast to a statement made in 2002 in a sermon at St. Patrick's Cathedral that equated homosexuals with pedophiles. The priest said, "This is why homosexuals should never be priests." From what we know now, that statement is not true, and I hope it was said in ignorance and not malice. We cannot equate pedophilia with homosexuality. As Pope Benedict XVI said, there is a difference.

Just because an adult heterosexual man is attracted to adult women, that does not mean he is also attracted to pre-pubescent girls. Likewise, just because an adult homosexual man is attracted to adult men, that does not mean he is attracted to pre-pubescent boys.

If every time we see a gay man we assume he is a pedophile, we are wrong both in judgment and charity. Churches and individuals will have to change their presumptions about homosexuals or start questioning their own Christianity. Hate and Christianity do not belong together.

## Religion and Violence

Beware of the man who has a mouth that prays and a hand that kills.[6]

There are two things you have to do to win high public office in Texas: know how to lead a prayer session and how to shoot a gun.[7]

Is there a corollary between religion and intolerance, between Bible- or Koran-reading and violence? "Good church-goers" supported the Inquisition, the Crusades, anti-Semitism and slavery: all antithetical to the love of Christ. As we have seen, "good" churchgoers have been leading the discrimination against the gay community.

In Islam, the viciousness of the Muslim fringe sect of ISIS (or ISIL or Islamic State) is a current example of violence driven by religion. Unfortunately it is only the most recent example in a long, tragic history of religion's fueling

5. Plante, "Clergy Sexual Abuse," para. 7.
6. Eastern Proverb.
7. Christy Hoppe of the Dallas Morning News.

of hatred. Experience has shown that it is by no means the first, and I doubt that it will be the last of wickedness and evil performed in the name of God.

In Judaism, nowhere can you find more violence and mass killing than in the Old Testament, the Jewish Scriptures. An outsider could reasonably accuse the Jews, and thus God (who is said to be instructing them), of ethnic cleansing. In those scriptures are these "terror texts": God instructs the Israelites in battle, "do not leave anything that breathes." (Deut 20:16) And at Jericho, God commands, "destroy with the sword every living thing, every man and woman, young and old, cattle, sheep and donkeys." (Joshua 6:21) For instructions on how to carry out total war, very few books can match the Bible.

The Bible is a standard on which Christian morality is based. Historically, however, Christians have used the Bible to justify everything from floggings to war, religious persecutions to burning witches, from refusing to get medical help for dying children to the handling of snakes. You name the contentious topic; you can prove it with the Bible, from capital punishment to slavery. The common Christian refrain is, "The Bible says so."

My cynical repeating of "The Bible says so" is not a refutation of the Bible or of those exclusively Biblical churches. It is a refutation of the misuse of the Bible. It is not a rejection of the scriptures but a rejection of how we use the scriptures to justify our fear, hate, and cruelty, to justify our wars, bigotry, and persecutions. How many people have been killed or tortured because believers have convinced themselves that "The Bible says so."

The most tragic example of Christians using the Bible and religion to justify their hate and hostility toward the Jews is the misuse of a line from the Gospel of Matthew. At the trial of Jesus, the Jewish people are said to have shouted, "His blood be upon us and our children" (Matt 27:25). Matthew is the only evangelist who records those words. Mark, Luke, and John do not have them.

Throughout history, many people have used this passage to justify anti-Semitism violence. Christians saw that passage as affirming the collective guilt of the Jewish people for the death of Jesus, thus accusing the Jews of deicide. It wasn't until Vatican II that the church officially repudiated that "Christian" view—nineteen hundred and sixty years too late. Now Biblical scholars see evidence for doubting that those words were ever part of the original text. They are opposed to Matthew's general theme of Jesus' being, first of all, for the Jews. Therefore, they don't fit with the tone of his gospel.

For the first fifty years of Christianity, Christians saw themselves religiously as Jews, observing Jewish laws and attending the synagogue. They called themselves "Jewish Christians." Hostility soon arose between the two groups, which resulted in the break between Jews and Christians.

Scholars now feel that the mutual antipathy caused by the break was the reason for that passage being inserted into Matthew's gospel. Recently, Pope Benedict XVI in his book *Jesus of Nazareth* also questioned if that text was originally written by Matthew. That passage, which has caused so much suffering through the centuries, may not even be an authentic part of scripture! Unfortunately it was one of the passages that Christians have long used to justify their hate, saying: "The Jews are Christ killers. The Bible says so."

Another tragic example of the misuse of scripture is Christ's parable regarding inviting guests to a banquet, as found in Matt 22:9. The master in the parable commands his servants to compel, or force, the people to come in for the banquet. Centuries later, churchmen took those words to justify forcing people to come into the church, to become Christian. Jews and others were killed, or forced into exile, if they refused to be baptized. In 1492, Jews in Spain who refused to join the church were expelled from the country.

We ask ourselves today, how could Christians have so misunderstood the message of love imbedded in the scriptures? How could they have used those same scriptures to kill and harm people? It's the same situation today among those who hate, fear, and want to isolate homosexuals. They use scriptures to "prove" that God supports them in their bigotry. "The Bible says so," after all.

I studied Latin, Greek, and Hebrew to aid in my scriptural studies, which formally lasted seven years. Later, in the monastery, there was daily scripture reading. In church we prayed all 150 psalms every two weeks. In addition, we had scripture scholars come and give lectures. My background in interpreting and understanding scripture is adequate, to say the least. Yet, I still would be very hesitant to claim definitively what any particular passage means. Each passage must be read in its entire context and with an understanding of the particular literary form employed and the culture of the times.

I was privileged to have Dr. Brandon Scott as a teacher. Dr. Scott's book, *Hear Then the Parable: A Commentary on the Parables of Jesus*, is considered a standard in the study of Christ's parables. He said, "You can prove any position you want from scripture, even contradictory positions," and he warned against falling into the trap of quoting "proof texts."[8]

The following is an example of a "proof text." In Isa 6:3, Isaiah's prayer "Holy, Holy, Holy, Lord God of Hosts" proves there are three persons in God. Isaiah's prayer proves there is a father, son and Holy Spirit, because he said "holy" three times. Each time signifies a person. That is an example of reading a passage out of context. Isaiah speaking of the trinity would be meaningless, because Isaiah is in the Old Testament. The trinity was unknown in Old Testament times.

Recently, a man "proved" to me why women live longer than men. He said: "It's because women have one more rib than men. God took one rib from Adam and gave it to Eve." The Bible says so. His friends all agreed with his interpretation of the text. They are good people, doing good work, so I was not about to disturb their spiritual beliefs. It would have served no purpose to begin a scripture exegesis. Besides, a lack of knowledge does not mean there is a lack of holiness. I answered, "That sounds good to me."

However, literal interpretation of scripture officially preached from pulpits is harmful in two ways. First, it denies scientific truth, thus making the Bible look ridiculous. Fundamentalists say the Bible teaches that the world was created in seven days, five thousand years ago. But the Bible contains divine truth, not scientific truth. It is a religious book, not a scientific one. It teaches that creation is of God, not the details of that creation.

Truth is truth and, therefore, is of God. True religion never needs to fear true science. In fact, they both need each other, as Einstein insisted. Einstein said: "Science without religion is lame. Religion without science is blind."[9] Ironically, the evolving notion of creation is much more congruent with the dynamic life of God than is instantaneous, complete creation. The former provides a goal for all life, not just human life. All life moves, evolves toward some form of higher life, and ultimately to God.

The Scopes trial in 1925 may be amusingly understandable to us, but holding such a trial today would be sacrilegious. It is an insult to limit God's creative power to one time, especially since there is no concept of time with God. With God, everything is now; there is no before and after.

In the 1960s, I was teaching Christian evolution to high school students and adults using the decree of Vatican II, "The Church in the Modern World" and the writings of Jesuit priest Pierre Teilhard de Chardin. Never

8. Scott, *Here Then the Parable.*

9. Roy, "Rapture," 54.

once did I get a negative response. It is difficult today to hear people arguing over evolution. Will the Flat Earth people arise again, as well?

Secondly, and even more harmful, by insisting on the scientific accuracy of the Bible, the fundamentalists miss the spiritual accuracy. They miss what the scriptures intend to teach, because the religious truth gets lost in the scientific debate.

As an example, the true meaning of the story of Adam's rib is that men and women have the same substance, essence, or nature. Those words were too abstract for ancient people; such language would have had no meaning for them. Instead, they talk about understandable, relatable things like ribs, and these things (this essence, substance, nature) are in both men and women. Since Eve has the same stuff as Adam, men and women are of the same essence, unlike men and animals. Of all creation, only women and men share the same nature; they have the same rib.

The idea that men and women are equal in nature was not understood in primitive times. The common belief was that women were substantially, essentially inferior to men. In fact, some ancient peoples felt that their animals were worth more than their women. Scripture warns against avarice and the hoarding of valuables, and its listing of valuables actually places horses before wives. "The king should not multiply horses for himself, neither shall he multiply wives for himself" (Deut 17:17).

The inspired teaching of the text about God's creating Eve from Adam's rib is that the common belief of the inferiority of women is not so. For the ancients, it was divine revelation, and it should be for us, also. Men and women are equal.

Someone who takes the creation story as literally true is missing the truth of the Bible and its teachings for today. The "literalists" can be amusing, but sometimes dangerous.

In Texas, a school board was discussing teaching foreign languages in schools. A man objected, shouting: "No way! If English was good enough for Jesus, it is good enough for me." The Bible says so. And in English, no less. Corporal punishment is still used in the Longhorn state. Why? "Chastise your son with a rod! Thus says the Lord." I suspect any young witch or warlock caught reading Harry Potter in the Longhorn state would be in big trouble

Texas is one of the most church-going states in the country, yet it also is one of the most violently anti-gay states. Current Texas law allows that a gay teenager who engages in consensual sex can be imprisoned. The U.S.

Supreme Court declared that law unconstitutional. Texas paid no attention and keeps that state law on the books. When a gay person gets beat up or killed, the prayer from the self-righteous ascends to the heavens: "The wages of sin is death." The Bible says so.

Southerners are church-going people, much more so than northerners. Mississippi, along with Alabama, Georgia, Louisiana, North and South Carolina, Tennessee, Arkansas, and Texas, has the highest percentage of churchgoers in the country. The whole area is called the Bible Belt. Along with its church-going reputation, this region also has a long reputation of violence. Southern convicts were the most abused, enduring chain gangs and floggings. Blacks, Jews, Catholics, and even women were kept "in their place." Up until the Civil War, Mississippi and North Carolina had the "Rule of Thumb," which allowed a man to beat his wife if the stick he used was no bigger around than his thumb.

The present-day South is not the Old South, overall, and to stereotype it as such is erroneous and unkind. We may only hope that Georgia allowing confederate flags on their license plates, and a noose on James Meredith's statue at the campus of the University of Mississippi, and a fire chief in Texas displaying a picture of the president with a noose around his neck, and Floridians lining up to get an autographed picture, shake the hand of, and congratulate George Zimmerman—the man who shot and killed an unarmed black youth—are not typical of the modern-day South.

Unfortunately, there are new villains. People fear and vilify Muslims of any age or occupation, including third-generation chefs, cab drivers, and tailors. All are lumped together as anti-American, evil worshipers of a "false God"—whoever that may be. The entire country is infected with this anti-Islamic disease, but the South seems to have turned it into an epidemic. Again, religion often is fueling the fire of violence.

Recently in Murfreesboro, Tennessee, Muslims purchased land to build a mosque. The community responded as if they were planning on building a nuclear reactor. Here were people planning to build a place of worship, and other worshippers would not stand for it. Again, religion is fueling the fire of violence.

The South has a reputation, unfortunately often justified, of being severe toward those who dare to differ from the white, Protestant, male rule. Even more, the states with the most vocal anti-gay sentiment are in the Bible Belt. The South has long presented a double picture. The first is that it is a church-going, Bible-reading culture. The second is that it is intolerant and harsh toward anyone who differs from the norm.

From those two images come some obvious questions. First, is the strict religious atmosphere in the South the cause of its history of intolerance and hostility? Second, does such an atmosphere create suspicion, fear, and hatred of outsiders?

To burn people to death is a cruel punishment; yet, for centuries, Christians did so in the name of religion. Torturing people is inhumane, and yet "good Christians" have tortured other Christians. To one who feels commanded by God to preserve and protect a Christian society, causing death or pain to outsiders is not only irrelevant, but it is seen as the duty of a good Christian.

A person who blindly holds onto religious absolutes is insensitive to the pain of others. In dealing with a dogmatist, you can't appeal to our common humanity or to human compassion. Such a person feels he is dealing in divine realities, so human feelings are irrelevant. He sees himself as one who is called to make the world "Godly."

Does knowing that religion and dogmatic teachings sometimes leads to violence mean we should stop reading the Bible? Of course not! However, we must read the Bible gracefully. We must not look for passages that can be twisted to support our hate. If we turn to the Bible to justify our harming others or taking away their freedoms, we can be sure we are misusing God's word. The Bible and religion should not be used as a weapon against others. The gospel is good news, after all!

Today, we are aware of how Islamic zealots misuse the Qur'an to justify their violence. However, as Pope Francis said, "Authentic Islam and the proper reading of the Qur'an are opposed to every form of violence." We must not allow their misuse of their holy texts to be an excuse for our misuse of the Bible.

American religious extremists (be they Catholic, Protestant, Jewish, or Muslim) should get together and try to understand the others' positions. A perfect place for this meeting would be Amsterdam; it is a laid back, relaxed country. It would be a blessing for these religious groups to sit together at sidewalk cafes overlooking the city's storied canals and exchange views.

It is also a fitting place to meet because of its past. In the midst of this attempted fellowship would be an ominous reminder of what happens when communication and ecumenism die, of the result of division and hate—Anne Frank's house is just around the corner.

The house sits right next to a large Catholic church. In the movie *The Diary of Anne Frank*, you hear the ringing of those church bells. While walking through her house, those same bells still ring, breaking visitors' respectful silence. Are those bells ringing, or are they tolling? If they are tolling, for whom? For the dead or for the worshipers? For those who lived comfortably in their churches for centuries, next door to the victims of their religious crimes? Are they tolling for you, for me, for Christian promoters of violence?

A visit to that little girl's "house" is haunting and disturbing. How could such rabid anti-Semitism go on in the shadow of churches filled with worshipers? Walking through Anne Frank's house and hearing the church bells are a reminder: religion and violence can and often have lived side-by-side, just like Anne Frank and that church. Two thousand years of Christian anti-Semitism is captured in that small attic next to that big church. Size and power always win. Little girls are no matches against self-righteousness, religious or civil.

Throughout history, religion has not only lived next to violence, unfortunately it also has supported violence against the outsiders, those who are different, those who don't look like, worship like, or talk like they should. Violence and religion actually can support each other, as did the church and Spain's Francisco Franco. Have they supported each other in this country? Have the Indians, African-Americans, Jews, Italians, Hispanics, Irish Catholics, the immigrants, and the strangers, felt the wrath of the religious establishment?

This negative picture of Christianity's past must not overshadow or deny Christianity's positive contribution to humanity. Institutionally and individually, Christianity has benefited humankind. The church was educating and caring for the sick and poor long before the state undertook those projects. Individuals, inspired by the gospel's message of love, have dedicated their lives to the service of others. They often have served their neighbors to a heroic degree. While sinfulness is part of our history, it is not the only part, nor is it the most important part. Christianity has contributed to the betterment of humanity. That contribution must not be overlooked in the recounting of the past.

However, we have to also admit that nothing packs them in like a prayer meeting calling on God to defeat our enemies. This is one way that non-believers are more honest than we. Atheists don't drag God into their fights. They don't try to manipulate God so that they win. They are so laid back they don't even care who wins the Notre Dame versus Southern Methodist football game!

For believers, however, it is never doubted that our enemies are also God's enemies, and God is always on our side! We don't seem to recognize that asking God's help to kill is an oxymoron, problematic, to say the least. Yet year after year, decade after decade and century after century, there is always a younger generation coming along to be subjected to the often-told lie, "our enemies are God's enemies." Ambrose Bierce labeled such chauvinism "the dupe of statesmen and the tool of conquerors."

Statesmen of every age have used God to rally the troops. In every war, the theme is "God is on our side." Truly, that is "the dupe of statesmen," of politicians, and of generals, to say nothing of the clergy, up to and including popes. Pope Urban granted a plenary indulgence to anyone who was killed in the war against the infidels. In effect he was saying: "If you get killed in this war, I will guarantee your eternal salvation. You will go right to Heaven."

If anything could stir up saintly feelings, it was that! No politician could ever match Pope Urban for duping. In America's previous wars, using "God is on our side" presented some difficulties, because our enemies were also Christian nations: Spain, Germany, and Italy. So, in theory at least, God could also be on their side. Of course, we knew that was not so. "God is always on our side," because even though they may be Christian, they are bad Christians. We are good Christians; every American holds that "truth," that we are good Christians.

In the 1950s, at the height of the Cold War, the lines were clearly drawn. Our enemy was the atheistic communist. We were the godly people fighting against the ungodly people. At the time of the Crusades, the Crusaders put crosses on their shields making sure everyone, including God, knew which side they were on.

During the Cold War, we wanted all to know whose side we were on. What better way than to have every child daily recite the name of God? In 1954, Congress passed legislation to insert the words "under God" into the Pledge of Allegiance; a few months later, President Eisenhower signed the bill into law. "Under God" was neither in the original pledge from 1880, nor in the one introduced to Congress in 1944 at the height of World War II. In the midst of the anti-communist frenzy, however, Americans wanted to make sure that everyone knew we Americans were fighting "under God."

Until 1944, Ike was never formally a Christian. In that year, he was baptized into the Presbyterian Church. He was fifty-four years old at the time of his conversion and the blossoming of his Godly feelings. Ten years later, he was the person most responsible for including God in the pledge. Could that be the "zeal of the neophyte?"

Today we have seven-year old children saying "under God," whether they believe in God or not. Ike was a very good man, but it took him fifty-four years to publicly accept his faith. Isn't it presumptuous of our government to expect children to publicly profess their faith at age seven? Should a democracy require a person to publically profess either their faith or lack of faith?

God's aid has been solicited for everything: from religious persecutions to the German World War I engraving on soldier's belt buckles, "God is our help." The more bloodshed, the greater our need of God's intercession.

In World War II, before flying to their deaths, Japanese suicide bombers partook in a religious ceremony. Their mission was called Kamikaze, which means divine or godly wind. Once again, God was called into battle. Maybe God does not wish to be anyone's partner in a war; maybe God has nothing to do with war. For a chauvinist, that is utter blasphemy. But it is well to remember that Christ was accused of blasphemy; in fact, just about everything he did was viewed as opposing the religious establishment.

Religious people never doubt that God is always on their side, whether that happens to be the Japanese, German, or American side. That is one way non-believers are more honest than believers; they don't drag God into their fights. They don't try to manipulate God, as do we "believers." Praying armies can be an oxymoron. You can't be worshipping God when you ask his help to kill people.

On Christmas Day in a monastery in Belgium, there were two Masses going on simultaneously on opposite sides of the church. The German priest was saying one for the German soldiers; thirty yards away, the American priest was saying Mass for the American soldiers. The next day these Christian soldiers were killing each other. Do those mutual prayers and Masses for opposing sides put God in a bind?

I wonder if the German and American priests ever questioned themselves. I wonder if they considered the absurd contradiction they were perpetuating by leading the opposing armies in the same worship, in the same church and in the same language?

Each side was dedicated to killing the other, yet they were worshipping in the name of Christ, who said, "What you do to the least of these you do to me" (Matt 25:40). The first casualty in any war is truth. What greater evidence of truth being shattered than opposing armies "joined" in worshipping their mutual savior, yet dedicated to killing each other?

Christianity has a long tradition of teaching the necessary conditions before a Christian may be involved in war. The early Christians refused to join the Roman military, even refused to defend themselves. They were the first martyrs. We have gone from Christian pacifism to Christians who justify the atomic bomb. Has our thinking progressed or regressed?

In the fourth century, St. Augustine was the first Christian to fully develop the "just war principle." He laid down the conditions that must be present before a Christian could engage in war. He concluded that it is permissible for a Christian to be involved in war, however, only under those certain conditions. The most basic condition is that in any war, there must be a distinction made between combatants and non-combatants, between the military and civilians. Civilians may never be the objects of military attack.

In the thirteenth century, St. Thomas Aquinas further developed what is and is not moral in warfare. Traditionally, there are several conditions that must be present for a war to be considered moral. The first and overriding principle is that it is always immoral to directly kill civilians. The explanation of that principal and how, in practice, it is to be carried out is long and involved. We cannot fully develop it here. Suffice it to say that it is fundamental that in war a distinction must be made between combatants and non-combatants. Not making that distinction results in total war, which has always been considered immoral.

In the Second World War, this principle was violated on both sides. The bombing of London, Dresden, Hiroshima and Nagasaki are the most obvious, but certainly not the only violations of the rule against directly attacking non-combatants.

I was in my twentieth year of Catholic education before I learned the "just war principle." Until then, I felt, "you go to war and you do what you do. My country, right or wrong. All is fair in love and war. There is only one way to engage in war, and that is to win it." It was all very simple; no questions asked about what was moral or immoral. You wage war like General Sherman in the Civil War: scorched earth, total war, destruction, annihilation and death. That is war. There is no such thing as Christian morality, Christian law, in war. To win is the only law.

I was a 27-year-old Catholic before I realized that my thoughts about war were anti-Catholic, anti-Christian and anti-human. I was fascinated with my new knowledge and questioned why I had never been so taught before. I wanted to learn more about this "just war principle" and the church's condemnation of total war. I decided to write my philosophy thesis on the subject. I titled it "The Morality of War: A Christian Perspective." Up until that time in my Christian education, we wrestled with such weighty moral questions as the morality of French kissing or playing the Ouija board. While writing my thesis, I learned theologians were not the only ones who discussed the morality of war; popes discussed it, too! In the 1100s, at the Second Lateran Council in Rome, Pope Innocent II called the crossbow "an inhuman weapon, hated by God." The crossbow could shoot two bolts a minute to a distance of four hundred yards. The pope forbade the "deadly act of the crossbow against Christians," notice the "against Christians." You could fire away, however, at Jews, Muslims, Buddhists, Indians or Pagans. I don't know how Innocent would have classified Protestant Christians, four hundred years later. I'm guessing he would have justified using the crossbow against them, also. The point is that a crossbow was considered an evil weapon. We have moved from the Christian pacifism of the first century to the crossbow of the Middle Ages to the atomic weapons of the present. The "growth" of Christianity! This "progression" has prompted Father Richard Rohr to declare that the only response to modern warfare is not justification or pride, even in victory, but sorrow and repentance.

Father Rohr has been a spiritual writer for the past 30 years. He is a Franciscan priest, following the traditional pacifism of St. Francis. In the book *Jesus' Plan for a New World: The Sermon on the Mount*, co-written with John Feister, he writes: "I've told gatherings in Germany that because many Germans have never yet repented the Second World War, they're going to repeat it. It is as certain as the dawn that America will continue to be a militaristic, violent country because we have never repented any of our wars. Grief and repentance are the only appropriate Christian response to any war, never a victory parade. At very best, wars are a necessary evil, which we can never celebrate or romanticize. Perhaps we need 'wailing walls.'"[10]

On Sept. 5, 2014, the magazine Charisma posted a column entitled "Why I Am Absolutely Islamophobic," in which evangelical preacher Gary Cass called for genocide against the world's 1.6 billion Muslims. He called for a holy war, demanding that "we crush the vicious seed of Ishmael in

10. Rohr, *Jesus' Plan*, 108.

Jesus' name." Outcry over the column prompted Charisma to delete it from their site, but it remains on the site DefendChristians.org.[11]

When are we going to realize that Holy War is a contradiction of terms? The words should never be joined. War may be necessary at times, but there never is anything holy in the killing of a human being. Killing may be required, but it is sacrilegious to call it holy. We may never crush anyone in Jesus' name.

Notice that Rohr, in advocating repentance in war instead of victory celebrations, is not dishonoring soldiers who fight in wars. Nor am I! He is condemning a mentality that elevates and glorifies war, even in its most horrendous conditions. It is a common misconception that being anti-war means you are anti-soldier. Living in a military town, I daily see military personnel, male and female, active and retired, who are of moral and even noble character. A person may feel that Vietnam and the 2003 invasion of Iraq were not morally justified; yet still respect and honor those who fought in those wars.

It also should be noted that Father Rohr did admit that "war may be a necessary evil," therefore it may be permissible for a Christian to fight in a war. War may be waged, but only under moral conditions. If not, the good guys end up being as evil as the bad guys. What he is condemning is the incessant approval, the near sanctification of war. We romanticize the battlefield, we celebrate killing. Robert E. Lee expressed our dark fascination with war this way: "It is well that war is so terrible, lest we should grow so fond of it."

General Lee understood the human heart. There is something in the battle itself that our fallen natures find exhilarating. The real danger is what war may do to our spiritual selves—the damage it can do to our souls. The real danger is that we may grow to enjoy war, to be "fond of it," and, thus, we destroy ourselves. War is the ultimate Super Bowl experience, where half of the combatants win and half lose. In war, however, the gamble is higher, the risks greater. For the losers, for those killed, there is literally no tomorrow. What stakes! What stimulation! What exhilaration! Winner takes all! Life or death!

In sports, we give trophies to the winners; in war, we give medals. In President Reagan's 1983 "war" against Grenada—where nineteen Americans were killed—five thousand of our seventy-three hundred military involved received "Medals of Merit and Valor." Practically every solider,

---

11. Mosbergen, "Charisma News."

even those sunning themselves on the beaches, received a medal for "valor." I wonder how a veteran of Okinawa—where twelve thousand Americans were killed—would feel about those five thousand valiant warriors of Grenada. The United Nations voted to condemn our invasion of Grenada as an unjustified act of war. The United States used its veto power to defeat the vote. At that time, one American writer quipped, Grenada is "a lovely little war." There is a history to that.

In 1963, there was a musical on the New York stage entitled "Oh! What a Lovely War." The show's title was taken from its hit song. The song was written in 1917 during World War I, the "war to end all wars." It was a satirical and brutally sarcastic song about the senseless slaughter of that conflict. One line stated that it was so wonderful to be a soldier that "it is hardly right to take the pay."[12] World War I is remembered primarily for its deadly senselessness, and that its concluding peace terms so angered Germany that they swore to get revenge, which they did in World War II. The number of dead, wounded, and missing in the span of the war's four years totaled 37 million souls, according to the U.S. State Department. Thus, the satirical song, "Oh! What a Lovely War."

It was fitting to later apply that song to our "war" against Grenada, not because it was equally deadly, but because it was equally senseless. Both wars are easy targets for the song—World War I for satire, and Grenada for fact. Grenada was indeed "a lovely little war," fought in pleasant surroundings. World War I was neither lovely nor pleasant. In fact, it is the perfect example to describe this chapter on religion and violence.

The respected English military historian Max Hastings has recently published the book *Catastrophe 1914: Europe Goes to War*. He mentions the overriding religiosity of that war: "The merits of the Allied cause become tarnished by . . . the spurious religiosity with which the war was marketed."[13] Supporting his view, he quotes Beatrice Webb, the English economist and social reformer of the early 1900s. She criticizes that war's "disgusting misuse of religion to stimulate nationalism."[14] Nationalism tries to employ religion in its cause. If you go to the root of just about any war, you are likely to find religion. Ask the Israelis and Palestinians. Does their fight not go all the way back to Esau and Jacob? Or even to Ishmael and Isaac? Richard Aldington, in one of his novels, defined nationalism as "a

---

12. Dowd, "Birth of Oh!"
13. Hastings, *Catastrophe*.
14. Hastings, *Catastrophe*.

silly cock, crowing on its own dunghill."[15] Unfortunately, it always wants to drag religion onto its dunghill, usually with great success. Besides, war provides a great opportunity to grant medals, which we all love.

Religion and violence—as Kurt Vonnegut would say, "and so it goes." From World War I to Grenada, "and so it goes."

There is a dark, bellicose spot in the human psyche concerning war that we don't have the courage to acknowledge, even to ourselves. We are drawn to the awesome power and might of the military struggle. The male psyche is especially attracted to the power inherent in war. The word power, in Latin, is "potentia," from which comes our word "potency." Males desire potency, power. Being potent is inherent in men's survival instinct.

Today, females have shown that they, too, may be so inclined to hold power. Whether that impulse is a victory for equality has yet to be seen. Until modern times, it had been presumed that killing was predominantly a "male thing," that males had a natural taste for war. A young soldier said that before his first firefight, his first taste of battle, he felt excitement, even exhilaration. The adrenaline was flowing in anticipation of experiencing for real what he had been trained for in practice. He wanted to go into battle! Later, he admitted that his eagerness and euphoria quickly wore off. Young men are eager to fight; old men are reluctant. Young men often feel they have something to prove; old men grow tired of proving. Those who experience the most horrendous battles seem to be reluctant to talk about them.

The appeal that battle holds for young men who want to test their manhood is often exploited, especially in the case of war. This was brought home to me in 1952, during my first year of college. I was in the Air Force R.O.T.C. We didn't have many officers to salute, so we marched around campus saluting statues. Jesus and Mary were our commanding officers. You could do worse!

As you walked into the R.O.T.C. building, you faced a large picture of a jet fighter, going straight up through the white clouds into the brilliant blue sky. The caption read: "Are you man enough to go above and beyond?"

We were 18-year-old kids just three months out of high school. I thought to myself, "Those words, 'man enough,' are the same words our football coaches used on us: 'Are you man enough?'" The coach's battle cry for manhood was, "OK, we are done with this sissy, girly stuff. Today we are going to separate the men from the boys." I was always tempted to reply: "Coach, I am a 16-year-old boy. I am not yet a man. I just want to be a boy a

15. Aldington, *Colonel's Daughter*.

little longer and have some fun." I thought better of it. I was not a very good football player, and I doubt if I would have made a good soldier.

Football coaches and military recruiters are great manipulators. Both groups play into the young male psyche, to win, to conquer, to triumph. That conquering hero tendency is prevalent in males starting at a young age. I was eight years old when World War II began. All boys did was play soldier, play war. Before the war, we played cowboys and Indians. In both games, the "good guys" killed the "bad guys" with toy guns bought for us by our parents. They never gave our sisters guns.

I realize that circumstances are different today and young boys do not play "guns" as we did in the late 1930s and early 1940s. The Indians are no longer the "bad guys." Today missiles and atomic weapons have replaced rifles. Young males, however, are still attracted to conquering. They are attracted to combat and to war.

This attitude of war, when fully developed, is what General Lee warned against—lest "we become too fond of it." Today, with the modern weapons involved, war is a deadly fondness. We may no longer be "fond" of war. It is too deadly, too inhuman. Today, sorrow and repentance are the only proper response to war.

Instead of worshipping statues of generals with swords drawn, perhaps we need to ask for forgiveness. Perhaps instead of medals and parades and victorious flyovers, we need humility and sorrow. Perhaps instead of praying for victory, we need to pray for grace and love. Perhaps today we should ask for absolution for growing "fond of it."

Religious people never doubt that God is always on our side, and we continually pray to remind God of that fact. As the principal of a Catholic high school, I would put a dilemma before our students when we were playing against the Catholic school across town, which, of course, was praying just as hard as we were for victory. It would make them think about using God and wonder if God is really on our side. Like most of us when it comes to religion, they didn't want to think. They wanted pat answers, and they definitely wanted God on our side.

We "believers" pray to beat the other team, to cause the other team sorrow. The victor's locker room is filled with prayers, thanking God. The losers, who prayed just as hard, are crying their eyes out. Winning has become the Divine Command. Where in the gospel does it say we must win? I have seen high school kids who, after losing a football game, feel they have done something wrong. America's Eleventh Commandment, apparently, is "Thou shalt win." That makes life very difficult, because in any contest, someone has to lose.

Prayer is our most sacred privilege; we must not use it to bring sorrow to others. Besides, I don't think praying to win or conquer has ever worked. When the Christians of ancient Rome went head to head with the lions, the scoreboard read Lions 10, Christians 0.

At its core, Christianity is a paradox—self-emptying is the path to fullness; the path to victory is loss; eternal life comes through death. Prayer and competition don't mix, whether in sports or in war. The ultimate in competition is war, where the winner takes all. The ultimate in Christianity is love, where the winner gives all.

The French Cardinal Suhard stated, "To be a Christian does not mean engaging in propaganda or in stirring people up. Rather it means living in such a way that your life would not make sense if there were no God. It means living a mystery." Losers being the ultimate winners are a mystery. It is the mystery of the cross, the mystery of Christianity that the "losers" win. In the eyes of the world, Christ lost. But he won the ultimate victory.

Winning makes all the sense in the world, but Christianity is not of the world. For a Christian, winning is not the have-all and be-all that so characterizes our competitive society, and that makes the Christian the odd man out. We need more "odd" Christians today. Monks, too, living their non-competitive monastic existence, are odd. We need more monks.

God is never more in demand than in wartime. A priest even blessed the Enola Gay and its crew before they flew off to Hiroshima. If the old saying "war is good business" is true, it is even truer that war is good church business. Religious zealots love war, for fighting for a "just cause" is intoxicating. Christian, Muslim, and Jewish zealots alike can't kill enough of "God's enemies."

A good summary of how religious bigotry leads to violence is found in a 2013 issue of *Time*: "Every religion can be twisted into a destructive force poisoned by ideas that are antithetical to its foundation."[16] Religious extremists—be they Hindu nationalist, Muslim militants, ultra-Orthodox Jews, or fundamentalist Christians—all have been associated with violence.

Pope Francis has denounced violence, especially religiously supported violence in the Middle East, where religious wars have been raging for millennia. The Jews are faithful readers of the word of God as presented in their scriptures. The Muslims accept much of the Old Testament and call

16. Beech, "Face."

Abraham their "father in faith," as do Jews and Christians. They accept Jesus as a great prophet, honoring him and his teachings, along with his mother Mary. Christians accept the Jewish scriptures, in addition to Christ and his teachings.

Yet all three religious groups, Jews, Muslims, and Christians, have instigated and promoted war in its most violent and cruel manner. The more dogmatic the believers, the more prone they are to violence. This unfortunate truth raises questions about the role religion plays in promoting violence.

Sadly, it now seems that we can add Buddhists to that list. While I was in the monastery, the Dalai Lama and some Buddhist monks twice came to visit. Once, they stayed a week, praying and meditating with us. At the time I thought, "Well, there is at least one religious group that is non-violent— the Buddhists." Now it seems I was wrong.

In Asia, Buddhist monks are inciting bigotry and violence against minority religious groups, especially Muslims. In Burma, the monks are leading a bloody crusade. I guess the Buddhists have finally "gotten religion." I doubt that the Dalai Lama approves of that behavior; he appeared to be a good and gentle person. It is hard to control religious people in their zeal for God and what they see as God's righteousness.

The church is called upon to be the light of the world, leading all in justice and mercy. Too often, though, that light has been the taillight and not the headlight. In the battles for women's suffrage, for the abolition of slavery, and for civil rights, the church lagged behind. Once everything was safe and acceptable, the church then shined its light on the subject. In social advancements, the secular humanist often is ahead of the religious establishment.

Slavery is institutionalized violence. It is war that never ends. The Second Vatican Council and Pope John Paul II both condemned the church's historical acceptance of slavery, calling it one of the infamies in church history. That anti-slave position has not always been the case, even in religious circles. In 1866, three years after President Lincoln's Emancipation Proclamation freeing the slaves, Pope Pius IX said, "Slavery was not against divine law."

Some American bishops in the South continued to support slavery until the end of the war, shining the taillight again. Poor Pius IX—every time he opened his mouth he seemed to put his foot in it. He condoned slavery and condemned religious liberty in his *Syllabus of Errors*.

Those Christians should have been listening to Abraham Lincoln rather than reading those parts of the Bible that support slavery. In both the Jewish scriptures and the Christian scriptures, slavery is an accepted fact of life. The Bible says so.

In contrast to the churchmen, however, Lincoln said, "God has decided this question in favor of the slaves." It seems that Lincoln, who was never baptized, rarely attended church, and whose wife said was "technically not a Christian," had a deeper spirituality and sense of God than did the popes, bishops, and good Christians. Throughout history, there were too many times when that was not difficult to do. Some so-called non-believers had a deeper spirituality than believers but, because they saw churches promoting prejudice and violence, they stayed home on Sundays. If the Christian churches do not make an open commitment against all forms of violence, including and especially war, more and more people will look for peace elsewhere! Sad to say, after seeing, once again, the regular Jewish-Muslim slaughter in the Holy Land, they are not going to find it either in the synagogue or mosque. Unfortunately, religion and violence do seem to go together.

## Religion and Money

The love of money is root of all evil.[17]

You cannot serve two masters. You cannot serve God and money.[18]

The most sinful topic for the church, where money is concerned, is the admitted greed and corruption in the Vatican Bank. This evil is large and complex, and I am in no way qualified to discuss the bank scandal. We have been discussing the problems that Pope Francis is facing beginning his pontificate. Underlying most of those problems is money. Francis has been shockingly frank in pointing out the damage done to the social fabric as a result of making money being the goal of our lives. The pope does not feel that money will solve our problems. On the contrary, he feels that greed is the cause of our problems. Here, we will discuss just a few of these.

One of the biggest, if not the biggest moral problem we face today is climate change. Popes John Paul II and Benedict XVI, along with the U.S.

17. 1 Tim 6:24.
18. Matt 24:6.

Conference of Catholic Bishops, have spoken on this problem. Pope Francis has added to the topic. Glaciers melting, oceans rising—are these not man-made problems, resulting from human greed? Big business says, "All of our scientists, (both of them), say we are not warming the atmosphere." The right-wingers say, "This global warming nonsense is nothing but a perverted plot by tree huggers to take down capitalism."

Now they have to include the recent popes among those "tree huggers," because the popes have repeatedly spoken out against the deadly results of global warming. Benedict spoke of "waking up consciousness" about global warming and the necessity to change our way of life. Francis has confirmed Benedict words and is planning a new encyclical on the environment. Reportedly, it will drive conservatives to distraction. What is the basis for the disagreement about climate change? Money! Many people fear that if we try to slow down the heating up of our world they might lose money. They may be right! Undoubtedly, money is the main concern when global warming is the topic.

Some TV evangelists say, if I understand them correctly, "Jesus wants us to make money." Through history, there have been infinite ways the gospel has been perverted. However, I don't think there has been a greater perversion than, "Jesus wants us to be rich." "Blessed are the poor" got lost somewhere along the way. Thankfully, in the business world, there recently has been a reversal of the policy "my personal good surpasses the common good." The drug company CVS has announced that in the future they will not sell cigarettes because they are a health hazard. By their refusal to sell cigarettes, the company will lose two billion dollars a year. To give up a personal good for the sake of the common good is almost unheard of in the business world. Do you think the cigarette and gun manufacturers will follow CVS's example? I don't think so. Selfishness, be it individual or collective, is difficult to overcome.

As the song in the movie *Cabaret* says so vividly, "Money, money, money, money makes the world go 'round, the world go 'round." If you trace all of the world's problems back far enough, you will find greed at their source. St. Paul said, "The love of money is the root of all evil," so why is it that we don't hear a sermon on the root of all evil? Is the church so entwined with the wealth problem that it would rather not open that can of worms? It seems we now have a pope who is not afraid to open some cans.

We never hear a challenging homily on Mary's Magnificat, which actually speaks about money in damning ways. Mary's prayer always made me uncomfortable, and I never had the courage to give a homily on it. I also know some very fine Christian people who also are very wealthy, and I didn't want to offend them.

Mary, the Jewish peasant girl, used some of the most revolutionary, inflammatory, language ever uttered, even to the left of Karl Marx. "My soul magnifies the Lord . . . He has regarded the low estate of his handmaiden . . . He has put down the mighty from their thrones . . . He has filled the hungry with good things, and the rich he has sent away empty handed" (Luke 1:46–55).

No preacher in a capitalist society is going to touch that one; at least, not if he wants to keep his job. I also doubt if the Magnificat will ever be prayed at the opening bell on the New York Stock Exchange. Preachers shun the Magnificat and totally avoid the Sermon on the Mount, but the beatitudes are the heart of the gospel. They are what separates Christ's message from other ethical or moral teachings. Christianity is a mystical religion. There are two accounts of the Sermon on the Mount. Matthew has it on a mountain, whereas Luke has it on a plain. Luke's account is much more radical. He says, simply, "Blessed are the poor," and his words make us feel uncomfortable.

We find Matthew's account much more acceptable: Blessed are the "poor in spirit." That gives us more wiggle room. Matthew was a tax collector and felt more at home with the idea of money. I suspect that Matthew and King Solomon are the only two capitalists in the Bible. Not surprisingly, then, it is easier to identify with Matthew than with Luke.

The following are passages from Luke 6:20–21:

*Blessed are the poor.*

*Blessed are those who hunger.*

*Blessed are those who weep.*

(Do we feel that those who are hungry, poor, and weeping are blessed?)

*Blessed are you when men hate you and separate you from their company.*

(Do we feel that gay children must be blessed?)

*Lend, hoping for nothing in return.*

(The banks are going to go out of business.)

*Love your enemies.*

(How about that for foreign policy?)

*Woe to you that are rich.*

*Woe to you that are full.*

(Not great topics for *The Wall Street Journal*.)

How is a preacher in twenty-first-century America going to present those? They don't. When wars are being fought, I never heard "love your enemies." The beatitudes are not topics for Sunday sermons, but the priests and nuns working with the poor in Central America had the courage to pray Mary's Magnificat and teach the beatitudes.

Right-wing dictators, supported by our government, viciously opposed these teachings. In 1980, Bishop Romero of El Salvador was shot while saying Mass. Also in 1980, three female missionaries—two nuns and one laywoman—were raped and killed. Later, it was publicly admitted that government forces had killed them all. Two of the women were from my home diocese.

In 1989, members of the dictator's military killed six Jesuit priests in El Salvador. The U.S. trained the elite members of that military at The School of the Americas in Fort Benning, Georgia.

Sadly, when Pope John Paul II began the canonization process for Bishop Romero, it was met with strong opposition from some in the church. The wealthy Catholic landowners chose money over the gospel. Don't we all? I have, and that is why I have the blood of the poor on my hands. Certainly in those troublesome years in Central America, the United States had the blood of the poor on its hands.

I wonder if the Tea Party Christians ever think about those things? We all know how they feel about taxes, immigrants, and the minimum wage. How do they feel about the poor? The Tea Party people don't often mention the poor, whom Christ called "blessed."

I imagine that Samuel Gregg, author of *Tea Party Catholic*, was on the verge of cardiac arrest when he read Pope Francis' *The Joy of the Gospel*. Indeed the pope did criticize "those economic policies that defend the absolute autonomy of the market place and financial speculation and the logic of profit—that economy of exclusion and equality based on the idolatry of money." The church also has called for a larger role of the state in aiding the disenfranchised. The pope wants "a church that is poor and for the poor."

That kind of talk will cause any Tea Party member a heart flutter at the very least.

Believe it or not, there was a time when Republicans spoke out on behalf of the poor. Three months after taking office in 1953, President Eisenhower made his "Cross of Iron" speech: "Every gun made, every war ship launched, every rocket fired, signifies a theft from those who hunger and are not fed, those who are cold and not clothed." I like Ike. I did in 1953, and I do in 2014. He would be weeping that the Tea Party is claiming Republican roots. They are smudging a noble tradition.

Do we really want a church that is for the poor? I saw an editorial cartoon, drawn by Daryl Cagle that was published on July 14, 2014. It depicted a very overweight white American elephant, on his knees devoutly praying: "Dear Heavenly Father, I pray that you make Obama deport thousands of little brown children back to their awful countries as soon as possible, and I pray that no more little illegal brown kids cross the border into our blessed America, the greatest nation ever. In Jesus' name, amen."

One picture is worth a thousand words, and that one picture says it all. People in this country are caring less and less about the poor, about those in need, about those going to bed hungry. What ever happened to, "Give us your tired, your poor, your huddled masses?" May God have mercy on my indifference, have mercy on my selfishness. God have mercy.

U.S. Representative Stephen Fincher, a Republican from Tennessee who has received three and a half million dollars from the government on farm subsidies, wants to cut back on federal spending for food stamps. He uses scripture to support his callousness, saying, "The poor you will always have with you." The Bible says so.

Even worse, the political analysts didn't think Fincher's anti-food stamp position would hurt him politically. A U.S. congressman gets three and a half million dollars from the federal government, and Fincher wants the federal government to cut back on food stamps for the poor. This won't hurt him with voters? Shouldn't that paradox, in itself, be a problem for us?

Pope Francis has echoed his predecessors in their denunciation of unbridled capitalism. "In many respects, democratic socialism is close to Catholic doctrine and has in any case made a remarkable contribution to the formation of social consciousness," said Cardinal Ratzinger, the future Pope Benedict XVI.

Rush Limbaugh reacted to Pope Francis' *The Joy of the Gospel* by calling it "pure Marxism coming out of the mouth of the pope." I wonder what Rush Limbaugh would call the beatitudes coming out of the mouth of Christ? "Blessed are the poor . . . . Woe to you who are rich." Would Limbaugh call that pure Marxism coming out of the mouth of Christ? I suspect he would. As for myself, I am still waiting for anything that makes sense to come out of the mouth of Rush Limbaugh.

Adam Shaw, a news editor for Fox News and a Catholic, wrote that Pope Francis is "like Obama." In the context of how Shaw feels about Obama, this is like saying "Pope Francis is the anti-Christ."

In the next presidential election, I doubt that the pope's words "unfettered capitalism is the new tyranny unleashed on the world" from *The Joy of the Gospel* will be a major platform of either party's political convention. Sarah Palin said she was "taken aback" by the pope's words. I suspect that there will be many on the right who will be "taken aback," as she was. There will be American Catholics who feel uncomfortable with this pope, but isn't the gospel supposed to make us feel uncomfortable at times?

I am anxious to see how Shaw and many other Catholics are going to dance around the pope's words "unfettered capitalism is the new tyranny." I suspect Francis is going to cause some sleepless nights.

What would happen if either party had the eight beatitudes as one of its planks? Most people would walk out. I suspect only the "forty-seven percenters" would remain—and Jesus. After all, the beatitudes are Jesus' words, not Karl Marx's; Christ was most definitely among the forty-seven percent.

I am sure Congressman Fincher also votes against any increase in the minimum wage. With three and a half million dollars coming in from the government, you don't worry about what a minimum-wage worker gets. Is that a problem? It is probably not for most of us churchgoers. "If this is going to be a Christian nation, either we have to pretend that Jesus was just as selfish as we are, or acknowledge that he commanded us to love the poor and serve the needy without condition—and then admit that we just do not want to do it," said political satirist and TV personality Stephen Colbert. His words are all too true.

There are many problems we face today. Abortion is one problem we hear about from the pulpit, over and over and over again. That is understandable! Every year in the U.S., three to four hundred thousand abortions are performed. Taking innocent life is morally wrong. But why are other problems not also mentioned?

The pope asked, "How can it be that it is not a news item when an elderly homeless person dies of exposure, but it is news when the stock market loses two points?"[19] A poor person dying is not a concern for us, but a drop in the stock market is very troubling.

There are earth-shaking problems facing us. Instead of discussing these problems, the religious Right tells us to keep a check on homosexuals. We are told that God causes tornados, floods, rising oceans, shrinking ice caps, and hurricanes as punishment for our tolerance of homosexuals. New Orleans, with its gay population, "rightfully" felt the heavy hand of God's wrath in the form of Hurricane Katrina's destructive power.

Interesting, however, that the proclaimers of God's just punishments do not mention the tornados hitting the arrow-straight and Far Right state of Oklahoma.

I recently heard that the reason North Korea is aiming missiles at us is because of our tolerance of gay people. Such talk leads me to respect intelligent, honest, and compassionate non-believers. What comes over some radio and TV religious programs is horrifying and amusing, to be sure; unfortunately, it also may be highly dangerous. At least the non-believer does not use God to support his bigotry and hate. In that sense they are much more "Christian" than we who call ourselves Christians.

We have worldwide problems—many money based—that require a Christian response, and instead, we spend time discussing the sexuality of America's pre-pubescent boys, one of the few groups in America which is not caught up in chasing money.

For shame! May God have mercy on my hypocrisy. To borrow from Jesus in the book of Matthew: "Woe to me, hypocrite, I appear beautiful outside but within I am full of all uncleanness. Woe to me, hypocrite, I appear righteous, but within I am full of hypocrisy and iniquity." (Matt 23:27–28)

To the degree that we are judgmental, separating, and dividing, we are denying the message of both Vatican II and Pope Francis. The council—and now Pope Francis—is sending a message of acceptance and celebration. Do we really want to live the gospel of Pope Francis and Vatican II? Or will we just pretend to, thereby lying to ourselves and to everyone else? The challenge—that we must answer both individually and collectively—is for us to put into practice what they proclaim.

19. Chua-Eoan, "Pope Francis," 60.

# 5

# Conclusion

## Exceptions

IN THE INTERVENING YEARS between Vatican II and when I returned to parish life in 2000, we went from a church that chose people over policy, to a church that chose policy over people. Immediately after the council, the emphasis was on serving people. Gradually, that emphasis began to change, and by the year 2000, the cast was set. We had become a ruling church rather than a serving church. In the days just preceding Pope Francis, the church seemed driven by the idea that every rule—no matter how small or nonessential—had to be followed regardless of the negative effect it might have on people. As a result, people felt cut off from the church and started to leave, especially young people in Europe and America.

Dishearteningly, though, the church didn't seem to care. The attitude among the clergy and hierarchy seemed to be: "Let them go. They are not worthy of our standards." The well-known words, "We need a purer, smaller church," are attributed to Pope Benedict. There is some question as to just what they mean. A priest taking the words at face value said to me, "If we keep going the way we have been going, excluding people, we will end up a religiously right-wing cult."

It is an oversimplification to say that the church was not serving its people or that the church was dying. There are, of course, exceptions to the "exclusive club" idea of the church held by many of today's clergy—many dioceses have parishes and priests who are living that exception.

Shortly after I left the monastery, I went to Mass at Old St. Patrick's church in Chicago's inner city. It was a parish that had all but disappeared for lack of membership, but then the church was taken over and spiritually rejuvenated by a few priests. Now, you have to go early to get a seat—people are flooding in from the suburbs, driving past churches nearer to their homes to go to an inner-city church. Is it because of the positive message of the homilies? Is it because of the quality of the liturgy? At their Mass, I got the impression that these people knew they are the people of God, joyfully celebrating their identity. The homilies are filled with "do's" rather than "don'ts." The priests are obviously people priests, rather than law priests, and so people made the effort to be there.

However, those types of liturgies are not nearly as common as they should be. In fact in reading the statements of some bishops, I don't see how any parish in their diocese could have an uplifting liturgy. If those negative, punitive bishops would put more emphasis on being kind rather than being right, being positive rather than being negative, people would be more inclined to celebrate a joyful Eucharist.

Possibly you have seen T-shirts that say, "I'm a recovering Catholic." I have seen them in the most diverse places: on a retreatant at the monastery and on a young woman walking down a concourse at JFK airport. One time, a woman at a church service introduced herself as "a recovering Catholic." I replied, "I understand, and I am sorry." I don't think she knew what to do with that. It left her no one to battle. There are wounded people out there. Gratefully, there are priests and parishes who are trying to heal those wounds; there are other "Old St. Patrick's" around.

While at Old St. Patrick's we had an unexpectedly pleasant experience. The church has beautiful stained glass windows, and one depicts St. Anne—Mary's mother and Jesus' grandmother. My wife at times feels awkward and not included at Mass, especially where there is talk of "Catholics in good standing." But when my wife, Ann, saw that window of St. Anne, she felt at home.

The image of a small, centralized, controlling church that has been prevalent in recent years is now changing, and rapidly. Pope Francis has torpedoed that elitist image, and there is no doubt that he is setting a different tone than his predecessors; that tone is spreading. The pastor of a large church in Washington, D.C. said his crowds at Easter services were larger than ever. He added, "And that is because of Francis!"

I heard a lapsed Catholic say, "If Francis has his way and frees up the church, making it more caring and loving, I may find myself going back to church." What great things a little kindness can do in a short time. The pope's effect goes well beyond individuals and Catholicism—*Time* named him the "Person of the Year" in 2013. His appeal is universal.

## "Francis, Repair My Church"

I conclude this book quoting Pope Francis. His words touch on just about every topic we have discussed. I will not comment on them; I leave it to you to put the pieces together and understand how this pope is "truly opening the windows," as did Pope John. Under this pope, the essentials will remain, but there will be a broader discussion of what those essentials are and what they mean. There will surely be a greater emphasis on the spirit of the law, rather than the letter of the law, on people rather than policy.

Pope Francis made the following remarks in August 2013 to Jesuit Father Antonio Spadaro, editor of *La Civilta Cattolica*, an Italian journal:

- "We have to find a new balance, otherwise even the moral edifice of the church is likely to fall, like a house of cards, losing the freshness and fragrance of the Gospel.

- "The church sometimes has locked itself up in small things, in small-minded rules.

- "Those who always look for disciplinary solutions, those who long for an exaggerated doctrinal security, those who stubbornly try to recover that past that no longer exists—they have a static and inward directed view of things."

- Some Vatican offices "run the risk of becoming institutions of censorship. It is amazing to see the denunciation for lack of orthodoxy that came to Rome.

- "The church is the 'people of God' on the journey through history.

- "All the people, considered as a whole, are infallible in the matters of belief.

- "But this is not a forum of populism. It is the church as the people of God, pastors and people together."

- "The thing the church needs most today is the ability to heal wounds and to warm the hearts of the faithful. It needs nearness and proximity.

- "The church's pastoral ministry cannot be obsessed with the transmission of a disjointed multitude of doctrines to be imposed insistently.

- "We cannot insist only on issues related to abortion, gay marriage, and contraceptive methods. It is not necessary to talk about these issues all the time."

- The pope said he had been "reprimanded for failing to speak often of these things." Merton had similar sentiments: "One would certainly wish that the Catholic position on nuclear war was held as strictly as the Catholic policy on birth control."

His words are those that priests use talking among themselves, words that the laity usually does not hear. They are radical! No pope since Pope John XXIII has spoken so openly about the church's need to be people-directed rather than institution-directed! It may well be that no pope at any time has spoken so candidly about the need for reform.

I am grateful to have lived long enough to see the arrival of Pope Francis. For the past fourteen years, since leaving the monastery and experiencing the loss of the spirit of Vatican II, I have sympathized with the words of an elderly priest: "I had just about given up any hope that the church could purify herself. And then Pope Francis came along, and I was revived."

The priest's sentiments are understandable, but they lack historical perspective. The church has survived darker days. The church has seen illegitimate sons of popes fight over who will succeed to the papacy. Those were dark days.

In the thirteenth century, the humble Pope Celestine V resigned from the papacy after six months. His successor had him imprisoned, and he died ten months later of "complications"—darker days!

In 1203, papal armies in France massacred "heretical" men, women, and children. Before the slaughter began, a member of the papal army asked his commander—a monk—"How can we tell Catholics from the heretics to know whom to kill?" His commander answered: "Kill them all! God will know his own." About 7,000 people were killed—the darkest days, indeed.

In the winter 2013–14 issue of *Notre Dame Magazine*, Michael Garvey, a prominent Catholic layman, acknowledged that many have been disenchanted with the church through the past twenty-five years. The sex-abuse scandal, the church's treatment of women, and the misuse of power both in Rome and among the hierarchy—all have had a divesting effect. Nevertheless, Garvey sees a reason to stay in the church: "[I] have plenty of reasons to stay with this maddeningly human, redemptively divine social sacrament with people like [myself].[1] For me, that summarized it pretty well.

1. Garvey, "Still Catholic," excerpt.

I am a cradle Catholic and, God willing, I will be a casket Catholic. Like Peter answered when Jesus asked him, "Will you also go away?" I would say, "Lord, to whom shall I go?" (John 6:68)

In the 1970s, when some young people where leaving Christianity and looking toward Eastern religions, the Dalai Lama discouraged them. He said they instead should find a deeper spirituality within their own tradition, telling them, "Grow where you are planted." That is very good advice for spiritual seekers.

I have received six of the church's seven sacraments. The one remaining is the sacrament of the sick, formerly known as "extreme unction" or the last blessing. It is reserved for those about to die. At my age, the possibility of death is a daily reality, if not an actual expectancy.

I once heard a story about death that I find relevant. A man sent his suit to the cleaners to have a stain removed. The suit was returned with the stain still visible and a note from the cleaner, "I deeply regret having to return flawed goods." That would be a fitting epithet for my tombstone, "God, I deeply regret having to return flawed goods." On the other side of the stone should be chiseled, "He had fun!"

# Bibliography

Author's note: Twice a week, over a period of about five years, Thomas Merton gave 45-minute talks to the novice monks at the Trappist Abbey of Gethsemani in Bardstown, Kentucky. Those talks were taped and make up more than 350 hours. It took me about four years to listen to and assemble his talks into topics. This resulted in a collection of more than 800 quotations from his tapes and another 200 from his books. In the footnotes, I cite quotations from the tape collection using *Tape*, followed by the tape number.

Aldington, Richard. *The Colonel's Daughter.* Garden City, NY: Doubleday, 1931.

Anglican Communion. "Unity, Faith, and Order—Dialogues—Anglican Roman Catholic." 1971. http://www.anglicancommunion.org/ministry/ecumenical/dialogues/catholic/arcic/docs/eucharistic_doctrine1971.cfm.

Aquinas, Thomas, Saint. *Summa Theologica I & II.* http://www.munseys.com/diskthree/sumth.htm.

Augustine, Saint. *Confessions.* Edited by Sir Tobie Matthew. London: Burns & Oates, 1954.

Bash, Dana. "Ted Nugent Hits Campaign Trail After Calling Obama 'Subhuman Mongrel.'" *CNN Politics,* February 18, 2014. http://politicalticker.blogs.cnn.com/2014/02/18/ted-nugent-hits-campaign-trail-for-texas-gop-candidate/.

Beech, Hannah. "The Face of Buddhist Terror." *Time,* July 1, 2013. http://content.time.com/ time/magazine /article/0,9171,2146000,00.html.

Benedict, Saint. *The Rule of Saint Benedict.* Edited by Bruce L. Venarde. Cambridge: Harvard University Press, 2011.

Benedict XVI, Pope. *Jesus of Nazareth.* San Francisco: Ignatius, 2008.

Bowman, Rebecca. "Jefferson's Religious Beliefs." *Monticello.org.* http://www.monticello.org/ site/research-and-collections/jeffersons-religious-beliefs.

Brown, Dan. *The Lost Symbol.* New York: Anchor, 2009.

Buchanan, Patrick J. "Vladamir Putin: Christian Crusader?" *The American Conservative,* April 4, 2014. www.theamericanconservative.com/vladimir-putin-christian-crusader/comment-page-1/.

Chardin, Pierre Teildard de. *The Divine Milieu: An Essay on the Interior Life.* New York: Harper, 1960.

# Bibliography

Chua-Eoan, Howard and Elizabeth Dias. "Pope Francis, the People's Pope." *Time*, December 11, 2013. http://poy.time.com/2013/12/11/person-of-the-year-pope-francis-the-peoples-pope/.

Dacey, Liam. "Notre Dame Inspires (excerpt)." *Notre Dame Magazine* (Autumn 2013) 9.

DeCosse, David. "Imbalance between Francis, U.S. Bishops Undermines Religious Liberty Campaign." *National Catholic Reporter*, October 23, 2013. http://ncronline.org/news/politics/imbalance-undermines-bishops-campaign.

Dillenberger, John. *Martin Luther*. Garden City, NY: Doubleday, 1961.

Donne, John. *John Donne: A Selection of His Poetry*. Edited by John Hayward. Baltimore: Penguin, 1950.

Dostoevsky, Fyodor. *The Brothers Karamazov*. 2nd ed. Great Books of the Western World 52. Chicago: Encyclopedia Britannica, 1990.

Dowd, Vincent. "The Birth of Oh! What a Lovely War." *BBC News*, November 11, 2011. http://www.bbc.com/news/magazine-15691707.

Falk, Gerhard. *The Jew in Christian Theology: Martin Luther's Anti-Jewish Vom Schem Hamphoras*. Jefferson, NC: McFarland, 1992.

Francis, Pope. *The Joy of the Gospel*. Washington, D.C.: United States Conference of Catholic Bishops, 2013.

Freud, Sigmund. *Character and Culture*. Edited by Philip Rieff. New York: Crowell-Collier, 1963.

Garvey, Michael. "Still Catholic (excerpt)." *Notre Dame Magazine* (Winter 2013). http://magazine.nd.edu/archives/2013/winter-2013-14/.

Harris Interactive. "Harris Poll Finds Different Religious Groups have Very Different Attitudes to some Health Policies and Programs." October 2005. http://www.harrisinteractive.com/vault/Harris-Interactive-Poll-Research-New-Finds-Different-Religious-Groups-H-2005-10.pdf.

Hastings, Max. *Catastrophe 1914: Europe Goes to War*. New York: Knopf, 2013.

Hay, Malcolm. *Thy Brother's Blood: The Roots of Christian Anti-Semitism*. Oxford: Hart, 1975.

Jefferson, Thomas. "Letter to Mrs. Samuel H. Smith." http://www.let.rug.nl/usa/presidents/thomas-jefferson/letters-of-thomas-jefferson/jefl247.php.

———. "The Virginia Act for Establishing Religious Freedom." *University of Virginia Library*. http://religiousfreedom.lib.virginia.edu/sacred/vaact.html.

Küng, Hans. *The Council and Reunion*. Translated by Cecily Hastings. London: Sheed & Ward, 1961.

Kushner, Harold S. *When Bad Things Happen to Good People*. New York: Schocken, 1981.

Luther, Martin. *Luther's Works*. Vol. 47. Edited by Martin H. Bertram. St. Louis: Concordia, 1971.

Maurovich, Frank. "Humanae Vitae at 45: A Personal Story." *National Catholic Reporter*, July 25, 2013. http://ncronline.org/news/vatican/humanae-vitae-45-personal-story.

McClory, Robert. "The New Pope's Real Target: Clericalism." *National Catholic Reporter*, April 4, 2013. http://ncronline.org/blogs/ncr-today/new-pope-s-real-target-clericalism.

Merton, Thomas. *New Seeds of Contemplation*. Norfolk, CT: New Directions, 1961.

Mosbergen, Dominique. "Charisma News Takes Down Hateful Post Calling For Violence Against Muslims." No pages. Online: http://www.huffingtonpost.com/2014/09/08/charisma-news-islamophobic_n_5786942.html.

Newman, John Henry. *The Letters and Diaries of John Henry Newman.* Vol. 24. Edited by Charles Stephen Dessain et al. Oxford: Clarendon, 1973.

―――. "Letter to the Duke of Norfolk." In *Certain Difficulties Felt by Anglicans in Catholic Teaching.* Vol. 2. London: Longmans, Green, 1900.

Nugent, Robert. *Silence Speaks.* Mahwah, NJ: Paulist, 2011.

―――. *Thomas Merton and Thérèse Lentfoehr: The Story of a Friendship.* Staten Island, NY: Pious Society of Saint Paul, 2012.

Papesh, Michael. *Clerical Culture: Contradiction and Transformation.* Collegeville, MN: Liturgical, 2004.

Paul VI, Pope. *Gaudium et Spes.* Vatican, 1965. http://www.vatican.va/archive/ hist_councils/ii_vatican_council/documents/vat-ii_cons_19651207_gaudium-et-spes_en.html.

―――. *Humanae Vitae.* Vatican, 1968. http://www.vatican.va/holy_father/ paul_vi/encyclicals/documents/hf_p-vi_enc_25071968_humanae-vitae_en.html.

―――. *Lumen Gentium.* Vatican, 1964. http://www.vatican.va/archive/hist_ councils/ii_vatican_council/documents/vat-ii_const_19641121_lumen-gentium_en.html.

Pius IX, Pope. *Syllabus Errorum.* Papal Encyclicals Online. http://www.papalencyclicals.net/Pius09/p9syll.htm.

Plante, Thomas. "A Perspective on Clergy Sexual Abuse." *Psychology of Religion,* 2010. http://www.psywww.com/psyrelig/plante.html

"'Pope' Francis & Our Lady of Fatima." *Novus Ordo Watch,* 2013. http://www.novusordowatch.org/wire/francis-and-fatima.htm.

Rohr, Richard, and John Feister. *Jesus' Plan for a New World: The Sermon on the Mount.* Cincinnati: St. Anthony Messenger Press, 1996.

Roy, Jessica. "The Rapture of the Nerds." *Time,* April 17, 2014. http://time.com/66536/terasem-trascendence-religion-technology/.

Runciman, Steven. *A History of the Crusades.* Vol. 3. London: Folio Society, 1994.

Sartino, Richard. *Another Look at Newman.* Internet Archive, September 23, 2009. https://archive.org/details/AnotherLookAtNewman.

Scalfari, Eugenio. "The Pope: How the Church Will Change." Dialogue with Pope Francis. *La Repubblica,* October 1, 2013. http://www.repubblica.it/cultura/2013/10/01/news/pope_s_conversation_with_scalfari_english-67643118/.

Scott, Bernard Brandon. *Hear Then the Parable: A Commentary on the Parables of Jesus.* Minneapolis: Fortress, 1989.

Spadaro, Antonio. "A Big Heart Open to God." *America,* September 30, 2013. http://www.americamagazine.org/ pope-interview.

"Voice of the Faithful's Conclusions about the John Jay College Report: Causes and Context of Sexual Abuse of Minors by Catholic Priests in the United States, 1950–2010." *Voice of the Faithful,* October 11, 2011. http://www.votf.org/Govt_reports/VOTF_Conclusions_Report.pdf.

Wald, Matthew. "Woman Becomes First Openly Gay General." *New York Times,* August 12, 2012. http://www.nytimes.com/2012/08/13/us/army-woman-is-first-openly-gay-officer-promoted-to-flag-rank.html.

Ward, Wilfrid. *The Life of John Henry Cardinal Newman.* Vols. 1–2. New York: Longmans, Green, 1912.

Watts, Alan. *Behold the Spirit: A Study in the Necessity of Mystical Religion.* New York: Random House, 1971.

Wilson, George. *Clericalism: The Death of the Priesthood.* Collegeville, MN: Liturgical, 2008.

Winfield, Nicole, et al. "Rebel Pope Urges Catholics to Shake Up Dioceses." *Huffington Post*, July 25, 2013. http://www.huffingtonpost.com/huff-wires/20130725/lt-brazil-pope/?utm_hp_ref=world&ir=world.